The Journey to Enterprise Agility

Daryl Kulak • Hong Li

The Journey to Enterprise Agility

Systems Thinking
and Organizational Legacy

Daryl Kulak
Westerville, OH
USA

Hong Li
Westerville, OH
USA

ISBN 978-3-319-54086-3   ISBN 978-3-319-54087-0 (eBook)
DOI 10.1007/978-3-319-54087-0

Library of Congress Control Number: 2017937541

© Springer International Publishing AG 2017

This work is subject to copyright. All rights are reserved by the Publisher, whether the whole or part of the material is concerned, specifically the rights of translation, reprinting, reuse of illustrations, recitation, broadcasting, reproduction on microfilms or in any other physical way, and transmission or information storage and retrieval, electronic adaptation, computer software, or by similar or dissimilar methodology now known or hereafter developed.

The use of general descriptive names, registered names, trademarks, service marks, etc. in this publication does not imply, even in the absence of a specific statement, that such names are exempt from the relevant protective laws and regulations and therefore free for general use.

The publisher, the authors and the editors are safe to assume that the advice and information in this book are believed to be true and accurate at the date of publication. Neither the publisher nor the authors or the editors give a warranty, express or implied, with respect to the material contained herein or for any errors or omissions that may have been made. The publisher remains neutral with regard to jurisdictional claims in published maps and institutional affiliations.

Printed on acid-free paper

This Springer imprint is published by Springer Nature
The registered company is Springer International Publishing AG
The registered company address is: Gewerbestrasse 11, 6330 Cham, Switzerland

We dedicate this book to Robert Rosen and W. Edwards Deming for their contributions to systems science, the workplace and society. Each man forged a new path, even though they were often marginalized and misinterpreted during their lives and even afterward. Each of them saw derivative works that claimed to represent them, but often fell far short. We hope to guide the conversation back to Rosen's and Deming's original material, where the real value still lies.

Preface

I remember Hong's frantic phone call back in 2003. I was busy trying to get a new solo consulting venture off the ground. Hong wanted to talk about some "systems thinking" nonsense. He wanted us to write a damn book about it. I had just finished the second edition of my first book and, quite frankly, was in no mood.

Three years later, the ever-persistent Hong had convinced me this was a book that needed to be written.

Hong warned me this would be a long journey. I had much to learn, because I had to catch up on his 3 years of (full-time) research. We then agreed to meet every Sunday morning at around 10:30. In 2006, we started writing in earnest on evenings and weekends.

So, we began in 2006. Eleven years ago, as I write these words.

It took me a long, long time to understand systems thinking as Hong was teaching me. It took even longer to apply it to day-to-day life in a software team. I am a slow learner, apparently. Glacial. But, eventually, it came together in my head. I began to feel like we had something big.

Around 2008, Hong and I trashed what we had and rewrote the entire book once we realized that our audience might not want to know every thought, meal and fart of our systems scholars. We rewrote it again the next year to incorporate more storytelling into the text, rather than dry bullet points of principles and concepts. We figured out better, clearer ways to state our message. Another rewrite. And another. The versions are there in Google Docs if you want to see them (it was called Writely back then).

Every year, I would think that next year would be the year. We would finish it, damn it. I would even update my LinkedIn status to show that my next book would be released in 2011, I mean, 2012, I mean 2013... This was getting embarrassing. I started dreading that question at parties, "So, how's the book going?"

But now it's 2017. We've finished it. So there's a fair bit of work sitting here in front of you. We've talked about these ideas with all our clients over these 11 years, and they've helped us refine them. We've had dialogs over lunch and drinks with our colleagues and fellow travelers. We've done presentations at conferences. Fortunately, we joined a consulting company, Pillar Technology, who encouraged everything we were doing and actually incorporated a lot of our ideas into the company's way of managing projects. And we've used the ideas day-to-day in our consulting work to continually improve the execution of every project we've led over these years. Many other friends and coworkers have helped us understand how this book needed to be written.

We won't say that it works. We can't say that. It isn't a set of best practices. But we hope we can help provide a new worldview and yes, some practices that could be helpful to our readers as you try to push some software out the door.

Westerville, OH
January 2017

Daryl Kulak

Acknowledgments

We've been working on the ideas in this book for a long time and, thus, have had many collaborators. We will inevitably miss some names and, for that, we are sorry.

Thank you so much to Chris Davis, Geoff Wilhelm, Yvonne Weller, Mike Miller, Naum Sayfullin, Conal Thompson, Joe Sjostrom, Diane Roquemore, Jodi Cannon, Rob Richardson, Zach Guisinger, Andy Secrest, Chris Beale, Patrick Welsh, Gary Baker, Justin Searls, Kelly Allan, Sanjiv Augustine, Rick Neighbarger, Angelo Mazzocco, Ben Blanquera, Kermit Morse, Justin Foley, John Griffin, Jim Hertzfeld, Anita Shankar, Rich Diers, Bill Gray, Sip Reyes, Rachel Howard, Mike Cottmeyer, Mark Davidson, Mark Walker, Joe Hammond and Tax Commissioner Joe Testa.

Thank you to the readers of Daryl's first book and everyone who gave us encouragement to write another one.

Thanks to our colleagues at ISSS, who continually encourage us to progress in our understanding of systems thinking, including Dennis Finlayson, Delia MacNamara, Debora Hammond, Jennifer Makar and many others.

A special thanks to Linda Farrenkopf, Brian Caldwell, Walter den Haan, Jeff Jamison and John Lavkulich for your enduring friendship and encouragement.

Thanks to everyone at Pillar for allowing us to try our ideas with so many clients, incorporating our work into the very fabric of how Pillar operates. We appreciate the conversations and feedback from many Pillarites, including Bob Myers, Matt VanVleet, Gary Gentry, John Huston, Katie Robinson, Allen Smith, Cheryl Smith, Nish Gandhi, Mary Kaufman, Dan Wiebe, Todd Flanders, Kevin Smith, Steve Yaffe, Rich Dammkoehler and Kevin McCann.

Thank you to everyone in the Java Guys program, organizers and inmates, at Marion Correctional Institute. You guys really inspire us with your continuous dedication to becoming great test-driven developers.

Thanks in particular to Gene Johnson for joining "The Church of Hong" those Sunday mornings and giving us specific, but always kind, feedback on so many parts of this book. You really helped us organize our ideas.

We'd like to thank Dr. Theodore Williams for creating the Purdue Enterprise Reference Architecture (PERA), for introducing Hong to the major players in enterprise integration, and for being a true gentleman in everything he did.

Thank you to Jason Kinsey for providing the creative illustrations for this book. Jason, you did a great job on a short time schedule. You are so very talented.

A big, amazing thank you to Springer-Verlag and especially editor Ralf Gerstner and his team. Thank you for giving us this chance to take our ideas to a worldwide audience under your guidance and leadership.

And thanks, of course, to our wives and families for supporting us and loving us through the trials and tribulations of writing this book.

Endorsements

A masterful, thought-provoking read for any business leader motivated to sustainably improve business value. Its delightfully entertaining but substance-rich style will readily guide you to "aha moments" on how to advance agile software development to enterprise scale!
Conal Thompson, CTO and VP of IT, Chemical Abstracts Service,
a Division of the American Chemical Society

At recent conferences of the International Society for the Systems Sciences (ISSS), I have enjoyed talking with Daryl, learning about his work, and witnessing the evolution of this book. I'm impressed with the way he and co-author Hong have effectively linked abstract concepts of systems theories with good, practical advice for software development teams. They've created a valuable bridge between academic scholarship in the systems field and the day-to-day functioning of software teams. A must-read for software managers.
Debora Hammond, PhD, Professor of Interdisciplinary Studies,
Hutchins School of Liberal Studies, Sonoma State University;
author of "The Science of Synthesis" and past president of ISSS

Dr. Li and Daryl have produced a very nice book in "The Journey to Enterprise Agility." This book integrates the highest priority ingredients that are necessary to achieve true enterprise agility. My favorite ingredient is human relationships. This book not only includes important teaching on process, technology, value, etc. but also on human relationships. It is no wonder that Hong and Daryl have not only written this excellent book but also that they have spent their careers successfully developing systems within an enterprise agility framework.
Angelo Mazzocco, CIO, Central Ohio Primary Care

This is a marvelous book! It only took a few pages to realize that the authors have created a sound basis for effective team performance. The Journey to Enterprise Agility provides a mindset, not a static formula, which is refreshing. Any software development organization that chooses not to embrace what this book offers probably misses an opportunity to enhance their performance.
Gene Bellinger, Director - Systems Thinking World (systemswiki.org)

Have you wondered how to improve the process of software product development? It's about changing your approach to leadership, your concept of professionalism, even how you see the world. But it's worth it. Daryl and Hong's book will give you details on how to make that shift.

Philip Pointer, VP Applications Development, Mednax National Medical Group

Contents

1 Today's Problems with Enterprise Business Software 1
   1.1   The New, New Thing 2
   1.2   Cheap Green Shirts 3
   1.3   Help! We're Terrible! 4
   1.4   Aristotle, Descartes and Disconnection to Business Value 5
   1.5   The Mechanical Business World 8
         1.5.1   The Question of Business Value 9
   1.6   Scalability and Sustainability 11
         1.6.1   The Story of Sticky LaGrange 11
   1.7   Yes, But What About the Illth? 13
         1.7.1   Agile Illth 13
   1.8   Our Software Industry Problems Can Be Overcome 15
   Reference 16

2 The Scholars of Systems Thinking 17
   2.1   Hard and Soft Systems Thinking 17
         2.1.1   Don't Worry: This Will Not Be a Complete
                 History of Systems Thinking 21
   2.2   Systems Thinking Forms the Basis 22

3 Worldview and Intentions 23
   3.1   Borrowing from the Buddha 23
         3.1.1   Right View 24
         3.1.2   Right Intention 28
         3.1.3   Right Speech 29
         3.1.4   Right Action 31
   3.2   Right View + Right Intention + Right Speech + Right Action ... 32
         3.2.1   A Worldview That Is Compatible with Success 32
   Reference 33

4 Seven Principles of Systems Thinking for Software Development ... 35
   4.1   So Many Principles! 35
         4.1.1   Systems Thinking Principle 1: Trust = Speed 36
         4.1.2   Systems Thinking Principle 2: Avoid Best
                 Practices 37

		4.1.3	Systems Thinking Principle 3: Beware the Immense Power of Analogies.........................	39
		4.1.4	Systems Thinking Principle 4: Blame the System, Not the Person............................	40
		4.1.5	Systems Thinking Principle 5: Treat People Like People, Not Like Machines...................	41
		4.1.6	Systems Thinking Principle 6: Acknowledge Your Boundaries..............................	42
		4.1.7	Systems Thinking Principle 7: Relation-ness Matters More Than Thing-ness.................	43
	4.2	Principles for Your Worldview.......................		44
	References....................................			45
5	**Redefining Professionalism**..............................			47
	5.1	Understanding What It Means to Be a Professional..........		47
		5.1.1	What Defined the Professionalism of the Past?.....	48
		5.1.2	Mechanical Professionalism..................	49
	5.2	The New Professionalism...........................		52
	5.3	The Principles of the New Professionalism...............		53
		5.3.1	New Professionalism Principle 1: Speak Up!.......	54
		5.3.2	New Professionalism Principle 2: Solving Communication Problems with Via Negativa......	59
		5.3.3	New Professionalism Principle 3: Be an Advocate for Weak or Absent Voices...................	63
		5.3.4	New Professionalism Principle 4: Proudly Display Your Dirty Laundry.......................	70
		5.3.5	New Professionalism Principle 5: Connect People to One Another...........................	70
		5.3.6	New Professionalism Principle 6: Challenge Your Own Assumptions as Much as You Challenge Others'.................................	71
		5.3.7	New Professionalism Principle 7: Be Accountable to Change...............................	72
		5.3.8	New Professionalism Principle 8: Manage Uncertainties Through Adaptive Practices and Stop Faking Risk Management....................	73
		5.3.9	The Worldview of the New Professional..........	78
	References....................................			79
6	**Scaling and Sustaining: Avoiding Mechanical Behavior**.........			81
	6.1	The Burning Question on Robert Rosen's Mind............		82
	6.2	Allow Me to Work Somewhere Fit for Humans............		83
	6.3	Are Humans Similar to Software?.....................		83
	6.4	But Agile Ain't Mechanical, Is It?.....................		85
	6.5	Conversations with a Terrible Coach...................		85
	6.6	Why? What's the Purpose?.........................		87

		6.6.1	Thin Knowledge Versus Thick Knowledge	87
		6.6.2	Why? Tell Me Your Thought Process	88
	6.7	What Type of Organization Do You Work In?		89
	6.8	Agile Practices and the "Why" Behind Them		90
		6.8.1	Be a Skeptical Empiricist	91
		6.8.2	Run a Process Experimentation Lab in Every Team Space	92
	References			93

7 Business Value, Estimation and Metrics ... 95

- 7.1 Do We Really, Honestly Need a PMO? ... 95
- 7.2 How an Idea Becomes a Project ... 96
- 7.3 The Problems with Today's Portfolio Management Processes Are ... 96
  - 7.3.1 The Annual Portfolio Management Cycle ... 96
  - 7.3.2 Projects Incur Unnecessary Costs and Risks ... 97
  - 7.3.3 Early Estimates Are Inaccurate ... 97
- 7.4 Ideas for Portfolio Management ... 98
  - 7.4.1 The Fleeting Concept of Value ... 98
  - 7.4.2 Value Stories ... 99
  - 7.4.3 The Cisco Rule ... 102
  - 7.4.4 Prioritizing Value Stories ... 103
  - 7.4.5 Slicing Value Stories ... 103
  - 7.4.6 The Real Day-to-Day Magic of Value Stories ... 104
  - 7.4.7 "Get Me a Black Truck!" ... 106
  - 7.4.8 Three Levels of ROI: Thin, Thick and "Thurmanator" ... 107
  - 7.4.9 Metrics ... 109
  - 7.4.10 Estimation ... 117
- 7.5 Meanwhile...Back in the Team Space ... 121
- 7.6 Portfolio Management Does Not Have to Be a Dinosaur ... 122
- References ... 122

8 Missing Deadlines Means Missing Market Opportunities ... 123

- 8.1 How to Miss a Deadline ... 123
- 8.2 Why Requirements Is a Bad Word ... 124
  - 8.2.1 Shotgun or Rifle Approach? ... 126
  - 8.2.2 Adding a Sponge to the Iron Triangle ... 126
  - 8.2.3 Acceptable and Unacceptable Responses to the Business ... 128
  - 8.2.4 The Steel Query Application ... 128
- 8.3 "How Much Will It Cost?" Is the Wrong Question ... 130
  - 8.3.1 Thinking in Buckets ... 131
  - 8.3.2 Short Sprints Really Help ... 133

	8.4	Stop Thinking Like an IT Person: Think Like a Businessperson	133
	8.5	Things Move So Dang Fast	134
	Reference	135
9	**Flipping the Run/Build Ratio: The Business Case for Software Craftsmanship**	137
	9.1	Just Keeping the Lights On	137
	9.2	Software Craftsmanship: How a Movement Among Developers Is Good for Business	139
		9.2.1 Software Craftsmanship Practices	141
		9.2.2 Software Craftsmanship with Commercial Packaged Software	147
	9.3	DevOps	149
	9.4	The Intention of Software Craftsmanship	150
	References	151
10	**Better Vendor RFPs and Contracts**	153
	10.1	Let's Put It Out to Bid!	153
	10.2	The Alan Shepard Principle	154
	10.3	A Better Way to Write RFPs	155
		10.3.1 RFPs with Value Stories	155
		10.3.2 Sprint Zero Contract with Follow-On	157
		10.3.3 Connecting Non-Agile Vendors to Your Agile Process	157
	10.4	Working with Vendors Is Not Always Easy	161
11	**Servant Leadership**	163
	11.1	The Basis of Servant Leadership	163
		11.1.1 Needs Not Wants	165
		11.1.2 Management and Leadership	166
	11.2	A Leadership Culture	167
	11.3	The Nine Leadership Principles	168
		11.3.1 Leadership Principle 1: Bring Decision-Making as Close to the Work as Possible	168
		11.3.2 Leadership Principle 2: A Leader Is Anxious When the Team Is Calm and Calm When the Team Is Anxious	171
		11.3.3 Leadership Principle 3: A Leader Is a Systems Scientist	171
		11.3.4 Leadership Principle 4: A Leader Understands the Benefits and Dangers of Measurement	172
		11.3.5 Leadership Principle 5: A Leader Negotiates	174
		11.3.6 Leadership Principle 6: A Leader Leads Across Team Boundaries Using Scouts and Ambassadors	175

		11.3.7	Leadership Principle 7: A Leader Organizes Field Trips...................................	177

		11.3.7	Leadership Principle 7: A Leader Organizes Field Trips......................................	177
		11.3.8	Leadership Principle 8: A Leader Is a Student of Corporate Culture.............................	178
		11.3.9	Leadership Principle 9: A Leader Respects the Psychological Contract.............................	179
	11.4	The Desolate Wasteland of Management Training..........		180
	11.5	Getting Started with Servant Leadership.................		181
	References..			182
12	**How Teams Keep Learning and Improving**..................			183
	12.1	Continuous Improvement with W. Edwards Deming........		183
		12.1.1	The Shewhart Cycle.........................	184
		12.1.2	The Trouble with Self-Reinforcing Feedback......	192
	12.2	Where's the System?..................................		193
	12.3	How Long Is a Sprint?................................		193
	12.4	Lightning Talks.....................................		195
	12.5	Learning, Improving.................................		195
	References..			196
13	**Getting Coaching That Really Helps**........................			197
	13.1	Fighting Poverty in Rural China........................		197
	13.2	How to Transform an Organization?....................		199
		13.2.1	Shu-ha-ri................................	199
		13.2.2	The Alternative to Shu-ha-ri..................	200
		13.2.3	Scrum and Done!...........................	201
		13.2.4	Aspects of a Transformation...................	202
	13.3	Coaches Who Just Coach: NO; Extensive Training Sessions: NO; Certification: HELL NO.........................		203
	13.4	Talker+Doer..		205
	13.5	Six Questions to Ask Your Agile Coach or Consultant.......		205
	13.6	People Don't Resist Change...........................		208
	Reference..			209
14	**Capitalizing Software Investments**.........................			211
	14.1	Will That Be CAPEX or OPEX?........................		211
		14.1.1	CAPEX and OPEX Activities in Software Development................................	212
	14.2	Why Capitalize?....................................		213
		14.2.1	Income Smoothing...........................	213
		14.2.2	Ratio Analysis..............................	214
		14.2.3	Reduced OPEX.............................	214
	14.3	Creating Financial Projections with More Confidence........		214

15 Integrating Enterprise Methodology and Architecture with Fast-Moving Development Teams 217
- 15.1 The Organizational Legacy 217
  - 15.1.1 Playing Nice: Avoiding Process Illth 218
- 15.2 How Development Teams Can Play Nice with Corporate Methodology Groups 218
  - 15.2.1 Stage Gates 219
  - 15.2.2 Project Plans 221
  - 15.2.3 Corporate Methodology Is Not the Enemy 225
- 15.3 How the Corporate Methodology Group Can Transform Its Worldview 226
- 15.4 How Development Teams Can Play Nice with Enterprise Architecture 227
  - 15.4.1 Architects: Come to Our Demos! 227
  - 15.4.2 Volunteer to Be an Early Adopter for New Architectural Capabilities 228
- 15.5 How the Enterprise Architecture Group Can Transform Its Worldview 228
  - 15.5.1 Architects Who Write Code 228
  - 15.5.2 Setting Standards 229
  - 15.5.3 Emergent Architecture 232
  - 15.5.4 What's That Sound? Is Your Architecture Screaming? 232
  - 15.5.5 Test-Driven Architecture 233
  - 15.5.6 Being an Architect Is Not the Desired Career Path for Every Developer 233
- 15.6 A Word About Bimodal IT 234
- 15.7 The Corporate Immune System 234
- Reference 235

16 HR Agility 237
- 16.1 Why Did Churchman Quit the Field He Pioneered? 238
- 16.2 Changing Your HR Worldview: People Aren't Your Resources 239
  - 16.2.1 The Neighborhood Nurses 240
- 16.3 Evaluating People 241
  - 16.3.1 Reduce the Document Focus 241
  - 16.3.2 Performance Appraisals 242
- 16.4 Rewarding People 244
  - 16.4.1 Goal-Setting and Specific Targets 244
  - 16.4.2 Tangible Rewards 245
  - 16.4.3 Work That Is Challenging, but Not Overwhelming ... 247
  - 16.4.4 The Fun Committee 249
- 16.5 Teams Competing Against One Another 249
- 16.6 Promotion Paths 250
  - 16.6.1 Leadership Promotion Paths 251

	16.7	There Is Only One Motivator	251
	16.8	Recruiting, Interviewing and Contracting	252
		16.8.1 Diversity and Inclusion	252
		16.8.2 Don't Fetishize Technical Skills in Interviews	253
		16.8.3 The Use of Contractors and Contracted Services	255
	16.9	Changing the Culture	255
		16.9.1 Look! I'll Change the Culture by Replacing the People!	256
		16.9.2 Being a Student of Corporate Culture	256
	16.10	How Team Roles Change	257
		16.10.1 Thinner Management Layers	257
		16.10.2 User Interface Designers	258
		16.10.3 Generalizing Specialists	259
	16.11	Allocating People's Time	260
		16.11.1 Competency Centers	260
		16.11.2 Time-Slicing People Is the Biggest Productivity Killer in the Known World	261
	16.12	HR Is a Big Part of an Agile Transformation	263
	References		264
17	**Buy Versus Build**		265
	17.1	The Character of Your IT Shop	265
	17.2	To Buy or to Build?	266
		17.2.1 What Business Are You In?	267
	17.3	It Might Not Be Buy Versus Build: It Could Be Buy and Build	270
	17.4	Where Are You on the Emotional Spectrum of Packaged Software?	271
	Reference		272
18	**A Brief Note About Using Offshore Teams**		273
	18.1	Mind-Body Separation	273
		18.1.1 Slice at the Thinnest Part	274
	18.2	High and Low Bandwidth Communication	276
		18.2.1 Those Tricky Metaphors	277
	18.3	Large Distributed Teams Can Work	278
19	**Highlighting the Differences Between Software Product Companies and Internal IT**		279
	19.1	The Role of Software in Your Organization	279
		19.1.1 Making Money by Selling Software Versus a Software Cost Center	280
		19.1.2 A Software Subsidiary	282
	19.2	Product Managers and Product Owners	282
	19.3	Selling Software or Just Using It	283
20	**Conclusion**		285

Today's Problems with Enterprise Business Software

1

Keys to Reading This Book

You'll notice that the chapters have certain common sections at the beginning and end. At the beginning of every chapter is "Test Drive Your Knowledge"—a quick, three question quiz to help you assess the state of your knowledge for what is in the coming chapter. A corresponding "Test Drive Your Knowledge Again" is at the end of every chapter, allowing you to see what you've learned by the end. These quizzes don't cover every point of the chapter but try to hit some of the highlights.

Certain chapters also have a section at the end called "Try This Next." This section provides summary action items for various levels of readers: executives, managers and individual contributors. Feel free to use these to implement the ideas you've just read.

And, finally, at the end of each chapter, we list the references of books and articles that we've mentioned within the text.

> **Test Drive Your Knowledge**
> Answer the following questions with the knowledge you have now. Then answer them again at the end of this chapter.
>
> 1. What does it mean for a team to be operating "mechanically?" In what ways is this helpful or harmful?
> 2. What problems do organizations have with scaling Agile practices?
> 3. What problems do organizations have with sustaining Agile practices?

1.1 The New, New Thing

I'm about to introduce you to the most amazing set of best practices. A few years ago, I was conducting a workshop using the "old techniques" and suddenly someone put up their hand and asked "How can you prove that this technique works?" I was embarrassed. I had no answer.

I set about measuring what the results were after each workshop. To my shock, I found out that the "old techniques" were not working at all. They weren't producing the results I had imagined. I began a search for some "new techniques." I stumbled upon them while working with some friends and began using them. Do you know what? They worked. I used them here, I used them there. I continually fine-tuned them until I was sure they worked in every situation. I passed them on to other people and they worked again! People said it was like magic! It was a "secret sauce!" And now I am presenting them to you! Finally, you have something that truly works. These best practices are proven to work!

This all sounded good. So, you, dear reader, tried these best practices. Proven to work, after all.

But they didn't work. False advertising? Lies, distortions and chicanery?

No. That can't be what it is. These are proven best practices, after all. It must have been some aspect you did wrong. Something didn't make the translation when you read that book. So, you get certified, read all the blogs, attend a bunch of conferences. You hire a consultant and he patiently explains what you're doing wrong. He leaves, but nothing gets better. You dive into more details. The devil is in the details, y'know?

You try and you try.

But you fail and fail.

Then, after a while, you give up.

You abandon this set of best practices for a new set. Far better than that old stuff! We fixed all the problems! Brand new name! Brand new website! Brand new meta-model! Brand new certification program (a bit more expensive than the last one, but totally worth it). To be honest, you knew all along that the old stuff didn't work; it was so stupid when you look back on it!

And the cycle repeats. Our industry has been doing this for decades now.

In the early 1980s, best practices came from places like IBM, Bell Labs, ITT, Harvard, P&G, James Martin, Texas Instruments, Software AG, Xerox, Cray, 3M and Lockheed. CASE tools! Inverted list databases! Supercomputers! Spiral development! That was where the innovation was happening. We were all sure of it.

In the 1990s, we unceremoniously discarded those former idols because now it was all about Intel, Microsoft, General Electric, Progressive Insurance, Rational, Stanford, Yahoo, Tata, Arthur Andersen, SAP and Motorola. These were our true thought leaders. Let's code like they code! Recruit like they recruit! Manage like they manage! Did you know their methodology takes up eleven binders!

Then Motorola suddenly shrank to a shadow of its former self. Yahoo lost its way. Microsoft and General Electric flattened out. Arthur Andersen disappeared overnight. The amazing cost benefits of offshore work became...less amazing.

Today, in 2017, there is an avalanche of videos, books and blog posts from companies like Amazon, Facebook, Spotify, Valve, Andreessen Horowitz, Y Combinator, MuleSoft, Pivotal Labs, Tesla, Uber, Netflix and, particularly, Google. If only we could align our practices with what these successful companies do, we'd really thrive!

Ah! But we've dated ourselves! If you're reading this book in 2027, whose best practices are we emulating now? Are any of these 2017 firms even still around?

Here is what we all must realize. Success in software development goes beyond frantically "copying the successful."[1] It goes beyond "best practices." There is more to it. In the course of these chapters, we'll try to explain what is missing.

There's another problem with best practice models. They tend to describe what we call "the city on the hill." They describe the end-state, the beautiful place where we'd all like to be. But they all miss one important piece. They miss the journey to the city on the hill. That's where we intend to help with this book.

1.2 Cheap Green Shirts

Once[2] upon[3] a time there was a clothing manufacturing company called CheapGreenShirts.com. The company had several Agile teams that were doing a great job and were highly productive. Their velocity was high, the teams were happy and the business was benefiting.

"I think we can juice these teams up even more," said one of the vice-presidents. "I've noticed that Team Antwerp is doing significantly better than the other teams, so we should take the best practices from Team Antwerp and give them to the other teams. That way, we'll have all teams performing at the level of Team Antwerp. And finally, we'll have some standardization around here. It will be great!"

---

[1] This best practices model goes far beyond software. The vast majority of business, career and self-help books have been presenting the same "copy the successful" idea since Tom Peters first wrote his book in the 1980s. For the record, almost none of Tom Peters' originally profiled companies are still around. The same is true for other books of this ilk (e.g., *Good to Great*, etc.).

[2] Reprinted with the kind permission of *Methods and Tools* magazine, Spring 2010 issue (author: Daryl Kulak).

[3] Thank you to Gene Johnson for this great example of separating the decision making from the work.

So the vice-president hired a group of Agile experts that he called a Software Engineering Process Group (SEPG) that was to advise the teams. The SEPG (pronounced seepage, seriously) experts carefully examined each practice used by Team Antwerp and the other teams, harvested them and chose the best of the best, then gave them back to the teams.

Surprisingly, the teams didn't use many of these redistributed practices. The SEPG experts were incensed. "These teams don't want to learn how to do things better, they're resistant to change" the SEPG experts groaned. "The SEPG dudes don't understand what we do," said the teams.

So the vice-president mandated that the groups use what the SEPG experts had come up with. Now with a gun to their heads, the teams dutifully used the new practices. At this point, velocity dropped and defects increased for each and every group, including Team Antwerp. How could this happen?

Stories like this one exist in many corporations, nonprofits and government agencies around the world. When we moved teams to Agile practices, including short sprints, cards on the wall, engaged product owners, we were supposed to rid ourselves of these problems. And yet, even with Agile practices firmly in place, organizations make mistakes just like the one above. Should vice-presidents just keep their great ideas to themselves? Should SEPG stick to being a plumbing term?

We'd like to look at how to improve our software development teams beyond the usual Agile practices. There is a whole world beyond product owners, user stories and burndown charts that is worth exploring, and we'd like to explore it with you.

1.3 Help! We're Terrible!

If any other industry had the problems of our software industry, they would have been taken out back and shot. But somehow we've managed to survive. We regularly slip deadlines. As a rule, not an exception. We often don't provide what our stakeholders ask for. We spend money lavishly but our results lack.

Certain Silicon Valley companies, like Google, Tesla and others, seem to be doing a pretty good job of advancing the software industry, but in the world of enterprise business applications, we are getting worse. Custom software projects, especially the large ones, fail regularly. Implementations of packaged applications, like SAP, Oracle, etc., should, in theory be more successful but, crazily, they are actually more likely to fail than the custom work, and getting worse each year (according to Panorama Consulting's ERP Report[4]).

And, in a way, Google and Tesla are making our job of enterprise software even harder, because now users have even higher expectations of what software can and

---

[4]bit.ly/PanoramaERP

should do. If we create a search function in our own enterprise application, it better be as intuitive and responsive as Google Search. If we create an on-board vehicle software, it will be compared to Tesla's Model S. Good luck with that.

We'd like to examine the various factors that are causing these failures. Some factors are big, some are smaller. But we hope to present a reasonably complete picture of the current difficulties and our suggested fixes.

We see two major aspects of the failure of enterprise software endeavors (custom and packaged) in our industry today:

- Software projects quickly become disconnected from the business value they should be providing.
- Improvement initiatives, including transformation to Agile practices, may succeed in the short term but are not sustainable. They backslide.

Instead of quickly jumping into discussions on how to fix things, we would like to do some homework on how these issues have become issues in the first place. We hope if we truly understand why the issues crop up, we can avoid memorizing volumes of best practices.

1.4 Aristotle, Descartes and Disconnection to Business Value

Aristotle, student of Plato and consummate philosopher himself, explored physics, metaphysics, biology, zoology, logic, ethics, poetry and politics like no other before him and probably none since. But he also examined something he called "systems" that dealt with relationships between factors crossing the boundaries of the other sciences. Central to Aristotle's view of systems was what he called the "Four Causes."

Aristotle's Four Causes theory states that every system must have four elements: efficient, material, formal and final. The efficient cause is the part of the system that gets things done; it represents the labor. The material cause is the raw material, which could be coal or wood or even more ethereal elements like ideas or organizations. The formal cause represents the design or "form" of the end product and the methodology of how to get there. And the final cause is the purpose of the whole endeavor, the end consumer or the essential reason for the existence of the system.

Aristotle created the Four Causes to answer the question "Why does a thing exist?" He found the following four reasons that a thing might exist.

If we use a chair as our example, the wood, nails and glue that went into the chair constitute the **material cause** (see Fig. 1.1). Why does this chair exist? Because it is made of wood, nails and glue.

Fig. 1.1 Aristotle's Four Causes—material cause. © 2017 by Daryl Kulak and Hong Li—reprinted with permission

Fig. 1.2 Aristotle's Four Causes—efficient cause. © 2017 by Daryl Kulak and Hong Li—reprinted with permission

The **efficient cause** for the chair is the labor that produced it, possibly handmade by a woodworker or maybe in a factory pumping out lots of identical chairs. Why does this chair exist? Because the woodworker (Fig. 1.2) produced it.

The **formal cause** for the chair is the form it took as well as the process the woodworker followed. See Fig. 1.3. Why does this chair exist? Because the woodworker took the correct steps to create something in the "form" of a chair.

1.4 Aristotle, Descartes and Disconnection to Business Value

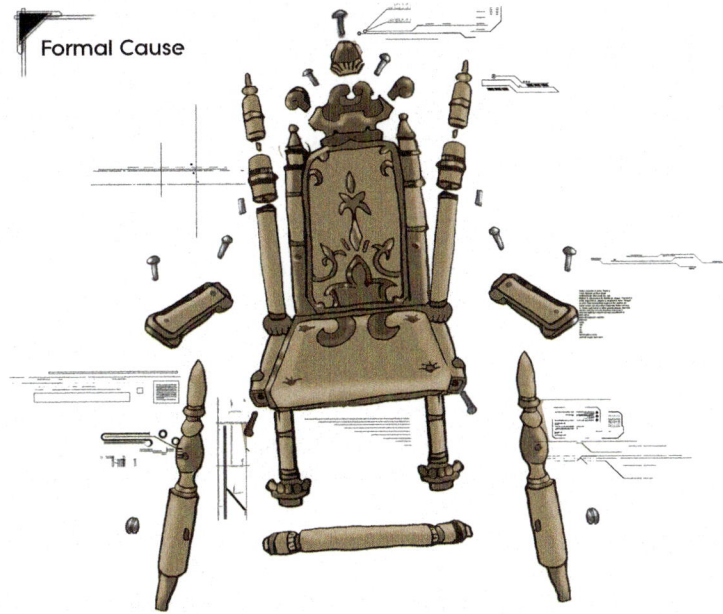

Fig. 1.3 Aristotle's Four Causes—formal cause. © 2017 by Daryl Kulak and Hong Li—reprinted with permission

Fig. 1.4 Aristotle's Four Causes—final cause. © 2017 by Daryl Kulak and Hong Li—reprinted with permission

And the **final cause** for the chair is the purpose. This can be general or specific. The final cause for a chair might be that people need it so they can sit (general). Or it might be that the chair is needed to ornament a cathedral for the pope's visit next year. See Fig. 1.4.

You can see how this could relate to a software system as well. The user stories, ideas and opinions are the material cause (material causes don't need to be "materially physical"). The team (including the product owner) creating the software is the efficient cause. The methodology the team follows as well as their software architecture make up the formal cause. And the business value is the final cause, the "why" we need this software.

Aristotle's theory of systems served the Western world well for a long time.

Then, almost 2000 years later, another influential fellow came along named René Descartes, who is often called the "Father of Modern Philosophy." Descartes, like Aristotle, did not limit himself to one small specialty; instead he excelled across philosophy, mathematics and many branches of science.

Descartes pioneered what became called "dualism." Descartes saw that there was a problem with trying to understand the human body as well as the human mind. Where did one begin and the other end? So, he separated them. In his writings, he showed how the human body could be seen as a complex machine, digesting food, producing work and excreting waste. And he pushed the mind aside, and with it the soul. Descartes made this separation for a very important and personal reason. He saw the example of Galileo, several decades before him, who had pointed out that the earth revolves around the sun, not the other way around, and the powerful Catholic Church tried him and found him guilty of heresy. Galileo was put under house arrest until his death. Descartes did not want to raise the ire of the Church. The easiest way to avoid this was to find a compromise where he could give the Church its domain (the mind, the soul) and science its own domain (the mechanical human body). It was a stroke of genius and it helped to pave a road for science and medicine for centuries to come.

But what Descartes had also done was to tear Aristotle's idea of Four Causes apart. Descartes was saying that only three causes belong to science—efficient, material and formal. The fourth cause (final) must be left to the Church. Scientists could not discuss the "why" of nature. The church could define the final cause as "Everything exists for the glory of God" and Descartes was off the hook. It was a good career move for Descartes, to be sure, but it was not good from a systems perspective.

1.5 The Mechanical Business World

As useful as the Cartesian compromise was in his time, and as much as it accelerated progress throughout the Renaissance, it is now hurting our society, our economy, our natural environment and our very lives and happiness. By disconnecting the mechanical world from the world of ideas, morals, emotions and spirit, we create problems for ourselves. Climate change is a result of prioritizing the mechanical production of energy above the ethics of harming our planet. Viewing people who commit crimes as "sand in the gears" of our civilization causes us to discard people into prisons rather than seeing them as people who might have potential for rehabilitation. Viewing animals as machines causes us to build factory farms where pigs, cows and chickens live in their own excrement and get no exercise except walking down the plank to slaughter.

Descartes' compromise also contributes to many of our problems in software development. We disconnect our three scientific causes (efficient, material, formal) from the final cause. Here's one of the ways we do this.

Several highly-placed executives decide on the purpose of a particular software application to be built. They document a return-on-investment (ROI) statement to show that the project is worth doing. Then they pass on the ROI document along with a specification to a technical team who focuses on getting it done. The technical team often pays attention only to the specification given them by the executive decision-makers and does not follow back to the ROI or the original purpose. Thus, the technical team often loses their way and builds something that satisfies the specs, but does not really address the purpose. The ROI document stays on the shelf and doesn't have any effect on the software being built, except to get the thing kicked off in the first place.

We've naturally separated the mind (the executives) from the body (team doing the work), just as Descartes taught us.

We can see this again and again with software projects. Teams build stuff that turns out not to be useful. "It isn't my job to worry about business value. I build what I'm told to build."

Thanks a lot, Descartes.[5]

Throughout this book, we will look for ways to repair the damage that Descartes has done. But it won't be easy. Cartesian dualism is what we've all grown up with. It was in our education. It is endemic to our Western societies. It's in our blood. It runs through the foundations of our corporations. But we must try to undo some of the dualism that says that we can see people like machines, and we can disconnect the final cause, the purpose, away from the work being done. We should not disconnect them. The work being done and the final cause should be intertwined and connected as closely as possible.

1.5.1 The Question of Business Value

This book asserts that there is a fundamental error in many software development efforts. The error is to disconnect the day-to-day effort from *business value*. In any

---

[5]To be fair, if Descartes were alive today, he would probably challenge the status quo as much as he did during his lifetime. He would look at the problems created by the mind/body dualism and he'd set about to fixing them, as should we.

situation where we look at the business value question at the beginning "What is this thing worth?" and then we abandon the question soon after, we're causing ourselves a headache. The typical project management approach to strictly enforce controls to ensure "traceability[6]" to the business value does not usually work. It gets too complicated and we spend more time tracing things and less time building things. Instead, the question of business value should be on everyone's mind at all times throughout the lifecycle of creating good software. Every developer, tester, analyst, UX designer and manager[7] should be thinking "Is this thing worthwhile? Is it going to help people? Is it going to make money?" If we only think about the value question at the start and then we get busy "doing stuff" we run a terrible risk of forgetting why we're doing what we're doing.

The other side of this error is to segregate the question of business value to only a few people. We use the minds of experienced business executives to calculate the value of a piece of software and then, once we "know" it's valuable, the work moves on to the "doers" who take that assurance and make the thing work. This is wrong. Everyone involved, from the most gray-haired executive to the most wet-behind-the-ears intern should be part of the ongoing debate about the value of the end product. What can we do to make the product more valuable? How can we cut the cost of development but not lose any value? Are there alternative ideas that get us to the value faster? These are debates that should occur almost every day on every software initiative, but they don't always happen.

The improvements we've seen when this simple (but tough) change happens are astounding. We've seen product costs decrease by 80% in some cases. We've seen products being delivered earlier than expected. We've seen stakeholders given the freedom to dramatically redirect the team multiple times to improve the result. These are possible and favorable and even likely outcomes if we can make this change in our thinking.

We will present our ideas on how to help you change your thinking and that of your organization. We rely on the principles brought forth from the world of systems thinking, also called systems science. This realm has had a few glimmers of recognition in the software world, mostly from Six Sigma, Lean and the work of Peter Senge in *The Fifth Discipline* (Senge 1994). But the academic work being done in systems thinking bears little resemblance to these popular representations of it, as we'll examine later.

---

[6]What we normally see is that project managers ask every team member to create heavy documentation to establish "traceability" from the executive vision and value statements. This process, unfortunately, shifts the focus of accountability away from "creating value through software" to "creating paper documents." Team members worry less about "am I creating something valuable" and worry more about "did I check off all the documents on the list."

[7]The role of the product owner doesn't solve this dilemma by itself. It just delegates the "value thing" to one person, who must, by themselves, remember why we are building the software. But the job of business value must belong to every team member, as we will illustrate in the coming chapters.

We will also discuss many aspects of Agile software development. This term "Agile" (with a capital A) has become a very popular topic, but we have our own take on it as well. The most mainstream versions of the Agile idea are actually the source of a set of problems we see with today's software teams. We will show which parts of Agile are helpful and productive and which parts are red herrings, at best, and damaging to business value, at worst.

1.6 Scalability and Sustainability

Next, let's examine sustainability of improvements and scalability from small teams to the larger organization.

Organizations face two particular problems in trying to improve processes for software development.

The first is that they find that the new processes cannot scale. That is, things seemed to work on the first few small projects, but once we tried them on larger initiatives, perhaps packaged software implementations or with large, distributed teams, things fell apart.

The second problem is sustainability. Things improve for a while but then they degrade until things are basically back where we started. Improvements wash away.

These two problems—scalability and sustainability—are related. They happen for the same reason.

1.6.1 The Story of Sticky LaGrange

Once upon a time,[8] in a company called Neverland Insurance, there was a team and their Agile consultant. Together, they decided to try to build an application. The team was about ten people, and the Agile consultant had a really, really good reputation as a brilliant person and dedicated Agilist. The team felt lucky to have him. The Agile consultant's name was Sticky LaGrange.

Sticky helped the team get started and taught them all the Agile practices. The team carefully followed Sticky's words and asked him questions whenever they weren't exactly sure what to do. Sticky was helpful and patient. Not only that, but Sticky prided himself on writing more code than any other team member, even though he was spending so much time coaching people. Sticky was truly amazing.

At the end, the application was finished on time and within budget. Everyone at Neverland was so impressed. The team was justifiably proud.

---

[8]This story reprinted with the kind permission of *Methods and Tools* magazine, Spring 2010 issue (author: Daryl Kulak).

Then a wicked warlord of Neverland cut budgets and the team had to say goodbye to Sticky. Surely they could succeed without Sticky; he had taught them so well. So the team went on to another application and began work. They tried to remember everything that Sticky had told them. If in doubt, someone would inevitably ask "What would Sticky do?" The group would try to remember what Sticky would have done and then replicate it faithfully.

But things were falling apart. Different team members remembered Sticky's advice differently. And sometimes, inexplicably, Sticky's advice, remembered accurately, seemed to be wrong! When applied in this new situation, Sticky's advice broke down. How could Sticky's advice be wrong?

Some team members said that maybe they should go beyond Sticky's advice. But other people thought this was a terrible idea. "That's not True Agile!" they cried. Why deviate from Sticky's advice if it had worked so well the first time?

The team at Neverland Insurance had fallen into a rut where they had to follow the advice of an expert. Even when the expert was gone, the team had to recall exactly how the expert would have approached the new problem and try to replicate that exactly.

These experts are most obvious when they are consultants, but this can happen with books, articles, blog posts or industry-standardized practices or certification programs, such as Scrum Alliance or Scrum.org.

Whenever a team gets into this compliance mode, they will see problems with scaling and sustainability. They are performing **mechanically**. And teams that are doing "Mechanical Agile" (which we will explain more later) always get into trouble, because they will always hit a snag that falls in between the advice they received from the expert (consultant, book, alliance, etc.). And as soon as that happens, they will have to try to guess what the expert would do, instead of applying their own intelligence and doing the best thing they can think to do.

Mechanical teams will never be able to scale their work, as in adapt their practices to larger and larger efforts. They will also lose their sustainability, because as the environment around them changes, their processes will become more and more brittle and the good advice of yesterday will become the terrible advice of today.

Scalability and sustainability both arise from a mechanical approach to software process. In the rest of this book, we will examine the various flavors of this mechanical approach and, subsequently, ways to avoid them and prosper with more adaptive thinking and doing.

1.7 Yes, But What About the Illth?

John Ruskin was much more than just a "man about town." He was well-known throughout London, being the foremost art critic of his time, but also dabbling in artistic and writing endeavors himself. Ruskin traveled throughout the country a lot, as well as Belgium, Germany and Italy, even in his childhood. International travel helped give him a perspective that other British citizens might not have had.

Ruskin lived during the middle of the nineteenth century, and was able to see the industrial revolution unfold from the vantage point of its global center—London. He was amazed to see the factories springing up, mass-producing textiles, metals and new chemicals that would help many nations rise up from poverty and start to experience luxuries that only the rich had previously known.

But Ruskin was lucid enough to notice that the revolution was producing good things as well as bad things, and it worried him that the bad was getting ignored. He could see the factory generating great new products, but he could also plainly see the pollution caused by the factory, the concentrating power among the factory owners, the rapid unemployment of manual craftsmen like weavers and blacksmiths and other very significant problems. Why did so many people (those in power, particularly) only focus on the positive aspects of industry and practically ignore the negative side effects?

Ruskin, being the intellectual he was, put a word to it. He called these negative side effects "illth." This is a nice little word, because it serves as an antonym to "wealth." Those factories were causing great increases in wealth, but they were simultaneously causing illth, in terms of those problems with pollution, loss of livelihood, disruptions, etc.

Ruskin's word has lasted until today, even if it has been used only sparingly in recent times. It's a great word, and it applies to situations we see today. When a Walmart moves into town, it creates great wealth, certainly. New shoppers have access to those low, low prices. New jobs are available for workers in the community. However, the Walmart also creates illth. Traffic congestion happens around the store, depression of wages, lack of health benefits for workers, low quality goods, competition against local mom-and-pop shops, and others. Is the Walmart a good thing or a bad thing? Most people pick one side or another. But a systems thinker tries to take in the whole situation and learn about the "wealth" and the "illth."

1.7.1 Agile Illth

We need to see an Agile team the same way John Ruskin saw those factories. Yes, a new Agile team can produce some amazing results, but it also produces a fair amount of illth. Let's examine some of that illth, why don't we?

Agile Breaks Budgeting
Agile teams often cause problems with budgeting. If IT budgets are project-based, and those projects are often long, then an Agile mindset may run counter to the budgeting process. Agile teams that try to be adaptive, that allow requirements to flex as the business flexes, can be problematic for an inflexible, annual budgeting process.

Agile Breaks Metrics
Imagine being a program manager. You see ninety-nine projects that all report results in terms of person-hours and costs, but one project is giving you something called a burndown chart and talking about "storypoints." What help is that, exactly?

Agile Breaks Resource Management
Waterfall teams need business analysts and stakeholders at the beginning of a project, designers and developers in the middle and testers and business stakeholders at the end. Agile teams need almost all the roles all the time. How is that going to fit in with our enterprise resource plan??

Agile Breaks Performance Appraisals
Agile teams work best when people can fulfill multiple roles. For example, you may have a business analyst who can also function as a tester, or a developer who can easily play the role of architect or database administrator. This can cause problems with annual performance appraisals, because any appraisal is going to measure a person against the expectations of their "role," and if they've been spending time outside of that role, it will look bad come appraisal time.

Agile Breaks Risk Management
Although Agile teams tend to be inherently less risky than waterfall projects, they do not often produce the same written artifacts that we are used to seeing, like issue logs and risk logs. This is problematic for outsiders who want to know that the team has a grip on the issues and risks that they are facing and has a detailed plan for mitigating each problem or potential problem.

Agile Breaks Architecture Review Boards
Agile teams use a concept of "emergent architecture," which means that they do not try to think through their architecture completely at the beginning of a project; they start to code the solution and let the architectural needs surface before they rush to address them. This drives enterprise architects batty, because they want to have some assurance that the team understands the challenges in front of them and how to solve them in a way that won't cause problems for other applications, existing and under development.

Agile Breaks Downstream Processes
Agile teams may produce software on a much faster cadence than downstream groups, like release management, for instance, are able to handle (Fig. 1.5). Is that a fault of the Agile team or the release management team? Everything worked fine before this Agile team started causing problems!

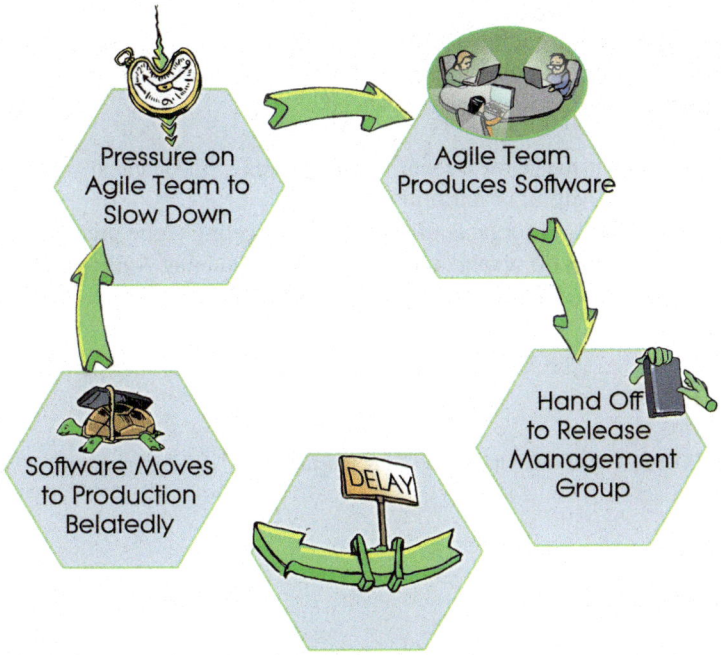

Fig. 1.5 Agile team and release management interactions. © 2017 by Daryl Kulak and Hong Li—reprinted with permission

Agile Breaks Everything

You name any external stakeholder, a new Agile team will cause problems for them. Executives who sign the checks, Program Management Office (PMO), Enterprise Architecture, Database Administration, Audit and Controls. It's unanimous. Agile teams cause illth.

Later in this book, we talk about how to address each type of Agile illth. At this point, our goal is to show that Agile falters in its scalability and sustainability in enterprises because it tends to focus too much on what's happening "inside the team room" and not enough with how that team is interacting with the groups around them. No amount of Scrum Certification classes will address this problem. We have to simultaneously have an inside and outside perspective when we're working in an Agile team room.

1.8 Our Software Industry Problems Can Be Overcome

Yes, the enterprise IT industry has big problems, and we've had them for years. But there are ways to address the problems. We'll just have to look a bit further than "best practices in a box" given to us by a consultant. It may, in fact, require a new way of thinking.

> **Test Drive Your Knowledge Again**
> Answer the following questions with the knowledge you have gained reading this chapter. Have your answers changed?
>
> 1. What does it mean for a team to be operating "mechanically?" In what ways is this helpful or harmful to the team?
> 2. What problems do organizations have with scaling Agile practices?
> 3. What problems do organizations have with sustaining Agile practices?

Reference

Senge PM (1994) The fifth discipline: the art & practice of the learning organization. Doubleday

The Scholars of Systems Thinking 2

> *What is a system? As any poet knows, a system is a way of looking at the world. A system is a point of view—natural for a poet, yet terrifying for a scientist!*
> Gerald Weinberg, *systems scientist and computer scientist*
>
> *Learn how to see. Realize that everything connects to everything else.*
> Leonardo da Vinci

> **Test Drive Your Knowledge**
> Answer the following questions with the knowledge you have now. Then answer them again at the end of this chapter.
>
> 1. What is the difference between hard and soft systems thinking?
> 2. Which school of systems thinking does Six Sigma fall into?
> 3. How long has systems thinking been with us?

2.1 Hard and Soft Systems Thinking

Systems thinking is often defined as the whole being greater than the sum of its parts. This is a simplistic view, but good enough for now.

The term "systems thinking" may seem quite odd. What, do we just sit around and think about systems?? No, it is more than that. What we've found is that, with the introduction of a few ideas about systems, our point of view in a situation can change dramatically, often to make the formerly most obvious course of action

Fig. 2.1 Hard and soft systems thinking. © 2017 by Daryl Kulak and Hong Li—reprinted with permission

seem entirely wrong. By changing our point of view, we can solve problems in new and unexpected ways. That is what systems thinking is all about.

Systems thinking[1] has many schools of thought. Advocates of familiar business topics like Six Sigma, lean manufacturing, total quality management (TQM), chaos and complexity theory all consider themselves to be a part of systems thinking. However, these represent only one branch which is called hard systems thinking. There is another branch called soft systems thinking.

Hard systems thinking refers to a type of system that can be reduced to an algorithm, or a set of algorithms. In order for hard systems thinking to be helpful, the system under study must operate mechanically and be predictable given a certain set of inputs. Figure 2.1 shows hard systems thinking as a set of gears, physical and mechanical.

---

[1] You may consider systems thinking and systems science as synonyms. Even in academic circles there isn't much difference between these terms.

2.1 Hard and Soft Systems Thinking

Soft systems thinking refers to systems that are not inherently predictable. This encompasses systems where people and perceptions are involved, where algorithms cannot accurately capture what might happen given a set of inputs. Practitioners of soft systems thinking do not see a system "out there" in reality. Instead, they think of reality as something that is socially constructed, constantly changing based on the stakeholders' perceptions.

Figure 2.1 shows soft systems thinking as a party on the beach. Think of the personal dynamics at play in any situation involving humans, whether at work or at play. Humans always bring with them human intentions, which make things much more complicated than the hard systems scenarios.

For many years, people have tried to use hard systems thinking with systems that involve people and perceptions. The resulting algorithmic models are not able to predict results and give us a false sense of security, as complicated mathematics often does.

The most useful of these two types for looking at software team dynamics is soft systems thinking. People cannot be reduced to machines and their activities cannot be reduced to algorithms.

The leaders of soft systems thinking are sometimes considered pariahs to the hard systems world. The hard side has a longer history and has many more conferences and methodologies. But, over time, soft systems are making inroads as people grapple with the limitations of the hard side.

From now on, when we refer to "systems thinking" you can assume we mean soft systems thinking.

Systems thinking has been with us since the days of ancient Greece, but it has experienced a renaissance of sorts since the 1930s. You can think of systems thinking as a rejection of Cartesian dualism, mentioned in Chap. 1. Systems thinking extends across[2] the typical scientific boundaries, because it applies to biology, physics, organizational theory, logic, operations research and business.

Systems thinking forms the backbone of this book. Our advice is a combination of our own experiences in decades of consulting combined with systems thinking principles. These principles and ideas come from a particular set of scholars who have been working hard to develop the best theories and practical usage for all of us in business, government and nonprofit.

Let us now introduce the systems science scholars who have influenced us so greatly (in chronological order):

---

[2] For this reason, people who are truly "systems scientists" often do not have a home on university campuses because no one can decide which building to put them in!

Aristotle
- The world's first known systems thinker, creator of the "four causes"

Kurt Gödel
- Austrian-American logician made famous with his "incompleteness theorem," which states that a human-constructed system that is consistent cannot be proven to be complete (including mathematics itself)

Karl Ludwig von Bertalanffy
- Austrian-American theoretical biologist and systems thinking pioneer who co-created "general systems theory" and charismatically led the systems movement in the twentieth century

W. Ross Ashby
- English psychiatrist and pioneer in the cybernetics field, creator of the "law of requisite variety"

C. West Churchman
- American systems thinker who helped to create operations research only to abandon it when he could see that his followers were turning it into a mechanical pursuit; moved on to become a systems thinker with von Bertalanffy and Ackoff

Russell L. Ackoff
- American cohort of Churchman in creating the field of operations research and then moving on to systems thinking, later wrote the book *Management f-Laws*

W. Edwards Deming
- American statistician who helped the Japanese perform their economic miracle after World War II; his theories and practices inspired the vast productivity improvements at Toyota, Honda and other companies

Peter Checkland
- English businessman and professor and creator of "soft systems methodology," an alternative to the mechanical disciplines of hard systems thinking

Peter Drucker
- Prolific American business author who coined the term "knowledge worker"

Edward de Bono
- Maltese philosopher and author, originator of "lateral thinking" and "six thinking hats" (generally not considered a systems thinker, but we owe a debt to his work nonetheless)

Werner Ulrich
- Swiss social scientist, one of the creators of "critical systems thinking" and boundary critique

2.1 Hard and Soft Systems Thinking

Robert Rosen
- American-Canadian theoretical biologist who created the "M-R model" and produced significant theories about the organization of biological and social organizations

Peter Senge
- American professor and consultant who wrote the book *The Fifth Discipline* and popularized cybernetics

Nassim Nicholas Taleb
- Lebanese-American trader and philosopher who wrote the books *The Black Swan* and *Antifragile*

Gerald Midgley
- English professor and practitioner who wrote the book *Systemic Intervention* and developed theories on boundary critique and methodological pluralism

These are writers, professors, researchers and practitioners who have heavily influenced our thinking. If your idea of "systems thinking" is limited to Lean/Six Sigma, you're in for a surprise. Our systems thinking scholars are part of a different branch of systems thinking away from the more popular business streams. We think you'll find that this branch of systems thinking is useful, fun and very human.

2.1.1 Don't Worry: This Will Not Be a Complete History of Systems Thinking

It would be easy (and fun—for the authors!) to dive into a giant historical chapter explaining how systems thinking came about and all the details it entails. But you are most likely a business and/or technology reader. You may or may not care about that. You are likely most interested in "what to do about it" rather than knowing all the twists and turns of the genesis of these ideas.

On the other hand, some of our readers will be interested in the history and the theories.

What to do? Here, we will make good use of the World Wide Web. We will minimize the systems thinking background in this book to describing the principles that serve as the backbone for the rest of our book. The practical IT reader can breeze through the Systems Thinking Principles chapter easily and jump straight into "how to" advice of the upcoming chapters.

For our readers who are intrigued by systems thinking and want to learn more, we've created a website:

EnterpriseAgile.biz

This site has all the information[3] we've gathered and/or written on our scholars (those listed above) and their theories, as well as our interpretations and mapping to ideas in this book. This site is not password-protected; it is free to all.

2.2 Systems Thinking Forms the Basis

We will refer to the scholars here and there in the upcoming chapters, even tell a few stories about them. But for the details on their theories and the connections to the ideas in this book, the website will be most helpful.

Systems thinking forms the basis for our book and our worldview. We will work to explain our ideas for improvements and connect them to the principles of systems thinking, as they relate to software development.

> If you find you are intrigued by our references to systems thinking and want to get involved and learn more, the conference series that will most interest you will be the **International Society for the Systems Sciences (ISSS)**. The Society holds an annual conference focused on soft systems thinking which rotates between a North American location and elsewhere in the world. Check the website for the next location and date of the conference. We've personally attended for years and greatly enjoy the camaraderie of other systems thinkers!
>
> isss.org

> **Test Drive Your Knowledge Again**
> Answer the following questions with the knowledge you have gained from this chapter. Have your answers changed?
>
> 1. What is the difference between hard and soft systems thinking?
> 2. Which school of systems thinking does Six Sigma fall into?
> 3. How long has systems thinking been with us?

---

[3]For those who enjoy the work of Jason Kinsey, our illustrator, we also include freely available files of the illustrations in this book that you may use under the Creative Commons license.

3. Worldview and Intentions

> *Systems thinking begins when first you see the world through the eyes of another.*
> C. West Churchman—systems thinking pioneer

> **Test Drive Your Knowledge**
> Answer the following questions with the knowledge you have now. Then answer them again at the end of this chapter.
>
> 1. Right action, right speech, right intention, right view. Which of these is the foundation of the others?
> 2. I can repeat what I did successfully on my last project. Is this a right view?
> 3. How can Agile teams follow all the practices perfectly and still fail?

3.1 Borrowing from the Buddha

In order to further explain why we should not reduce the success of an Agile project into a few mechanical and deterministic procedures, we'd like to borrow some wisdom from the Buddhist philosophy. Professor Gerald Midgley, one of our systems scholars, and some of his students have compared systems thinking and Buddhism. They found Buddhism could help the dialogue and learning in systems thinking. It might seem strange that we are bringing religious teaching into this technology book, but Buddhism has the best explanation in layman's terms that we've found to tell the stories about how we can make impact on the nondeterministic world.

Buddhism has something called the Noble Eightfold Path to instruct its followers on how to live a good life. Here are the four parts of the path:

Right view
Right intention
Right speech
Right action

There are other parts to the path (four more, to be precise: livelihood, mindfulness, effort and concentration) but we'll focus on just the four we've listed above.

If you look at the four folds of the path, you can see that today's Agile and Scrum experts focus almost entirely on the last two—right speech and right action. Today's experts think about what we should call things (ScrumMaster, sprint, product owner, user story, etc.) and try to choose the right words and meanings (right speech). They also have extensive advice about picking certain "best practices" (right action). This is what methodologies have always been about. "Can you please tell me what to do?" is the question that most methodologies and experts try to answer as best they can. But these two parts are not enough!

Think of the four folds as supporting one another, as shown in Fig. 3.1. *Right worldview* is on the bottom; it is the foundation for all the rest. Next is *right intention*; without the proper intention, our words and actions are lost. Next comes *right speech*; we must choose our words carefully. And finally, and truly least of all, we have *right action*.

Let's examine each fold of the path.

3.1.1 Right View

Right view is the foundation to all the rest. If your team members' views are oriented towards success, the other pieces will fall into place. If not, nothing else will work.

Let's define "right view" as having a **worldview** that is helpful to a successful team. If you have a worldview, for example, that people cannot be trusted and it's a dog-eat-dog world, you cannot be successful for long. Your internal demons will tear down any temporary success you create. Think of the rise and fall of Bernie Madoff or Martin Shkreli. They saw the world cynically and thought they could profit from it. They had a worldview that justified their personal agenda...for a while, until that worldview was challenged by jail time.

George Lakoff (Lakoff 2014) describes two prevalent worldviews in American politics as the "strict father" and "nurturing parent" models. The people holding the strict father worldview think that other people should be watched closely to prevent wrongdoing, and punishment should follow any incorrect action. Politically, the

Fig. 3.1 Right worldview and right intention support the rest. © 2017 by Daryl Kulak and Hong Li—reprinted with permission

strict fathers align quite well with Republican party politics. Nurturing parents are more likely to see the good in people and to assume that most people have the ability to be rehabilitated and we should care about the less fortunate. These folks associate with Democratic party politics more than the others.

Think of a worldview as the accumulation of all your experiences in your life up until this moment. Your friends in grade school contributed to your worldview. If you were beaten by your father, that contributed to your worldview. If you had an inspiring mentor in your first job, they contributed to your worldview.

Think of each of us carrying around this giant worldview, with this accumulation of experiences, biases and opinions. When we view the world, we can only view it through this stuff. That means that our viewing screen is dirty, cracked and distorted. We don't see what's really there. The same is true for everyone else. None of us see what is really there.[1]

---

[1] If indeed, *anything **really is there***, but that's a topic for another book.

Each of us perceives situations through our worldview; we simply can't help it. When someone offers their "unbiased viewpoint" on a situation, you should probably laugh at them, because each of us brings our biases with us.

So, in a software development team, how do we deal with worldviews? Obviously, each of us will have a different worldview, causing us to see each situation vastly differently. What do we do about it?

Your first reaction might be to fix everyone else's worldviews. "Let's just clean off that dirt and fix the broken glass!" But we can't do that. Worldviews are very difficult to change. In a way, our worldview is how we got to survive to this point, so we are hesitant to give it up. Each of us sees our own worldview as a great benefit. It takes a lot to convince us differently.

Instead of trying to "fix" each other's worldviews, we need to figure out how to work with them. For instance, there is an Agile practice called "Bring the work to the team." It means that, rather than pulling together a team to do a project and then disbanding them, we should try to keep the team together and feed them projects one after another. It is a different way of managing the work, but why is it better? The reason it's better is because the team members, just by virtue of working together for a few months, can begin to understand each other's worldviews. They can figure out ways to communicate that can be understood by their teammates, even through all that dirt and broken glass.

Another helpful tool is using worldview as a conversation topic. If it is okay for us to talk about each of us having a different worldview, you and I can compare our worldviews and figure out how to work around the problems. Not everyone might be willing to share their worldview easily. For instance, if part of my worldview is that I don't trust Canadians, due to several bad experiences in my life where Canadians let me down, I might not be willing to disclose this prejudice so easily. But if you are actively trying to figure out my worldview, making guesses and working closely with me to try to understand me, you might figure out my prejudice and be able to work around it (unless you're a Canadian[2] of course, in which case, forget it).

Group Worldviews

It is quite possible for a group of people to share a worldview. Certainly, religions such as Islam, Buddhism, Christianity, Hinduism, etc. help to provide a group worldview. But group worldviews can occur on a smaller scale as well. On several occasions, we've had the chance to work with startup companies that started small, just two or three partners, and then grew quickly once their ideas proved correct and their customer base mushroomed. Those original partners hired more workers and the workers stayed. Who doesn't like working for a fast-growing startup? After a few years, the entire staff shares a common worldview. They look at their amazing

---

[2]Daryl is a Canadian-American, so he ought to be allowed to make this joke. And honestly, who doesn't get along with Canadians?

success to date and assume that the way forward must be an extension of the past. Often, this is a good assumption. But sometimes, it is blatantly false. Blatant, that is, to outsiders looking in, but not to the staff themselves. Everybody in the company can be blind to horrible problems or missed opportunities because they all share the worldview of how to achieve success. And they are "sure" of it, because it has worked so well for so long. But suddenly, it stops working.

This is how startups burn out and die, unless they can bring people in from the outside to shake things up. And even that is a difficult task.

One of our systems thinking scholars, Peter Checkland, uses a German word Weltanschauung, which translates (imperfectly) back to the English "world view." He feels like it is naive to investigate a business process or to implement a software system without looking at the worldviews held by the people involved—the stakeholders, executives, end users and implementors. How do they see the world? How will that affect what we're trying to do?

In our work, we've found that having dialogue around worldviews is tremendously helpful. You cannot always flatten the mountains or evaporate the rivers, but it is good to have a map telling you where the obstacles are so you can plan around them.

What Is a Successful Worldview?
Okay, so if your worldview can limit or enable your success, what is a good worldview to aspire towards? Well, we have a good example right in our midst. It's called the Agile Manifesto.

> **The Agile Manifesto**
> *We are uncovering better ways of developing software by doing it and helping others do it. Through this work we have come to value:*
>
> *– Individuals and interactions over processes and tools*
> *– Working software over comprehensive documentation*
> *– Customer collaboration over contract negotiation*
> *– Responding to change over following a plan*
>
> *That is, while there is value in the items on the right, we value the items on the left more.*
>
>   agilemanifesto.org

In most cases, Agile coaches or consultants try to translate the Manifesto directly and immediately into practices. "Okay, great, that's the Manifesto, but here is what you need to do." But let's hold back from that immediate translation. What if these Agile values can form our worldview instead? What if we can really take these into ourselves and allow them to penetrate how we see the world?

We believe the originators of the Agile Manifesto meant for these values[3] to be treated as a change to our worldview, and not just as instruction for different practices.

What is surprising is that our current Agile and Scrum processes, books and articles generally do not make an attempt to discuss worldviews. Team member's worldviews, and our knowledge of each other's worldviews, can make or break projects. It is also worth saying that we could perfectly follow the "actions" of Agile or Scrum and still mess things up. One reason for that is that the team members may have worldviews that conflict or that prevent the work from getting done.

Often our clients ask us "Which projects are not compatible with an Agile approach?" They are probably expecting us to reply that package implementations, mainframe technology, highly regulated industries or break/fix teams should not use Agile. But any project effort is compatible with using an iterative/incremental approach like Agile. What are not compatible are people. When people cannot adapt their own worldviews to something compatible with the Agile Manifesto, then failure may result. But it won't be the technical situation or the business needs. It will be the people.

Another reason the team might follow the Agile practices and still fail is a case of incompatible intentions.

3.1.2 Right Intention

"Right intention" refers to the reason you are doing what you are doing. If you, as a manager, are executing the practice of daily standups, let's say, think about why you are doing it. If your intention is to use the daily standup to have a tighter control on your team, then you will fail at the practice, no matter how well you execute the details of the practice.

> *But we kept it to exactly fifteen minutes, we always have it at 8:30 every morning, and we used a talking stick, and we didn't try to solve detailed problems, yet everyone hates the standup. What are we doing wrong??*

Intentions[4] are different for each of us. They spring from our worldviews. If I've noticed that people always disappoint me (worldview), then I want to ensure that I have controls in place to make sure they won't disappoint me this time (intention).

---

[3] Let's leave the principles from the Manifesto aside for this discussion.
[4] One aspect of the Agile movement that truly embodies "intention" is software craftsmanship. Many practitioners talk about setting intentions to be proud of the code you write, which has such a

Intentions can be tricky. Most of us hide our intentions. We might be embarrassed by them, or we might realize that our intentions do not match what our bosses or team members want, so it is advantageous to keep them out of sight. But they still influence our behavior. They change the way we execute the practices and can make those practices ineffective.

Managers make the most common intention problem when they endeavor to control their team. The managers have learned that they shouldn't openly "want" to control their teams in their Agile classes, but that is still their intention. The goal for these managers then becomes to find ways to use the Agile practices, as written, as tools with which to control their team. The managers will likely plaster a lot of right-sounding words and practice names onto everything, but their intention shows through. No amount of training on speech and/or action can change that intention, especially if the intention arises from painful incidents in the past when a lack of control led to disaster.

It is best not to see intentions as "good" or "bad," but rather as compatible with success or not. We all think of ourselves as having good intentions, but that value judgment is made in the context of our own worldview. Using someone else's worldview, they may look at our intention and see it as a bad intention, doing a thing for the wrong reason.

Intentions are also difficult to change. They are hard to change within ourselves and they are very hard to change in other people. But examining intentions is very helpful. We can examine our own intentions and figure out whether they are helpful or harmful. We can discuss intentions with each other and help ourselves improve. Try to make intentions part of the conversation. "What are you trying to achieve when you run standups in this way? Maybe I can help you achieve that goal if I know where you are headed?"

Rather than seeing people as enemies or friends of an Agile transformation, we can instead see that each person has their own unique set of intentions, which they formed for perfectly good reasons in reaction to good or bad events in their lives. No good or bad people or even good or bad intentions, just compatibilities and incompatibilities. Those are things we can always work with.

3.1.3 Right Speech

> Your own words are the bricks and mortar of the dreams you want to realize. Your words are the greatest power you have. The words you choose and their use establish the life you experience.
> Sonia Choquette, inspirational author

---

massive impact on the quality of a software application. More about software craftsmanship in Chap. 9—Flipping the Run/Build Ratio.

Words matter.[5] Words can heal. Words can hurt. Words can change a person's life for the better.

Just by walking into a team space and listening to some of the conversations, you can tell what's going on by the language being used. Language can be positive or negative. It can be empowering or controlling. Language is a big part of how we communicate, so it is worth paying attention to the words we use.

Right speech is often addressed by Agile experts and coaches. Most people know that, in order to change behavior, it is helpful to use better words. If you call a part of a project a "phase," that has certain preconceptions that come with it. A phase sounds long. It sounds like we will produce some documentation and will pass it on to another set of people who execute the next "phase." The word phase seems inherently waterfall. So we invent a new word, perhaps calling a part of a project a "sprint," which sounds very fast. These changes in terminology are helpful.

However, changes in terms can also be deceiving. We've all been part of organizations that stop calling their people "employees" and decide that "associates" is a much more empowering word. However, if the actions of actually empowering people do not come along with the word, the word "associate" can have a negative connotation because it reminds everyone that the company pretends to empower its people but really doesn't. When a big company, like Walmart, does this, it can ruin that word for the rest of the companies, because people think of Walmart's treatment of its employees and connect it to the word they use instead of employee—"associate."

Similarly, if a company changes from "phase" to "sprint" but the sprints are still an entire month long, people will see the terminology change as nothing more than window dressing.

So the words have to be connected to real workplace changes. Often you will hear "I don't care what we call it, just get the work done." But words take on a life of their own. You can care or not care what we call it, but each person who hears the word will have some preconceived notions about it. Why not make those preconceived notions work for you instead of against you?

Even in the Agile world, we've seen that word choice can be pretty sloppy. For example, let's look at the term "ScrumMaster." This is a popular role name in the Scrum framework. What does it mean? It is connected to a set of responsibilities. But look at the word. It has two parts—Scrum and Master. It implies that your goal, playing this role, is to *master Scrum*; to get as good at Scrum as you possibly can. This is a problem. We now have people who are focused on being really good at

---

[5]Our colleague, Bob Myers, has a great habit of looking up the etymology (language origin) of words to more deeply understand the historical meanings. It's a good way to be sure that the meaning you're assuming today relates to the original meaning of the root of the word from Latin, Greek or whatever.

Scrum, becoming super Scrum experts, rather than focusing on solving business problems. What happens when we include parts of other processes, other than Scrum, into the workplace? The ScrumMaster will be lost. "I shall defend Scrum to the very end!!" This incorrect focus can be traced right back to the name of the role—ScrumMaster.

3.1.4 Right Action

You've probably seen and read lots of Agile books. How many of them are about Right Action? **Probably all of them.** Book after book after book focuses on answering the question "What should I do?"

This seems logical. But it's not smart. Right actions (practices) actually have the smallest impact on producing value. Right view and right intention are all more important. Have you heard people say "Just give me the right people and I can accomplish anything with any methodology"? That is what they're talking about.[6] If you have people who already have the right view and right intention, the process matters less.

Is process irrelevant? No. It still helps to have a set of steps, some advice. But that is not where we are at in the world of Agile books and articles. The vast majority of what is written about Agile falls into the right action territory. "Follow these steps and you will be successful." This is the philosophy of "best practices."[7] Hey, if you take the practices that were performed by a successful team or a successful company, and copy them to your team, then you can't go wrong. By experience, we all know this is bullshit. Practices are fine, and useful, but they aren't the whole picture. They aren't even half or a quarter of the picture. Right view and right intention come first.

The problem is when we treat the practices like a religion. "Why aren't we following Scrum completely? Let's get into compliance, dang it!" This is where the best practices mentality goes wrong. Even books with titles including words like

---

[6]The idea of "hire quality" has its own problems. See the related article at **EnterpriseAgile.biz**.

[7]You could compare our "Journey to Enterprise Agility" approach to the Agile frameworks, like the Scaled Agile Framework (SAFe), Large-Scale Scrum (LeSS), Lean Enterprise, Disciplined Agile Delivery, Modern Agile, GROWS, etc. We do not have any arguments against these frameworks, but they are simply bundles of "best practices." They do not supply guidance towards a new worldview or compatible intentions. Additionally, they only show the "end game," as in how your organization should look once you are "done" transforming. They do not delve into the dirty, messy job of being half-way through transforming, and how you deal with those situations. The dirty, messy part is what this book is all about.

Having said all that, none of the things we advocate go against the industry frameworks we've mentioned here, and we heartily endorse any of them as compatible with what we are suggesting here. They're actually very helpful.

"Agile mindset" or "Agile culture" tend to immediately dive into practices without providing enough guidance at the worldview or intention levels.

All of this is understandable. It's much easier to write a book about practices.

Many books provide massive amounts of details on seemingly simple practices, like retrospectives or user story writing. It seems like we are trying to provide enough detail to get past the problem where Agile goes wrong.

But we're looking for details in the wrong places.

3.2 Right View + Right Intention + Right Speech + Right Action

In order to get it "right," we have to have these four pieces. We need to find ways to improve our own personal view, intention, speech and action. The most powerful are view and intention, but it can help to improve every piece.

We need to look for the ways that our worldview shapes our intention, our intention shapes our speech and our speech shapes our action. We need to spend significant time trying to understand other people's worldviews and intentions, hidden or obvious.

The rest of this book will hopefully work to shape your worldview, intention and speech. Yes, we've included actions/practices here and there, but they serve mostly to reinforce a worldview or intention.

Quite frankly, this approach, by the way, caused us no end of grief in writing this book. How could we write a practical book, nontheoretical, when we know clearly that "best practices" are so unimportant? What we've decided is that we will write a "how to" book on setting the right worldview, intention and speech. "How to" have a worldview that is more consistent with speed-to-market. "How to" set your intention for creating a team that will produce fewer defects. "How to" speak in a way that does not encourage mechanical behavior.

Are there practices in our book too? You betcha. But we promise not to treat them like a religion. And you shouldn't either. The practices we are suggesting aren't guaranteed to work. You've got to adapt them to your situation. You've got to figure out your own (and your team's) worldview and intentions. Then you have a shot.

3.2.1 A Worldview That Is Compatible with Success

Here is some minimum worldview and intention setting you'll need to succeed with an Agile project or an Agile transformation:

> *Talking person-to-person is always going to convey a richer set of information than handing a document to someone. And we need the richest possible information passing from each of us if we hope to succeed.*
>
> *The more we get caught up in filling out documents and the further we get from the act of writing really good quality code, the worse off we will be.*
>
> *The relationship between the business customer and the IT team must be collaborative, congenial and familiar if real results are going to be achieved.*
>
> *Being humble is important.*
>
> *I can almost never repeat what I did on my last successful project. Every new situation is different. Success isn't ever mechanical.*
>
> *I cannot specify everything up-front in detail.*
>
> *I cannot predict worth shit. No one can.*
>
> *It is important to trust people easily and quickly.*

You can see view, intention, speech and action as being in order of importance. Right view and intention are hugely important—nothing can be accomplished without them. That is not to say speech and practices are irrelevant. They are helpful. Certain practices can even help to reinforce certain worldviews and intentions, which is a nice benefit. But when you're problem solving, look at the worldviews and intentions involved as much as you examine the practices.

> **Test Drive Your Knowledge Again**
> Answer the following questions with the knowledge you have after reading this chapter. Have your answers changed?
>
> 1. Right action, right speech, right intention, right view. Which of these is the foundation of the others?
> 2. I can repeat what I did successfully on my last project. Is this a right view?
> 3. I can use the Agile practices to control the work that is done on my team. Is this a right intention?

Reference

Lakoff G (2014) Don't think of an elephant: know your values and frame the debate, 2nd edn. Chelsea Green, White River Junction, VT

Seven Principles of Systems Thinking for Software Development

> **Test Drive Your Knowledge**
> Answer the following questions with the knowledge you have now. Then answer them again at the end of this chapter.
>
> 1. What current trends in software development are good examples of systems thinking?
> 2. When there is a problem, how do you decide who to blame?
> 3. When are analogies useful? When are they harmful?

4.1 So Many Principles!

Because this book is focused on changing your intentions and worldview, we rely on principles as much as practices. For this reason, we've ended up with three sets of principles:

- **Systems thinking principles**—helping to guide all your thoughts, ideas, speech, intentions and worldview
- **Professionalism principles**—defining what it means to be a professional in the new world
- **Servant leadership principles**—explaining how it looks and feels to be a true servant leader

In this chapter, we'll examine the systems thinking principles. In many ways, these principles are meant to bring us back to the foundations of our worldview and intentions, rather than focusing too much on practices. All four parts of the path are important, but world view and intention are the most important.

These principles are not codified by academic systems thinking scholars. While we (the authors) are certainly guided and inspired by the scholars we referenced in Chap. 2—The Scholars of Systems Thinking, we do not attribute these principles back to them as a whole. Instead, we've created a new set of principles to guide the application of systems thinking to the field of software development. Principles to help correct the ills (and illth) of today's problems in our beloved field.

The use of principles can help to elevate your thinking away from "What should I do?" practices towards "How can I see differently?" views and intentions.

1. Trust = Speed
2. Avoid best practices
3. Beware of immense power of analogies
4. Blame the system, not the person
5. Treat people like people, not machines
6. Acknowledge your boundaries
7. Relation-ness matters more than thing-ness

4.1.1 Systems Thinking Principle 1: Trust = Speed

> Trust and control are incompatible because the core of trust involves freedom. To trust people is to count on their sense of integrity, believing that they will choose to act in a trustworthy manner, while recognizing the possibility that they may choose to betray the trust.
> Robert C. Solomon and Fernando Flores (Solomon 2001)

In a flurry of methodologies, practices, team structures and manifestos, we often forget one factor—**trust**. If we don't trust the members of our team, it doesn't really matter what processes we use, we're never going to be very good. And we're never going to be fast. It's amazing how much you can strip away in terms of documents and processes when you trust each other.

Too often, we have a kind of persistent "hurt feelings" in the workplace. "Well, I did trust someone once, but they let me down, so now I need everyone to fill out this twenty page form before I can do anything." It is true that when we have an environment of trust, certain people will take advantage of that. But piling processes and documents on top of a functioning team to ensure that no one can ever "get away" with things is not the answer.

Having a team that trusts one another improves everything—quality, speed, happiness at work. We've worked in situations where the product owner truly trusts the team to execute on his wishes. The results are nothing short of magical. Things get done quickly. Quality is through the roof. In one case, a product owner said "It's like the team is inside my head. They know exactly what I want even before I can communicate it completely."

Trusting someone is a risk. Anyone who has worked for more than a couple of months out of school has had their trust broken by a coworker, boss, client or vendor. There is no magic to shielding yourself from broken trust. But the benefits that you gain from trusting people far outweigh the problems that happen when your trust is broken. Your goal should always be to find ways to trust people more and sooner, in whatever way possible.

4.1.2 Systems Thinking Principle 2: Avoid Best Practices

> If anyone were to study without theory such a company, i.e. without knowing what questions to ask, he would be tempted to copy the company, on the pretext that "they must be doing some things right." To copy is to invite disaster.
> W. Edwards Deming (Deming 1994)
>
> Much of what currently passes for IS theory is nothing more than "what works in practice.
> Peter Checkland, Sue Holwell (Checkland 1997)
>
> Adapt. Don't adopt.
> Timothy Lister

"Best practices" is a term we use persistently in software development, and especially in consulting. It implies stuff that's been tried before and proven successful. It worked for those guys, and it'll work for you.

But it's a dirty lie. You try the best practice and it doesn't live up to the advertising. So, you ask for your money back. The expert's response? "You did it wrong." You made some small mistake in the application of that best practice that prevented you from getting value from it.

The truth is that best practices should not, should never, be followed blindly. They are, at best, interesting stories from someone who experienced success. They are, at worst, a crutch or a set of handcuffs that cause teams to do stuff that they know is wrong, but "the consultant told us to do it." There are no "best practices."

There are, as Tom and Mary Poppendieck (Poppendieck 2003) say, only "good practices in context." We would add "...in context of the right worldview and intentions." Don't get caught up with what the industry best practices are. Treat them with curiosity and good humor.

Mike Myatt, executive advisor and *Forbes* columnist, has a twist on best practices that might be useful. He says that best practices are never "best," but in fact we should be looking for "next practices," ways to take what we learn from elsewhere and apply it to our own situations, projects, teams, companies.[1]

Most purveyors of best practices talk about the need to "adopt" their particular method. They want you to buy into it, to take on that mantle and become an evangelist of it yourself. There is a certain extent to which you should use the set

---

[1] bit.ly/bestpracticesaint.

of practices without questioning it. "It works for everyone else, why should you be different?" is the expert's question. But we'd like you to question the experts, to try to understand whether these "best practices" are really valid in your circumstance or not. Do you need to change them? Do you need to "adapt" them to what is unique about your world?

Probably the reason most experts are fearful of people adapting (rather than adopting) is that there might be a tendency to change the new practices to be as similar to the old practices (that definitely weren't working) as possible. This is not a good goal, of course. But it does happen. But rather than saying "Let's adopt this new process without question," we can distinguish between good ways to adapt and bad ways to adapt. It comes down to intent. If you are adapting the new process to make it like the old one, question yourself. What is your intention? Are you just afraid to change? Are you being lazy in your thinking? Are you trying to create a "hybrid" of your old way and the new way just because you're afraid to make the leap? Instead, find ways to adapt that help the new process work better in your environment. Are you making the adaptation because of some special element in your environment? Is there a business reason you are adapting it? If so, great. That's a good reason to adapt.

One of our systems thinking scholars, Peter Checkland, showed how our thinking can be flawed when we "adopt" new processes. One of Checkland's students came up to him after a lecture one day and said that he had used Checkland's soft systems methodology and it worked. Checkland immediately scolded the student. "How do you know it was the process that worked? How do you know it wasn't your team that worked?" The student was taken aback, of course. (He was trying to compliment the guy, after all.) But Checkland was trying to tell him that a process cannot "work" on its own, it depends on the context of who is using it and the particular situation. It is impossible to say that, once you have a success, you "have evidence" that the process worked. You have no evidence. All you know is that with that team, in that circumstance to solve that particular problem, using that process, it worked. That's all you can say.

It comes down to one fact: *success never comes from within the practices themselves. The success is in the relation between the people and the practices*, as we show in Fig. 4.1.

Taking this point of view is problematic to consultants. What do consultants do if not box up best practices and sell them to clients??

We have a lot of work to do to explain what a "post-best practices world" would look like. We promise to talk through many of these issues in this book. For now, let's just leave our advice as "avoid best practices.[2]"

---

[2]When we talk about avoiding blind adherence to best practices, you might say "Well, sure, but no one really thinks like that, do they?" Yes. Yes, they do. We've seen many speeches, articles and books that make this very mistake. Here is a recent example of an Agile blogger and coach offering

Fig. 4.1 The relation between people and the practices is where success truly lives. © 2017 by Daryl Kulak and Hong Li—reprinted with permission

4.1.3 Systems Thinking Principle 3: Beware the Immense Power of Analogies

> All metaphors…offer ways of not seeing as well as ways of seeing.
> Michael C. Jackson, systems science pioneer

First of all, it is certainly true that analogies (and metaphors) can be very useful in explaining concepts to people. But we want to point out that they can also be dangerous. Analogies run rampant in our software world. Maybe because software is so ethereal, but we love to construct analogies to explain why we're doing what we're doing. Most prominent is the "house building analogy." "You see, if you're building a house, you need to start with the foundation, and only then can you start on the framing and the electrical circuits."

Other people tend to use more organic analogies, like a gardener and her garden. Plant the seeds, watch them grow, don't yell at the seeds to grow faster, etc.

---

exactly the rigid "best practices" advice we are talking about here. His post is called *"**Modifying Scrum—You THINK You Know Better**…"* Now, it's bad enough that one so-called expert thinks this way. But his blog post was uncritically linked to by a number of other Agile coaches. Mechanical thinking is prevalent among Agile "experts." And why not? Being mechanical about Agile "best practices" makes life a whole lot easier…for the coach. (This is a real blog post…we did not make it up…swear to God.)

bit.ly/scrumknowbetter

At one level, these analogies seem harmless. Analogies can make whatever you're saying sound right. If you like a waterfall software model, you can use lots of physical building metaphors: house-building, bridge-building, road-construction. They work great in getting a point across.

But, we tend to take analogies too far. Analogies break down easily. If software is like building a house, and the architectural framework is the house's concrete foundation, then what is the equivalent to the sidewalk in front of the house? What is the connection of the analogy to the cedar siding? They don't relate, of course. Analogies can be very brittle and you never know when they will cause you problems.

Think of the house-building analogy again. In a waterfall lifecycle, it makes sense to complete the foundation, and only then move on to the frame. That is the only way to build a house. But is it the only way to build software? No. We can create "just enough" foundation and build a bit of value on top of it. You probably wouldn't build a house that way. So our house-building analogy fails us.

The biggest example we have of an analogy taken too far in our software world is Lean[3] software development. We try to make a comparison of how software is "similar to" producing automobiles at the rate of demand. The analogy breaks down almost immediately (is one feature equal to one car or one part?), but surprisingly, it has made great inroads and has many prophets.

In systems thinking, there is something stronger than an analogy. Ludwig von Bertalanffy (Bertalanffy 1968) provides us with examples of analogies and their more powerful cousin, the **homology**. He talks about how the flow of electricity and the flow of fluid can be studied using the *same set of laws*. All the physical equations that govern the flow of water through a tube work the same way for the flow of electricity through a cable. This is a super-powerful alternative to the analogy. It is an analogy that doesn't break down, it doesn't have exceptions, it's just *the same*.

The homology is very refreshing, compared to what we try to do in the software world "It's sorta like steering a cruise ship but it's also sorta like renting a backhoe." Whaaaa?? Instead, software development needs a good **homology**. We intend to supply one in this book with Robert Rosen's M-R model (Rosen 1991).

4.1.4 Systems Thinking Principle 4: Blame the System, Not the Person

In systems thinking we are always, naturally, trying to "think about the system." If we are developing software, we're trying to think about how a sprint proceeds, who does what, how we make progress, how we recover from missteps, how to move

---

[3]More about Lean at **EnterpriseAgile.biz**.

faster and how we figure out what it all means. When we're hiring people, there is a hiring system. You might also call it a "hiring process." But the process is just part of the system. A process diagram, showing the tasks, handoffs and responsibilities is a small part of the overall system. A system involves the people. Not people as interchangeable automatons, but real live people—with attitudes, emotions, personal goals, hidden agendas, relationships, worldviews and intentions. The system has to take all this into account.

Within a system, there are lots of interconnections. That means that you can fix what you think is the problem, and it can cause additional problems elsewhere. That's why we use causal loop diagrams. But it also means that the person who is sitting right directly where the problem occurred may look like the culprit, but they're really not. The problem likely originated elsewhere. In fact, W. Edwards Deming (Deming 1992) said throughout his life that almost all the problems that corporations encounter are a problem with the system, not a problem with a particular person. This seems so counter-intuitive at first. We all want to know "Who's to blame?" But it doesn't help to figure that out. It helps more to "blame the system."

Blaming the person comes directly from our best practice mentality. "I told you to use this Scrum best practice, which is guaranteed to work! You screwed it up, so you must have done your job poorly. Get out!"

4.1.5 Systems Thinking Principle 5: Treat People Like People, Not Like Machines

> How is it, then that our organizations are less adaptable, less creative and less inspiring than we are? Because they are hostages to an ideology that is, in a real sense, inhuman.
> —Gary Hamel (Hamel 2012)

In systems thinking, we try to find ways to affirm that people are more than just machines set up to do a job. They are people—complex, thinking, feeling, relationship-building, unpredictable, ambitious people.

Are you, as a manager, treating your people like people? If you are managing your team "by the metrics" or managing by results, you are probably treating them like machines. If you have tightly defined roles and responsibilities, you are treating them like machines. If you expect the team to follow a set of best practices (Do Scrum or else!), you are treating them like machines.

Machine-oriented teams are obvious by the number of "yes people" you can observe. "Yes sir, you are right. In fact, you are always right!"

Management problem solving in a machine-oriented team looks like replacing defective parts (people).

Most American corporations and teams are mechanical today. This is not necessarily a problem, as long as everyone knows that the organization is a machine. The executives must admit "we've created a machine." In this environment, any professions of "We deeply care about our people" or "Our people are our greatest asset" should be avoided. You've created a machine organization, you do not care about your people. The other thing that should be avoided is the expectation that people will think for themselves. It is very difficult to think for one's self in a machine organization. This type of organization can work in two circumstances. The first is that the work must be simple. The second is acknowledging that the machine will wear down over time. It will achieve some level of efficiency, and perhaps even success. Then the "money machine" will wear down and will stop working. Trying to get it started up again will be hard or impossible.

Look at the music industry, for example. Music executives have, for decades, seen new artists as "money machines." They look to squeeze profits out of the artists and then throw them away. That's a perfectly fine business model, but it will not last. The music labels are seeing the destruction of their businesses today, and are seemingly helpless to stop it. They cannot. The machine has worn down. It will never be back the way it was. Those executives must move on to the next opportunity.

The machine organization must obey Newton's laws of thermodynamics. Everything must eventually yield to entropy and disintegrate from year to year. It will wear out and run down.

In the software industry, we often hear terms like the "software factory." A name like this may indicate that people see the team mechanically, like a money machine. Running a machine-model organization can be a successful and dignified endeavor. But everyone involved needs to acknowledge that it is a machine, and any part of it is dispensable, and sooner or later will need to be dismantled and replaced.

The opposite of machine-model management is treating people like people, also known as *servant leadership*. This means acknowledging the fuzzy side of people. It does NOT mean having cake parties, throwing confetti, giving awards or other "fun committee" ideas. It means providing people with control over their own work. It means connecting people with a shared vision and common purpose. And giving them a chance to get really, really good at what they do. Autonomy, purpose, mastery (Pink 2011). Now that's a party!

4.1.6 Systems Thinking Principle 6: Acknowledge Your Boundaries

Boundaries are an important part of systems thinking. Scholars like C. West Churchman (Churchman 1979), Werner Ulrich (Ulrich 1996) and Gerald Midgley (Midgley 2000) have dedicated their lives to this concept.

Boundaries are part of our mental models. They are certain limits that must not be crossed. And they are often problematic. They keep us from seeing the whole picture. They cripple us from acting on information in a sensible way.

Let's look at an Agile example.

> A team is producing software quickly and it is exactly what the product owner (PO) wants. The communication between product owner and other team members is clear, instantaneous and precise. At a demo as the software nears a production release, some other executives from the company attend. The president of the company looks shocked. "This software isn't right!" he exclaims to the team. The product owner is as surprised as anyone.
>
> The team assumed that they should communicate with their product owner AND ONLY their product owner. Sure, the PO made a mistake by not asking the right questions of the company president. But the team also erred by assuming that they should not need to look beyond their product owner. This is a boundary built right into the Scrum framework.

You can see this situation as a problem with seeing a boundary in the wrong place. The team saw the boundary of their user community as one person—the PO. They did not think they needed to see past the PO into the broader user community, other stakeholders, executives, and potential end users who may not have had perfect communication with the PO. The team's boundary caused them to miss their goal completely, even though succeeding beautifully with their Scrum compliance.

Each of us needs to constantly look at the boundaries we've placed around us and listen hard when someone tells us those boundaries are wrong. The impossible happens to some industry, project and person every day. The worst reaction is to think it's still impossible when it's already happening, as we've seen with so many companies who have been blown out of their leadership position by one of their competitors actively and currently doing "the obviously impossible."

4.1.7 Systems Thinking Principle 7: Relation-ness Matters More Than Thing-ness

> The aim of science is not things in themselves but the relations between things; outside these relations there is no reality knowable.
> Henri Poincare

What do we mean by "silos" in an organization? Silos are when people and groups have tightly defined roles and their communication with other people/groups is formal and regulated.

A deeper meaning of silos is that it is a **lack of relations between people and groups**. The highest functioning organization will have the richest relations. If people inside a company know and trust each other, that company will be able to operate efficiently. And if the people inside the company have rich relationships with the customers, they will also be effective in the long term serving those customers. As they say, it is all about who you know, and also how rich your relationship is with them.

The richness of relationships on a team is also important. But something we get from Robert Rosen's M-R model (Rosen 1991) in systems thinking is this: the relations in an organism (fields, connections, etc.) are actually more important than the things (cells, organs, etc.). Rosen shows how the "life" is in the relations, not in the physics or chemistry of an organism (or organization).

This goes against all of science thus far, and it is also a slap in the face for our usual methods of leading people. What do we do when we have a problem? We try to figure out "who is the problem?" Once we know that, we can get rid of "the problem" and everything will be right again. But what if the problem is in the relations between the team members? Something in the embedded culture of the team? Then, getting rid of a "problem person" won't be the solution, it will have to be a deeper change.

Many soft skills consultants talk about changing the culture of a team. But it isn't easy. It definitely won't result from some classroom exercise, or knowledge of additional concepts, or, god forbid, a ropes and ladders adventure in the wilderness together. Soft skills consultants have tried many things, except to actually work with teams in real life to fix the problems of a bad culture. As far as we know, this is the only way to fix a culture.

4.2 Principles for Your Worldview

Use these principles to guide your own worldview. The systems thinking principles can be effective reminders in conversations as your teams are moving to more productive processes. "Are we acknowledging our boundaries in this case?" "Are we being mechanical with this best practices approach?" Principles are more effective tools to enforce intention and worldview than are practices. Hew more to the principles than to the practices whenever possible.

We've created a poster of the "Systems Thinking Principles" for you to print and use on our website **EnterpriseAgile.biz** if you think it will help your team connect to a helpful worldview and intention for transformation.

> **Test Drive Your Knowledge Again**
> Answer the following questions with the knowledge you have after reading this chapter. Have your answers changed?
>
> 1. What current trends in software development are good examples of systems thinking?
> 2. When there is a problem, how do you decide who to blame?
> 3. When are analogies useful? When are they harmful?

References

Bertalanffy L (1968) General systems theory: foundations, development, applications. George Braziller, New York

Checkland P, Holwell S (1997) Information, systems and information systems: making sense of the field. John Wiley and Sons, Chichester

Churchman CW (1979) The systems approach and its enemies. Basic Books, New York

Deming WE (1992) Out of the crisis. MIT Press, Cambridge, MA

Deming WE (1994) The new economics for industry, government, education. Massachusetts Institute of Technology Center for Advanced Educational Services, Cambridge, MA

Hamel G (2012) What matters now: how to win in a world of relentless change, ferocious competition and unstoppable innovation. Jossey-Bass, San Francisco

Midgley G (2000) Systemic intervention: philosophy, methodology and practice. Kluwer Academic, New York

Pink D (2011) Drive: the surprising truth about what motivates us. Riverhead Books, New York

Poppendieck M, Poppendieck T (2003) Lean software development: an agile toolkit. Addison Wesley, Boston, MA

Rosen R (1991) Life, itself: a comprehensive inquiry into the nature, origin and fabrication of life. Columbia University Press, New York

Solomon RC, Flores F (2001) Building trust in business, politics, relationships and life. Oxford University Press, New York

Ulrich W (1996) Critical systems thinking for citizens: a research proposal. University of Hull, Hull

Redefining Professionalism 5

Orthodoxy, of whatever colour, seems to demand a lifeless, imitative style.
George Orwell *(in his paper Politics and the English Language)*

Test Drive Your Knowledge
Answer the following questions with the knowledge you have now. Then answer them again at the end of this chapter.

1. What is the best way to handle weak stakeholders?
2. What does it mean to be accountable?
3. What is an alternative to creating yet another meeting when there is a communication problem between two groups?

5.1 Understanding What It Means to Be a Professional

Throughout this book, we've emphasized that practices cannot stand alone. Using a set of practices or actions may work or it may not, depending on the foundations of those practices. Those foundations are the speech, intention and worldview of the people involved inside and surrounding the team.

In the business world, a big part of how many of us describe our worldview is called "professionalism." Professionalism defines "This is how we are supposed to act around here." What does it mean to be a true professional inside and outside an Agile team space? If we hope to challenge our own worldview, we have to tackle our conception of what it means to be a professional.

The current definition of professionalism evolved in a very different era. Men made up almost the entire white collar workforce. Manufacturing made up more than half the workforce. Command-and-control management was not only accepted, it was expected.

A professionalism tailored for the ease of command-and-control management is disruptive to the self-managed Agile team. Well-established executives and managers often look at Agile team members and accuse them of being "unprofessional." We'll examine those accusations and how to change the tone and intention of the conversation.

It is actually the meaning of professionalism that must change. But first let's examine the downsides of today's version of professionalism.

5.1.1 What Defined the Professionalism of the Past?

If you research the principles of professionalism, you might encounter academic definitions like the following:

- Ability to work autonomously
- Belonging to a professional association, guild or licensed status
- Adhering to a code of ethics, including respect for fellow workers
- Public service and altruism
- Accountability

But the real practice of professionalism goes far beyond these standard abstract ideas. We've observed the following additional but seldom stated definitions of professionalism:

- Multitasking is important and impressive; always try to take on more and more responsibility even though you might be less effective
- Respond to emails, text messages and voicemail messages as fast as you can, even if that requires interrupting in-person conversations
- Don't be overly emotional; don't show too much anger, sadness, crying or laughing out loud
- Treat scheduled meetings as being more urgent than informal hallway conversations
- If you can tell the meeting you are in does not require your presence, stay anyway out of respect for the organizer (especially if the organizer is ranked higher than you are)
- Don't express your creativity through clothing, hairstyles or jewelry; dress similarly to your coworkers and your managers
- Don't bring a problem to your supervisor unless you've already got a solution to it
- Stay busy and look busy; it is very important to be busy all day every day; do not take time for reflection

- Don't be sloppy; get things right the first time; don't show people work that is half-done

It is unlikely you will read the above advice in any book about professionalism. These are the "unstated" principles of the professionalism of the past. We think it is how all of us have interpreted professionalism and it is how we translate it into daily life. To codify this current reality, we'd like to give it a name: **mechanical professionalism**.

5.1.2 Mechanical Professionalism

We're calling the current practices "mechanical professionalism." A corporate culture that says "Do what you're told" is one where you are being asked to fit in with the machine. Remember back to Systems Thinking Principle #5—Treat People Like People, Not Like Machines. With mechanical professionalism, we are treating ourselves and others like machines, expecting people to be "the same," not ruffling any feathers, going with the flow. Mechanical professionalism is a direct blocker to innovation and collaboration, as you'll see in the following pages.

The "Multitasking Professional"
In mechanical professionalism, you must be able to do multiple things at a time, juggle phone calls, emails, meetings, in-person requests and paperwork. Get it all done. Be a professional. To focus on one thing, put all your mental energy towards something, is not only unprofessional, it is...lazy. Why can't you multitask like the rest of us?

Edward Hallowell, psychologist and author of the book *CrazyBusy: Overstretched, Overbooked and About to Snap* (Hallowell 2006) says that multitasking is a myth. Your brain can only do one thing at a time. By multitasking between the phone call and the email you're writing, you are switching at high speed between one and the other. And every switch-over has overhead. Most people call it "context switching cost." So you are not as efficient, not nearly, as if you did them one at a time. However, there is a little rush of adrenaline that comes with multitasking, says Hallowell. And that makes us want to do it, to get the rush.

A study conducted at Stanford University[1] and published in the *Proceedings of the National Academy of Sciences* in 2009 found very conclusively that multitasking doesn't work at all. In the words of Clifford I. Nass, the leader of the study, "Multitaskers were just lousy at everything."

---

[1] bit.ly/MediocreMulti.

Overfilling the Task Bucket
In today's business world, you must not only be busy but instead "crazybusy," says Hallowell. It is not enough to have the right amount of work to do, but you must be committed far past anything that you could actually do. Then you must struggle valiantly to get it all done, sacrificing other aspects of your life.

But in reality, overfilling our task buckets isn't healthy or helpful. We become so tightly scheduled that we simply miss important deadlines. And when everything is tight, any small problem or slippage causes inevitable delays. And most importantly, without some built-in "slack" in our schedules, we won't have the opportunity to build a capacity for change into our organization.

More Meetings
Meetings are either the heartbeat of a humming, efficient workplace or the poison of every organization, depending on your perspective.

One way of judging the mechanical professionalism of a new manager is to look at what happens when they first take on a new position (or move into a new company). Often the first acts of a new manager will include setting up a new battery of meetings to show that they are firmly in control and know exactly what needs to be done.

As Gene Johnson, an insightful Agile consultant, once said to us "I have seen managers 'over collaborate' to such an extent where they have fifteen or more touchbase meetings every week."

"I am just so busy." There is a certain status to this statement. The person saying it is implicitly saying "There are so many people who need my input and guidance that my calendar remains full day after day." Do we need this status statement, at the expense of our productivity?

"Don't Do Sloppy Work"
"This document doesn't look professional. You shouldn't be showing it to people."

Truly, one of the biggest roadblocks to changing software development processes in a large corporation is mechanical professionalism.

An unwritten rule of mechanical professionalism is "Never let anyone see your dirty laundry." Dirty laundry includes partially-written emails, not-yet-first-draft documents, partially completed software and unvarnished ideas.

And yet, that is exactly what we need to expose to each other in an iterative/incremental lifecycle. We set up short sprints to showcase not-yet-completed code to businesspeople! Eeek! We work together in a room where other people can hear us having trouble with our test script construction! Gaak! We "pair up" with other people who can see the sloppiness of our code! Ulp!

We've got to learn to be okay with this. Professionalism shouldn't be about hiding your work until it is pretty. It isn't about pushing mistakes under the carpet.

We can't accomplish our work this way at all. Our work, warts and all, needs to be stuck out in the air. Sunlight is a great disinfectant. But it can be painful. But more useful than painful, especially after you get over the initial pain of coworkers knowing your weaknesses.

Creativity Corralled
Another part of mechanical professionalism is "knowing when to be creative." Mechanical professionalism does allow for creativity, but it must happen at the right place and time. There is a feeling that, yes, we can be creative, but could you please wait until we hold the brainstorming session on Wednesday afternoon to do that?

If you observe carefully, you may see that the least creative managers and executives are the ones who insist on getting people together to have "brainstorming[2] sessions." Why is that? We think it is because the term "brainstorming" provides a neat boundary around an activity that the group can start, do and quit. It segments the messiness of creativity into a time-bounded meeting without letting it escape into the rest of our worklife.

Please Speak and Write "Professionally"
What is today's version of speaking or writing professionally? Mechanical professionalism sounds something like this:

- In the third person—"leadership has decided" rather than "I've decided"
- Passive verbs rather than active verbs
- Crammed with the latest clichés
    - "at the end of the day…"
    - "socialized" (rather than "talked to")
    - "…don't want to try to boil the ocean"
    - "resources" (instead of "people")
- Devoid of emotion
- Devoid of humor

But what's the actual goal of communicating, in writing or speaking? To be clear. To be understood. This list above contributes more towards fuzziness than to clarity.

Business clichés are a symptom of mechanical thinking. It's easier to mechanically insert a cliché into a sentence rather than thinking about what the right words should be.

Can You Keep a Secret?
Mechanical professionalism is about keeping secrets among the management layer and away from the great unwashed masses. Knowledge is power.

---

[2]bit.ly/FCBrainDumb.

But professionalism should be about treating information as food for the organization. You must nourish your organization by providing them information so they can improve their own work. Find new ways to give them data, publish it often, keep it up-to-date, put it out there.

Managing by the Numbers

A mechanical professional will often feel like they can manage anything as long as they have "the numbers." Metrics are helpful, it's true (for more, see Chap. 7—Business Value, Estimation and Metrics), but mechanical professionals seem to be overly confident that they can manage things with nothing else except these figures.

We once worked with a program manager we'll call Budva who, as part of the PMO (program management office), was meant to manage a multimillion dollar project to develop a set of mobile apps. Budva felt she could effectively manage the team with nothing more than the status reports, GANTT charts and estimates-to-actuals given to her by the team. Week after week, she routinely spent less than one hour with the development team in the team room. Her disconnection to the team became very obvious. Her only interactions were to demand accurate hours per task tracked in reports and criticize small problems or inconsistencies she noticed on the reports. Being so out-of-touch, her subsequent status reports to executives did not represent the reality of the project. Unfortunately, she very quickly lost the respect of the development team and the executives. She was gone from organization after less than 1 year.

5.2 The New Professionalism

Okay, so our current mechanical professional is a mess. What do we need to change about mechanical professionalism to make it a new professionalism?

> **How Can I Change Anything? I'm Not in Charge!**
>
> *It's easy to think that, because you are not a CEO, there is no way you can change things in your workplace. But the truth is quite different. Professionalism starts with the individual. There is a lot you can do. If you make a small change in the way you act and you get away with it, this tells the people around you that they can do it too, and the behavior may spread quickly. And if you do not get away with it, that's okay too. After all, you picked a small change and you can revert back and try something else instead.*
>
> *Almost any time we speak publicly on changing culture, we are asked the following question during the session:*

(continued)

> *"I like what you're saying and I'm already on board. But the people I work with just don't see things this way. How can I convince them to improve?"*
>
> *There are several things at work here. The person asking this question assumes they themselves are already acting perfectly well, and that the real problem exists in "those people over there." This is an easy path. If only those other people would change, things would be a lot better.*
>
> *The more difficult path, and, as it turns out, the more productive, is to look at ourselves. How can we improve? Once we see a better future, how can we model this and change our own behavior to make it happen? It isn't about trying to win people over, but instead about changing ourselves to fit in with our new imagined workplace. This path is much harder and may seem to miss the point. We feel that we are mostly good, so how does it help for us to get a tiny bit better? Wouldn't it be most productive to take those really terrible people and improve them, because that's where the real problem is?*
>
> *This message might seem hard to swallow. But it can also be encouraging. If your focus is always in trying to change other people, you will live a frustrated life. People are hard to change. But you have complete control in changing yourself. Nobody can stop you. And you might be surprised at how your inward focus can change others.*

5.3 The Principles of the New Professionalism

1. Speak up!
   - It is your responsibility to speak up when you see something wrong. It doesn't matter if it is your boss' idea, or even an executive far above your boss. You have to say something. It's unprofessional not to.

2. Use Via Negativa to solve communication problems
   - We don't have to add new meetings, rules or roles to solve communication problems. Usually the best thing we can do is subtract things—meetings, silos or even the space between the two groups.

3. Be an advocate for weak or absent voices
   - You, as a professional, must blow the whistle when you see decisions being made that will hurt an important stakeholder, even if that stakeholder doesn't hold the purse strings.

4. Proudly display your dirty laundry
   - Collaborate with people at all levels, and don't be afraid to let them see early drafts of your code, written documents, important emails, diagrams or ideas. Pride of ownership needs to be at a team level, not an individual.

5. Connect people to one another
    - A true professional takes great joy in connecting people with one another, and in connecting disparate ideas together to make new ones.

6. Challenge your own assumptions as much as you challenge others
    - Critical thinking includes the ability to critique other people's ideas, but much more difficult is the ability to question our own long-held assumptions.

7. Be accountable to change
    - We do not need to be accountable to a plan that assumes scope and schedule have been precisely prescribed for the project. Accountability refers to our commitment to change with the business, to adapt and to thrive as chaos comes our way.

8. Manage uncertainties through adaptive practices and stop faking risk management
    - The best way to manage risks is not with a risk/issue list. Instead, you must embed real risk management into your everyday processes, assuming that there are black swans out there waiting for you and you have no ability to know what they are until they happen.

5.3.1 New Professionalism Principle 1: Speak Up!

> I decided it was better to scream. Silence is the real crime against humanity.
> Nadezhda Mandelstam, Russian writer

5.3.1.1 The Stanford Prison Experiment

It started as an experiment. In August 1971, several Stanford research scientists decided to create an experiment[3] to replicate the experience of being imprisoned. Solicited by an ad in the school newspaper, students volunteered to be part of the experiment to pick up some extra cash. In the pool of volunteers, students were chosen at random (flip of a coin) whether they would be prisoners or guards.

The mocked-up prison was actually the basement of a campus classroom building with the hall exits blocked. The experimenters mostly left the guards and prisoners alone, allowing them to decide how to respond as things moved along.

The experimenters asked the guards to perform several specific activities as they brought the prisoners into the prison, resulting in a dehumanizing of the prisoners. Each prisoner was strip-searched and dressed in a smock without undergarments. Each prisoner was given a number and referred to only by that number (not his name) for the rest of the experiment.

---

[3]bit.ly/StanfordPrisonX.

The prisoners' experience began with an establishment of routine meals and exercise. But on the second day, several prisoners staged a rebellion, and things went downhill quickly. The guards responded with violence, including spraying fire extinguishers at the rebelling prisoners, damaging the skin on their arms and faces.

Each day brought more and more sadistic treatment for the prisoners at the hands of their guards. Soon the prisoners, who were often not allowed to eat or even visit the bathroom regularly, were living in their own urine and defecation and some were sobbing uncontrollably.

The experiment was brought to an abrupt halt after only 6 days, because the guards became violent and abusive.

Strangely, even though any guard or prisoner could have left the experiment at any time, none did. All the participants seemed to have believed the illusion that this was a real prison and that the guards really were all-powerful.

5.3.1.2 Just "Go Along"

> If you see fraud and don't say fraud, you are a fraud.
> Nassim Nicholas Taleb (Taleb 2012)

Although the comparison seems like a stretch, try to think of the Stanford prison experiment in your own workplace. How often do you just "go along" with bad decisions being made by your superiors? It is certainly easy to do so. But by doing this, you are part of that bad decision. As the prison experiment, and several subsequent experiments, showed, we will do surprising things simply because we are instructed to do so. We have to speak up when we see something wrong.

The response you get will depend on the personality of the leader you are dealing with. People in executive leadership can often surround themselves with people who agree with them, so-called "yes men." This causes the executive to begin to think they are right all the time, because the people around them are so agreeable. This isn't because the executive is a bad person; it can happen to anyone who is surrounded by sycophants. So if someone speaks up to point out a problem, it can be surprising to the executive. But it also might be thought-provoking to the executive as well. "Who is this person? Why are they telling me I'm wrong? Do they have a point?"

It is your duty as a professional to tell them when they are wrong. Of course, how you manage the message is important. You don't need to be disrespectful. You don't need to call them out in public. There are lots of subtle ways to provide the message. But it is your duty to speak up.

The reason the executive is promoting their blatantly bad idea is not because the executive is stupid. It is because the executive does not have all the information that you, as an individual contributor, have. You are privy to people's complaints about day-to-day problems. The executive is probably not privy to that. You can sense the mood of the team. The executive probably isn't there often enough to have that sense. Managers and executives, by definition, are out-of-touch with what is happening at the worker level. It is your job to get them in touch with the problems they need to be aware of, and the ways their decisions are incorrect.

New professionalism cannot be about being a "good corporate soldier." If you are a person who follows the directions of your managers without hesitation, you cannot consider yourself to be one of the new professionals. The opinions of all managers must be held suspect, to a certain extent. Held suspect by the people who report to them as well as the managers themselves. The managers aren't the ones doing the work, writing the code, in the details. They/we are removed from the day-to-day work, therefore they don't know the details as intimately as the team members do. We're not saying managers are always wrong, just that it helps for managers to have awareness of their own fallibility. Managers may have seen more situations which might be similar to the one the team faces right now, and they might have good advice and perspective. But they also have to listen to the team members and encourage people to speak up if the team members hear something that seems wrong coming out of the manager's mouth.

Each manager should think about Principle 5—Treat People Like People, Not Like Machines. Is there a way we can focus on the creativity and humanity of our employees rather than seeing them as machines here to do the work and then be deactivated?

5.3.1.3 You Know What? I'll Just Become a Monk!

Honda has become a legendary company since its humble beginning in the aftermath of World War II. And, of course, each legendary company often has an equally legendary founder. For Honda, it was Soichiro Honda, who created first motorcycles and later cars that were the envy of the world. He also created a company that was very different from the mechanical cultures that were so prevalent in those years.

This is a story about Honda's early days that shows how the founder began to create the culture that would help the company succeed for so many decades, as documented in (Scott 2013).

Takeo Fujisawa was an engineer who knew Soichiro Honda personally and worked together with him to build the engines. They worked collaboratively for several years, but one day, they began to argue. Honda held the view that the motorcycle engines needed to be air-cooled, but Fujisawa thought that water-cooling was the answer. The argument continued for days and then weeks. Finally, Soichiro Honda shouted "It's my company and we will use air-cooling!" Fujisawa abruptly left the company that he had helped to prosper and dropped out of sight completely.

Honda continued to engineer his motorcycles using the air-cooled approach, but ran into problem after problem. Several months after Fujisawa's departure, Honda

Fig. 5.1 Studying at the monastery. © 2017 by Daryl Kulak and Hong Li—reprinted with permission

concluded that his loyal engineer had been right—water-cooling was the best direction. But Honda, in his ignorance, had driven the one person from the company who had the courage to stand up to him when he was wrong. And what a precedent he had now set for everyone else who worked there! Honda felt ashamed.

But what Soichiro Honda did next was truly extraordinary. Honda searched for Fujisawa around all of Japan and finally found him. Fujisawa was worshipping at a monastery. The argument had such an effect that the engineer was seriously considering leaving his professional (and personal) life behind and becoming a monk (Fig. 5.1). Honda took Fujisawa aside and apologized to him for treating him disrespectfully. (Remember, this was the Japan in the 1950s, not exactly a paradise of enlightened company policy.) Honda also told Fujisawa that he was going to create a culture at Honda where anyone was able to speak out about the problems they could see, without suffering punishment.

The happy ending is that Fujisawa rejoined the company and he and Honda together developed a culture so revolutionary and successful that very few large corporations, even today, could duplicate it.

To this day, Honda gives us a vision of how a company can operate with a culture where speaking up is encouraged. Countless consultants have studied Honda's practices and labels (kaizen, kanban, muda, etc.) and tried to export them to other companies and countries with very little success. If we instead can look to Honda's worldview and intentions, as visible in the story about Honda's argument with Fujisawa, we might understand their success at a deeper level.

5.3.1.4 Building Trust

As we said in Systems Thinking Principle #1—Trust = Speed. But how do we gain people's trust?

If you are a manager or executive and you want people to speak up, the way to help foster that behavior is to build trust.[4] When people trust that they will not be castigated for voicing their thoughts, they will be more willing to say what they think is wrong.

Building trust is easier said than done. It won't happen by putting up a bunch of colorful posters that say "Trust Each Other!" No, it is reflected in your every action, your every word. Since the corporate environment has been coercive for so many years, people are naturally suspicious of trusting their managers. You must get past that. Building trust takes time. Losing trust takes no time at all.

Much has been written about the diesel scandal at Volkswagen during 2015. The automotive company was caught engineering its on-board software to fool the emissions testing done by government agencies. The executives at Volkswagen claim they knew nothing about the "defeat devices." That may well be true. But the Volkswagen CEO, Martin Winterkorn, was known as a hard-driving competitor who didn't want to hear about problems. Even if he had declared an "open door policy" and placed "Trust!" posters on all the walls you can be sure that his employees wouldn't be eager to tell him about problems they observed, especially a problem that could potentially take down the company. The chairman of Volkswagen had the same reputation. Ferdinand Piëch said he viewed the widespread use of corporate funds on prostitution as simple "irregularities" during a corruption trial that eventually sent one VW worker to prison. During the trial he commented on one of the lawyer's mispronunciation of Lamborghini by saying "Those who cannot afford one should say it properly." Probably not a guy you're going to approach to talk about problems in the company.

It is likely that Winterkorn and Piëch built a culture at Volkswagen that encouraged competitive, illegal, immoral behavior. But how did they build it? They built it with their decisions, their speeches, what they said and didn't say, who they promoted, who they neglected and what they emphasized. Just like they built a negative culture, you can build a positive culture using the same tools. Consider the culture you are building with each decision, each comment. When you encourage an employee to take a dangerous shortcut "just this once," what kind of

---

[4]Building trust effectively is a big topic. If you'd like to read more about it, we suggest *Building Trust in Business, Politics, Relationships and Life* by Robert C. Solomon and Fernando Flores (2001).

5.3.2 New Professionalism Principle 2: Solving Communication Problems with Via Negativa

> Everybody complains about the weather, but nobody does anything about it.
> Charles Dudley Warner

In the 1990s, after our own employer merged with another larger consulting firm, we were invited to an offsite meeting of the executives of the new entity. There were over 200 people included, so the company rented a hotel ballroom for the occasion. We went through the usual rah-rah involved in a new merger, and then proceeded to a facilitated session probably meant to bond the disparate group of executives.

In this session, the facilitators broke us up into 12 groups and asked us to diagnose the problems with the new combined company. Then we went around the room and presented the findings of each group. Surprisingly, the first three groups all agreed on the top problem—communication. Then the next group—communication.

Fifth group—communication.

Sixth group—communication.

Seventh group—communication.

And so on. Right through to the last group, each group stated that the number one problem with the company was communication.

We were amazed. How could this be? We took one of the facilitators aside and asked her about it.

"We've seen that with other companies too," she said.

"Seen what? Some of the groups mention communication problems?"

"No. Every group in every company has communication problems as their number one."

It took us a minute to understand what she had just said. Every group she had ever worked with (it was several dozen companies, she told us) had prioritized communication problems as the biggest issue.

What is going on?

We think there are several possibilities. One is that communication problems are a smoke screen for other types of problems. Another is that each of us is in our own bubble, unable to see why people leave us out of certain communications and blind to when we forget to communicate to others.

Many of the "communication problems" are truly just innocent oversights. "How could you include the Director of Planning on the CC list without including me, the Director of Operations??" Well, sorry! I was rushing to get the email out and I guess I forgot?

The worst things about communication problems are often the solutions. What are the usual solutions? More meetings. More conference calls. More roles. More intermediary groups.

"Hey, it seems like IT and Marketing don't communicate very well."

"Okay, we'll create an IT-Marketing Intermediary Group."

Now IT and Marketing have someone else to complain about. The IT-Marketing Intermediary Group. Well, those guys are t-e-r-r-i-b-l-e about communication!!

5.3.2.1 Via Negativa!

In his book *Antifragile* (Taleb 2012), Nassim Nicholas Taleb uses the phrase "via negativa." It is a Latin term and it means "to deny." Roman Catholics have used the phrase to better define what God is, using ways to say what God is not, rather than what God is.

Taleb posits that we can benefit more often by removing things than by adding things. Have high blood pressure? You can either subtract your habit of smoking or you can add certain drugs to reduce your blood pressure. Subtraction of your smoking habit will be more lasting and also less dangerous. The addition of the drugs will have side effects. Quitting smoking will improve your health but is not likely to endanger it in other ways.

Steve Jobs was famous for a Via Negativa (although he did not use that phrase) approach to the design of computer hardware. When his engineers insisted on requiring multiple buttons on the Macintosh mouse, he pushed back. "How can we get by with only one button?" (Eventually, Apple got rid of the single button completely with the zero-button mouse.)

5.3.2.2 A Different Way to Solve Communication Problems

Can we use Via Negativa to solving communication problems?

Developers are not understanding and obeying the standards being created by enterprise architects. Can we get rid of some of the standards? Can we give ownership of the standards directly to the developers?

Our instincts probably tell us the opposite. We want to add, not subtract. Let's add a new weekly meeting to improve communication. Let's add a "National Communications Director" who will be in charge of fixing communication. But it doesn't usually work. Communication problems persist. New problems emerge from the additional layers of bureaucracy.

5.3 The Principles of the New Professionalism

Two development teams are constantly bickering and pointing fingers on botched deployments. Rather than more meetings, more checkpoints, how can we subtract? Can we subtract the physical space between the groups? Have them sitting in the same area of the building? Or even have team members pair with each other from the different groups?

Always look first at how to subtract to solve communication problems. How can there be fewer:

- Meetings?
- Checkpoints?
- Columns on the card wall?
- Ceremonies?
- Handoffs?
- Roles?
- Boundaries?
- Different budget buckets?
- Layers of management?
- Standards?
- Rules?
- Metrics?
- Orientation hoops?
- Mandatory training sessions?
- Less money?

Here are some examples:

Problem:
An Agile team is constantly being derailed by a PMO who is asking for a bunch of non-Agile deliverables (detailed design spec, test strategy, etc.). What should we do?

Addition Mentality:
Let's have weekly meetings with the Agile team and the PMO representatives and report on the status of the deliverables.

Via Negativa:
Let's move one project manager from the PMO into the team room full-time. They don't necessarily have to work on that team's deliverables full-time, but they can be there to answer questions about what the PMO requires and how compromises might be made. They can observe day-to-day life for the team and have some skin in the game. We are subtracting the space between the PMO and the Agile team.

Problem:
An upstream team is not producing what the downstream team needs in a timely enough way. There is waiting and frustration as a result.

Addition Mentality:
Let's have both groups work through the program manager to surface their complaints and to be more proactive about delays. We are adding (or reinforcing) an intermediary to solve the problem.

Via Negativa:
Let's rotate team members monthly between the upstream and downstream groups so they can start to understand the problems the other team is facing, and think of possible solutions given their new perspective.

These Via Negativa solutions make sense when we're dealing with people. People have perspectives, emotions, creativity and build relationships with each other. Machines parts are not like this. There would be no need to rotate parts of one software program with another program so they could "gain perspective." But for people, it can be smart.

Via Negativa is kind of like an opposite to best practices. Remember from our Principle 2—Avoid Best Practices, that we don't want to blindly copy from other organizations just because it "worked for them?" Practices are most often not very transferrable, although we can certainly often learn from other companies. We just must keep from having the expectation that a "best practice" will always work by adding additional layers of management or control. It depends on our intention and worldview as much as anything else.

Via Negativa is a way to say "What practices can we get rid of to grow a stronger team from within?"

5.3.2.3 Addition Often Has More Bad Side-Effects

Even within a team space, our instincts often tell us to put people into specialties because that seems more efficient in the short term.

"We can just add more roles."

Ed can be the authentication specialist. Praveen can do the GUI work. Ellen can handle the data access. We are using "divide and conquer."

But specialists within the team room will automatically cause mini-waterfalls, which will always cause bottlenecks.

Any time we have any big problem, managers will want to add something to ensure that the thing never happens again. New rules! New standards! Anything that, on the surface, could make things mechanical and simple as if the team was a programmable machine. But instead, we should look to subtract. Fewer meetings. Kill some regulation.

Often, after a disaster has occurred, managers (and politicians) have an irresistible urge to "do something." Most of the time, it leads to new rules, new restrictions, new structures, new meetings. Pretty soon, there grows a build-up of these rules meant to fix a one-time event that clatter against one another and prevent productivity from happening. But why not try the opposite? What can you reduce or eliminate?

5.3.2.4 Via Negativa for Retrospective Follow-Up Items

Via Negativa applies to the action items that come out of our retrospectives as well. When a problem is voiced during a retrospective, our automatic response is to "do something" or "create something" to fix the problem. But the PDSA cycle (discussed in Chap. 12—How Teams Can Keep Improving) can help us towards a Via Negativa mindset. Define the problem. Find a measurement that will tell you whether you are improving or not. Make a change, preferably subtracting something rather than adding. Measure. Look at whether things improved. Do the cycle again.

5.3.3 New Professionalism Principle 3: Be an Advocate for Weak or Absent Voices

A key to transforming into a "new professional" is to focus on giving voice to people who are not represented when important decisions are made. In this section, we will look at why this is important and ways to manifest this intention.

5.3.3.1 General Motors Calculates Loss of Their Customers' Lives

General Motors[5] built trucks from 1973 to 1989 that had a specially-designed gas compartment called a "side-saddle" tank. These tanks were alleged to result in the death of 17-year-old Shannon Moseley of Snellville, Georgia. Shannon was killed while driving a GM truck with this type of gas tank, which was said to produce more deadly explosions when the truck was involved in side collisions.

Several families sued GM over this issue. A whistleblower, Ronald Elwell, a former GM engineering analyst, was quoted at one of the trials as saying that there was a memo written at GM titled "Value Analysis of Auto Fuel-Fed Fire-Related Fatalities." In this memo, Elwell stated, GM analysts had calculated the cost of fighting legal battles over dead drivers of their trucks to be $2.20 per vehicle, while the cost of prevention of these fuel-fed fires to be $2.40. The memo makes no recommendation and ends with a disclaimer: "It's really impossible to put a value to human life. This analysis tried to do so in an objective manner but a human fatality is really beyond value, subjectively."

---

[5]bit.ly/GMLawsuits1
bit.ly/GMLawsuits2
bit.ly/GMLawsuits3

The customer was not in the room when people at General Motors were making this decision between the $2.20 and $2.40. If they were, they probably would have been horrified.

So the customer was a "weak voice" in this case. The customer's interests (in this case, not dying) were poorly represented.

This isn't about ensuring that no one ever gets hurt by any product. It is about making good business decisions. Do you think that GM really only paid $2.20 per vehicle after it was clear that they were at fault? Maybe in legal costs, yes, but what is the cost of a tarnished reputation? Did these actions play a part in GM's bankruptcy only a few years later?

It is true that you cannot put a price[6] on a human life. But it is also likely that the price GM arrived at did not take other factors into account that would help to bring down the entire corporation in the next few years.

5.3.3.2 Sony Builds a Back Door for Itself...and Hackers

Here's another story about weak voices.

In October 2005, Mark Russinovich,[7] a blogger, revealed that Sony BMG Music Entertainment had been secretly installing a hacker tool onto people's computers whenever they tried to play a Sony music CD. With no notification to the user, insertion of the CD caused a tool called a "rootkit" to be placed onto the person's hard drive. A rootkit is a tool that hackers and virus writers use to open up a "hole" in a person's computer and be able to get in and out later without being noticed. The rootkit was meant to send information about your activities back to Sony, which Sony felt was necessary to prevent music pirating and song sharing.[8]

Imagine the conversations at Sony. The problem of music piracy was discussed. Ways to prevent piracy were considered. But, at no point in time, obviously, did the rights and needs of their customers come out on top. A Sony executive said it was okay to put a hacker's tool, a rootkit, onto each and every Sony music CD going out the door, knowing that it created a gaping hole in the user's computer, knowing that, not only Sony, but any other ill-intentioned being, could easily gain access and make changes unnoticed by the user.

Where was the "voice of the customer" in this decision? It was absent. Sony wasn't thinking about its customers, they were obsessed with protecting against piracy. The cost was damage to their customer's computers. What did Sony gain?

---

[6]This story probably gained more publicity for the fact that the TV program *NBC Dateline* created a rigged explosion of a GM truck as footage in their story on these lawsuits. This was, of course, bad behavior by NBC, but it doesn't diminish the fact that GM was also acting improperly in knowingly selling products that would kill their users.

[7]bit.ly/OriginalSonyDRM.

[8]bit.ly/SonyDRM.

5.3 The Principles of the New Professionalism

Sony has faced a similar story to what GM experienced after their decision on the gas tanks. Sony's stock has drifted downwards and has not yet recovered to the level seen shortly after the hack was discovered.

As a professional at Sony or GM, would you be risking your job by bringing up the problems with these decisions? Quite possibly. But would you also be doing something to protect your employer from millions in liabilities and lost trust a few months down the road? What is the role of the professional? Are you an order-taker or do you need to apply your own wit and wisdom to your job?

For the professional, the lesson here is to speak up when you see the customer's voice is not represented. The lengths to which you go with that are your own decision. You might stop short of becoming a whistleblower or a street protester, or you might not stop short of that.

For the manager, it is your role to listen when your team members bring up issues like this. Certainly, you will probably not see an issue at the level of an exploding gas tank or a rootkit in your career, but you will see lesser issues. What will you do when those come up? Ignore the whistleblower? Shoot the messenger? If you have created a mechanical team, where your team mechanically follows your orders and nothing more, your team will miss these warnings every time. But if you can create a change-ready team, your team members will bring up these problems and you will have the chance to address them and ensure that your company puts its best foot forward instead of stepping in a puddle.

Please understand, we are not advocating that you take this to the extreme. It doesn't mean that every time a team member has a guilt complex about leaving out a feature or "getting it right" that you must stop the train and forgo the schedule. It is up to your own judgment. Do not act mechanically on the advice we've just given you. Your behavior needs to be situational. But pay attention to those weak or absent voices.

5.3.3.3 Sorry, But Here's One More Story About Weak Voices

We could tell these stories all day long (but we'll stop after this one). There is no lack of material.

After the amazing success of Apple's App Store for its iPhone, Google quickly went into action to create an app store for their own Android mobile operating system. Eventually, the Google app store was named Google Play.

Samsung, the Korean technology company, began building mobile phone hardware to run Google's Android operating system and rose to become the runaway best seller of Android phones (indeed, all smartphones) worldwide.

Samsung, like their competitors Motorola and HTC, created their own unique version of the Android user interface, to avoid becoming too much of a commodity. This made sense, although it turned out that the software engineers and designers at Samsung, Motorola and HTC (among others) seemed to be less capable and innovative than the Google team building the original Android UI. In general, most customers preferred the "stock Android" UI to any of the modified, supposedly improved, UIs provided by the hardware companies. Customers would even agree to pay extra to get the stock Android "Google Play" version of the UI on phones, which starkly illustrated the value of the Samsung, Motorola and HTC interface designs ("We built software that is worth negative $60 per unit!"). Sorry, but we find that friggin' hilarious.

But Samsung went even further with this differentiated business strategy. Samsung created their own app store where customers could download Samsung-specific apps. These apps included S-Planner, a calendar and S-Voice, a voice recognition platform. S-Planner was almost identical to the Google Calendar app and S-Voice only worked with Samsung apps, no other.

What benefit did Samsung have in mind for its customers when creating the Samsung App Store and these "me too" apps like S-Planner and S-Voice? There was no conceivable advantage for customers to have two app stores[9] with certain apps only available here or there, different UIs for each app store, etc. There was absolutely no benefit for the customer. And yet Samsung persisted. They pre-installed their redundant apps[10] on every Samsung phone and tablet and added restrictions so that the apps could not be removed.

In Samsung's case, no one died. No blatant security holes were created. But, once again, the voice of the customer was absent. Someone decided to create a redundant, useless app store and nobody inside the company stopped them. Samsung's separate app store makes life worse for the customer in every way. From the customer's viewpoint, Samsung should have sold or given away their own apps in the Google Play store and allowed customers to choose whenever a Samsung app had the same functionality as a Google app (or not built the redundant apps in the first place, for heaven's sake).

As a team member on a software team, or middle manager, or fellow executive, it is your responsibility to look for these disconnections from customer value and to point them out, repeatedly if necessary. Companies should not knowingly be placing gas tanks in a way that is very likely to burn customers to death. They should not be creating holes on customers' computers for hackers to exploit. And they should not even be frustrating customers with duplicate app stores in a vain attempt to differentiate themselves.

5.3.3.4 Weak and Powerful Stakeholders

As noted in the GM, Sony and Samsung stories, there is something to say about weak and powerful stakeholders providing requirements for your software

---

[9]Amazon also created a special app store, but they had at least a superficial reason in that they were releasing the Kindle devices which would require their own platform and app store/walled garden.

[10]Each successive year, there seem to be fewer Samsung apps preinstalled, which is good.

application. Sometimes an internal IT shop can be a bit like the GM analysts who were making decisions that heavily affected their customers and yet not involving or even "valuing" those customers, to the point of not worrying whether they lived or died. Your team is probably not making this level of value judgments, but you are making decisions that will make someone's job easier or harder. It is still worth it to pay more attention to your requirements gathering process and try to incorporate some humanity into it; it may not save lives, but it may reduce boredom, tediousness or stress.

Among your stakeholders, you will notice that some are powerful and some are weak. This can be the result of position in the organization, but it can also be the result of the force of personality.

Which requirements are more important? Those of the powerful or those of the weak? Some may say that the positionally powerful have more important requirements, because they are the ones who hold the purse strings. Others may say that the positionally weak have more important requirements, because they will be the clerks who need to use the software application day-to-day.

But let's add some texture to this viewpoint. Yes, you need to pay attention to the people who pay the bills. Yes, you need to give the people who will be "hands-on" users what they want and need. But what happens when there are conflicts? Who wins?

Teams we've seen have taken multiple approaches with requirements conflicts. Some teams say that the powerful should always win. After all, follow the money, right? Other teams say, if you have stakeholders who have conflicting requirements, get them into a room and let them hash it out. The Joint Requirements Planning (JRP) session is an example of this.

The situations where the powerful always win will cause problems. In some cases, the weak should actually win over the powerful, and when that does not happen, it will mean problems with the application in production and possibly its catastrophic failure. As professionals, we should have some sense of when that is happening.

When we ask our stakeholders to "fight it out" together, what are we doing? We are acting as "logical, objective" facilitators who try not to have a stake in the game. We are just outsiders who are not taking sides and are just allowing the requirements to emerge with a type of "survival of the fittest." And whose requirements will survive? Those belonging to the most powerful, of course. Either those of the positionally powerful or of the powerful personalities. Either way, there won't be a correlation to the "best requirements" coming out of it.

Remember Aristotle's Four Causes? For many years, hundreds of years, actually, we've been perfectly content to focus on our particular job and not worry too much about the consequences of our actions down the road.

> "Hey, I'm just a developer. It isn't my role to find bugs. That's why we have testers."
>
> "Hey, I just assemble the car door handles. If it comes off in a customer's hands, that means that the quality checkers didn't do their job."
>
> "Hey, I'm just a biologist. You can't hold me responsible for knowing **why** organisms act like they do. I just catalog what is happening."
>
> "Hey, I'm just the facilitator. The results you guys come up with are your responsibility."

As new professionals, we can no longer let go of the final cause—the end purpose—of the system we're in. We have to keep it in our minds constantly. What are the needs of the weak stakeholders? What can I do to build quality into the product right now? Will I speak up loudly enough when I see that our product is part of something bad in the world?

Being connected to the final cause of the system is not optional for the New Professional.

5.3.3.5 Well I, For One, Would Never Do That!

It's easy to read the stories of corporate malfeasance and exclaim "Well if I was in the room I would never do that!"

Not so fast, there, pardner.

Denny Gioia was a management professor at Penn State who went to work for Ford and then later went back into academia. During his time at Ford, he was the coordinator of product recalls in the early 1970s. Yes, during the time of the Ford Pinto. The Pinto had a design flaw that caused its gas tank to blow up, similar to GM's trucks. (We'll tell the full story of the Ford Pinto in Chap. 16—HR Agility).

Gioia was part of the team who elected not to recall the Pinto. In Gioia's words "Before I went to Ford I would have argued strongly that Ford had an ethical obligation to recall. I now argue and teach that Ford had an ethical obligation to recall. But, while I was there, I perceived no strong obligation to recall and I remember no strong ethical overtones to the case whatsoever."

Amazing! So, as a professor observing the industry, he would have called on Ford to recall the Pinto, before and after he worked there. But while he was on the team and had the authority to do so, he didn't feel the same way. We can all get caught up in strange, insular cultures that cause us to do the wrong thing, whether Gioia at Ford, Sony executives creating a dangerous rootkit, or Samsung saying "Hey, what we really need is another app store!" The trick is to be able to dig out of the culture around us and see the perspectives of the weak stakeholders before it is too late.

None of us are better than Professor Gioia. We shouldn't fool ourselves into thinking that we are.

5.3.3.6 The New Professional as Advocate

> When it comes to the design of social and societal systems of all kinds, it is the users, the people in the system who are the experts. Nobody has the right to design social systems for someone else. It is unethical to do so.
> Béla H. Bánáthy (Bánáthy 1997)

As mechanical professionals, we are often told that we need to be objective. "Stay out of the battles" between stakeholders. "Don't take sides."

This may make sense if you are interested only in keeping your job, but it won't actually produce the best software.

We see the best professional as sometimes being an "advocate" for the weak stakeholders. There are ways to get involved without overly compromising your own job or with alienating the stakeholders you are possibly arguing against.

Think of the subtle ways that you can advance the needs or wants of a weak stakeholder in the presence of a powerful one. You might pay extra attention to getting the weak person's agenda on the table, even while the powerful person is trying to crowd them out. You might jump in to rephrase the weak person's requirements in a way that might be more acceptable to the powerful person. You might quietly try to find powerful advocates for the weak person's case.

None of these tactics need to be abrasive, harsh or combative. Find a way to advocate for the weaker party's position in ways that aren't harmful to you, your stakeholders or the requirements process.

Does this mean you should always advocate for the weak and against the powerful? Not at all. But in the situations where you do believe the weaker person has a good point, don't hesitate to step away from your "neutral, objective" position and into a friendly advocative position.

This may not be advice you get in any professionalism training you've ever received, but don't you think it makes sense? In our experience, these steps are extremely helpful towards building a better software application. And they also help increase the trust you have among your stakeholders, weak and powerful, when you show that you are interested in their needs and wants beyond the level of an objective observer.

5.3.3.7 Representing Those Without a Voice

To summarize, think of your role as a professional as an advocate. Advocate for the weak in the presence of the powerful, when necessary, and also an advocate for those who do not have a voice in the debate at all. This may be a customer who is not represented, or it may be something like the people who will benefit from (or be victimized by) your software in the future, maybe people not even born yet.

How can you advocate for them? Think about the unseen stakeholders when you are participating in decisions. Your stakeholders might not only be the people in front of you in meetings, they might not be invited at all.

What do you do about unseen stakeholders? You can try to reach out to them, of course. There may be limits placed on that, which is understandable. But you can try to involve them.

5.3.4 New Professionalism Principle 4: Proudly Display Your Dirty Laundry

The new professional does not try to hide her unfinished product. Instead, she shows it to as many people as possible, trying to get alternative perspectives.

For mechanical professions, rework is a dirty word. We have to avoid it at all costs! Let's get it done right the first time.

The mechanical approach is okay if you are doing tasks that are simple and repetitive. But most of software development is neither simple nor repetitive. (If it was truly repetitive, we'd automate it.) So, the "get it right the first time" is quite dangerous advice. It causes us to fall quickly into an "analysis paralysis" mindset.

Much better to take a whack at the problem, write some code, knowing that you're probably wrong. Then demonstrate what you've built, get people's perspectives, and improve.

The same holds true for written documents. Write something quickly, get some opinions on the direction, then correct and proceed. It is a bit uncomfortable at first, but the frequent course corrections are invaluable in saving the "big bang" failures, even when writing a simple document.

5.3.5 New Professionalism Principle 5: Connect People to One Another

The new professional must be able to identify and build connections between ideas and people. More importantly, we must have a curiosity for learning about connections and finding joy in discovering them.

Angelo Mazzocco, a good friend of ours and a person who embodies new professionalism, takes the greatest joy in connecting people to one another. Walk by the hottest lunch venue in Columbus, Ohio, and you will likely see Angelo inside at a table helping a marketing graduate student meet a member of the local hockey team. Angelo's curiosity for connecting people and his joy in making it happen can be an inspiration to all of us in the importance of connections.

Connections apply to ideas too. Most ideas are not new; they are just borrowed from other situations. Finding an idea that exists in another industry and looking for ways to apply it to your own will always feel a lot more like innovating than "appropriating."

Systems thinking, the theory behind this entire book, is really the science of relationships. The field is full of tools that help people discover and understand connections, including behavior-over-time graphs, causal loop diagrams, rich pictures, Strategic Choice and many others.

5.3.6 New Professionalism Principle 6: Challenge Your Own Assumptions as Much as You Challenge Others'

> I am a skeptical empiricist. I hold all knowledge, including my own, suspect.
> Nassim Nicholas Taleb

> It ain't what you don't know that gets you; it's the things you know that ain't so.
> Mark Twain

> Be your own enemy.
> C. West Churchman, systems thinking pioneer

Do you feel comfortable challenging other people? Good. That is a good skill to have. Some people call it "critical thinking." It means not taking other people's ideas at face value, but being able to think about them critically and accepting only those ideas that make sense to you. This is a good example of Professionalism Principle #1—Speak Up.

But there is another type of critical thinking that is even more valuable. That is the ability to hold your own beliefs as suspect. Much tougher. Much, much tougher.

If you've made the transition from a waterfall lifecycle to Agile, think of the ways your thinking had to change. Plan the work and work the plan? Yeah, that was a mistake. The boss decides who does what? Wrong again. So many assumptions of what we thought was exactly right suddenly became obviously crappy ways to do things.

So what assumptions are you holding onto right now that you'll find out are wrong later? An exercise we like to use is to think of all the things we used to do 20 years ago that we would laugh at today. Writing code without test driving? Ha! Crazy! Taking on a project that doesn't release anything for 18 months? No friggin' way! Hard to believe we used to do things that way.

So, now apply it to today. Wonder what things you are certain must be correct that you will laugh at 10 or 20 years from now. It may be somewhat humbling, but it could be helpful to allow you to be self-critical.

Self-critical, by the way, doesn't mean being critical of yourself as a person. Restrict your criticisms to the views you hold and the practices you hold dear, but don't criticize yourself. "I'm a bad person" or "I don't deserve happiness" are not the types of criticism we are advocating here.

5.3.7 New Professionalism Principle 7: Be Accountable to Change

Accountability means keeping your promises. If you say you're going to do something, then you'll do it. You hold yourself accountable.

But it is worth asking "To what are you holding yourself accountable?" Let's look at a manager. You could say that the manager should create a plan of which stories the team will build in the next few months and then "hold himself and the team accountable" to do it.

But what does that accomplish? This means that when the businessperson comes to the team and says "I need this change to happen," the team will actually say no, or will put the businessperson through some set of hoops to make sure the change doesn't impact their execution of the plan. Is this actually being accountability? Or is it just stubbornly sticking to the plan endorsed by command-and-control management, assuming that everything should be prescribed accurately in this plan?

A more up-to-date definition of accountability might be that it means "promising to work with your business partners to achieve what they want, and tracking to that goal even as things change."

In this version of accountability, the team holds itself accountable to the business, making sure that they are consistently available to do what the business wants, and being adaptive enough to shift their work around to meet the new wants when things change. This is the new accountability in the new professionalism.

People new to Agile software development often talk about the lack of accountability in the Agile lifecycle. What they are really asking about is "individual accountability."

If YOU screw up, how can I hold YOUR feet to the fire and blame YOU for the problem?

In reality, this is nothing more than a type of "cowboy accountability." Once again, it is every man or woman for themselves, which guarantees that each will pursue their own goals (to prove their own accountability) and will ignore the needs of the other team members or groups.

5.3.8 New Professionalism Principle 8: Manage Uncertainties Through Adaptive Practices and Stop Faking Risk Management

> As the complexity of a system increases, our ability to make precise and yet significant statements about its behavior diminishes until a threshold is reached beyond which precision and significance (or relevance) become almost exclusive characteristics.
> Lotfi Zadeh, mathematician and creator of fuzzy logic

Professionals are expected to manage risks. As a new professional, you need to re-examine your perceptions of what risks are and how to handle them effectively.

Risk is when we do not know the outcome of a certain situation, but we are able to understand the probability of things moving in one direction or another. Uncertainty is where we don't even know enough about the situation to understand the odds. Risk involves small, knowable randomness. Uncertainty involves wild randomness.

As professionals, we are expected to manage risk. How do you manage risk? Why, you create a list of the risks you are aware of, then you proceed to learn as much as you can about those risks and you take steps to mitigate them. Right?

Not exactly. This might be the preferred approach among mechanical project managers, but it misses some important aspects of risk.

5.3.8.1 Mediocristan and Extremistan

In Nassim Nicholas Taleb's book *The Black Swan* (Taleb 2007), he goes into great detail to describe two worlds that we all straddle, which he calls "Mediocristan" and "Extremistan." This takes a bit of explanation, but, trust us, it's worth it.

Mediocristan is a land where things are different from one another, but not too different. An example might be if you rounded up a large group of random adults into a sports stadium. You weigh each person and then consider average weights. Sure, some people are heavier than others. (Embarrassing!) Let's say that your sample included one of the heaviest people in the world, weighing in at 1,000 pounds. So you've got some tiny folks, weighing no more than 100 pounds, and then you've got someone at 1000 pounds. A factor of 10 separates the lightest from the heaviest.

If you are able to fit, perhaps, 50,000 people into that stadium, your average weight doesn't change much no matter who you add to the sample. If your average weight of the 50,000 people is 150 pounds, and then you add Mr. 1000 pounder to the list, he may change your average by 0.02 pounds, up to 150.02 pounds as the global average. Not much of a change.

Mediocristan has randomness, but it plays nicely within a predictable set of boundaries.

Now let's move to Extremistan. Let's fill the stadium with people again, but instead of weighing their physical bodies (embarrassing thing to do anyway) we calculate their individual net worth (also embarrassing, really). Net worth is the amount of assets a person owns (bank accounts, stocks/bonds, houses, cars, etc.) less their debts (mortgage, loans, credit card, etc.).

Let's say our global average net worth was $300,000 for the people in our 50,000 person stadium. Now instead of adding the heavy guy, this time we add Bill Gates, the richest person in the world. Bill Gates' amazing net worth is $80B (at the time of this writing) so he will change our global averages. But, unlike the big-boned guy in Mediocristan, Bill will bump our average much more significantly. Without Bill, our average net worth is $300,000. With Bill included, our average jumps to $1.9M.

Adding only one more variable in Extremistan can result in a surprising jump in the average (mean).

So if you are analyzing things and you miss one detail (big-boned guy), you are still okay as long as you are in Mediocristan. But if you are in Extremistan, you might have missed the one detail (Bill Gates) that means everything.

As Taleb notes, the financial markets exist solely in Extremistan. Crazy changes can occur that are predicted by no one. (These are the "Black Swan" events that Taleb focuses on.) American banks predictably make money year after year and then BLAM! they lose every penny that they've earned in their entire history in one quick jump. The market analysts who successfully predicted those quiet years are shown to be worthless because they could not predict the only event that really mattered (the 2008 subprime crisis, as an example).

Software Development: Which 'stan Do We Live In?

Which country do you think we live in, with software development? We live in Extremistan, every day. We pull one storycard from the wall, get it done in 4 h. The next one takes 8 h. The third takes 2.5 h. Suddenly, along comes a storycard that takes eight people 13 weeks. Who saw that coming? But it happens. It is not even rare, this stuff happens all the time. An innocent little storycard sitting on your card wall right now represents some huge percentage of the work, dwarfing all the other cards combined. The Black Swan card is sitting there, waiting to pounce. Which one is it? Can you predict?

As managers, we tend to think we can predict the flow of a project, the patterns within which work gets done.

Next time you hear someone say "It all averages out" remember that that's only true in Mediocristan. In Extremistan, if we miss one important element, our average will be completely messed up.

What's surprising is how people and corporations get the predictable boundaries of games in Mediocristan so confused with the Extremistan of real life risks. Even those who deal with risk and games every day...

A Casino Misses Its Losses

In *The Black Swan*, Taleb tells a story of a speech that he gave about risk and uncertainty at a casino. When he did some research into the casino's business, he saw very clearly that they had done a tremendous amount of research, calculation and surveillance to avoid incurring large losses to gamblers. They had their risk and issue log!

But the four largest losses that the casino suffered that year had zero to do with gambling. First, the casino lost about $100M when one of their top performers in their nightclub was mauled by a tiger (Siegfried and Roy). The casino had no prediction of this. The tiger was, of course, very emotionally attached to both performers. The casino had all types of insurance for the show, even predicting the possibility that the tiger might jump into the crowd. But nothing that covered one of the performers being hurt this way. The tigers slept in the same bedroom as the human performers! How could this have happened?

Secondly, a contractor was hurt during the construction of an annex to the main hotel. The casino made a typical settlement offer to him which the contractor apparently considered an insult. His rage at the offer caused him to make an attempt to dynamite the casino, putting explosives around the pillars in the basement. He was caught before he completed his plan, but the losses would have been immense.

Thirdly, casinos need to file forms with the Internal Revenue Service (IRS) whenever a particular gambler wins more than a given amount. Inexplicably, the casino employee who was supposed to mail the forms instead hid them in boxes under his desk. This continued for years. When the IRS came calling, the casino was forced into paying an extremely large fine for the mistake. Could the casino have predicted this?

Fourthly, the casino owner's daughter was kidnapped. Unfortunately, the owner was so intent on getting the money to pay off the kidnappers that he dipped into the casino's bank accounts.

The risks the casino faced with just these four Black Swan events were more costly than the risks they were studiously trying to avoid in their gambling enterprises by about a factor of 1000 to 1 (according to Taleb's calculations).

Taleb uses this example to illustrate that we should not be teaching risk using gambling examples or gaming theory. Risk and uncertainty are so much more complex than a pair of dice.

5.3.8.2 Risk Management for Software Development

> Avoiding danger is no safer in the long run than outright exposure. The fearful are caught as often as the bold.
> Helen Keller

When you are creating the typical risk/issue lists, you are like the casino tracking the gamblers, monitoring them going in and out of the gaming areas, making sure that they don't bet too much or count cards or hack the software. That is important work to be sure.

But you will be missing the big uncertainties. You will be missing the tiger mauling the performer. You will be missing the daughter getting kidnapped and the owner acting rashly to get the ransom payment.

Knowing that, what should the conscientious professional do? Let's examine the answer to that question.

5.3.8.3 Managing Uncertainties with Adaptive Practices

What we cannot tell you to do, of course, is make a list of all the things you don't know will happen. You don't know them! It isn't possible. What is possible is to take certain precautions that make you more likely to ride out those nasty future events. To be, in the words of Taleb, "antifragile."

Let's take a quick survey of a very few of the nasty future event categories that might be waiting for you in the shadows—those "Black Swan events":

- A technology doesn't work out
- A stakeholder doesn't accept a deliverable
- Something bad happens to the team
- Something is wrong with your process
- Requirements change late in the release cycle

These categories are so general that you cannot plan for them, necessarily, but you can make changes to how your organize your work in a way that will help.

What if a technology doesn't work out? In this book, and advocated by other authors, we describe a concept called Sprint Zero, part of which is dedicated to doing short research projects on those areas of technical risk. This research is called "spikes" in Agile terminology, and spikes can occur during the early Sprint Zero part of a release, or any other time as well. It is a hands-on way to tamp down a risky technical assumption.

What if a stakeholder doesn't accept a deliverable? You can reduce this risk by ensuring constant collaboration between the business stakeholders (particularly the product owner) and the technical team. No "throwing it over the wall." No prototypes, instead the team iterates on the real thing, the software to be built. Prototypes encourage confusion by creating a possibly unworkable facade in front of the "magic" of the back end. Frequent software demos at the end of each short sprint are the most helpful to show stakeholders what is really being built, bit by bit.

What if something bad happens to the team? Pair programming is a great way to ensure that no single developer exists as a silo of knowledge. Common code ownership goes hand-in-hand with pairing. Developers take pains to ensure that no code becomes the "private property" of any team member. This behavior applies to all team space activities, development, leadership, testing, etc.

What if something goes wrong with your process? In Agile teams, we have frequent retrospectives to improve our process. Don't fall in love with the process you have at present. Always be willing to adapt it once you can see it is not working.

What if there are late requirements changes? It's important not to put too much effort into the documentation of your requirements. Cards on a wall are not a big commitment of energy and effort. A thick "business requirements document" is a commitment. If someone wants a big change in direction right after you finish the last page of the thick document, you'll be upset. So don't put so much effort into them. They'll change. Embrace it.

As you can see, many of the normal Agile process—short sprints, retrospectives, card walls—help us manage risks. But they do more than that. They help to manage the known risks as well as giving us the mindset and openness to deal with the uncertainties—stuff we never saw coming. That is the great beauty of these simple practices—that they are deeply rooted in the worldviews and intentions.

The mentality with life in Extremistan that we need to have is:

We know we are terrible at predicting Black Swan events, so instead let's make the impact of those future events less damaging wherever possible.

This is such a different mentality than with mechanical professionalism:

We've had damaging events in the past. Let's get better at predicting them next time, okay?

Mechanical professionalism assumes that the future of a project is predictable in detail in terms of project plans and architectures, and therefore has always had a certain naiveté with randomness.

These Agile practices help us to be new professionals. They help us to ride out the inevitable uncertainties coming our way, and to do it in a dignified, manageable way.

Next time someone asks why you're using Agile practices, tell them you're simply doing risk management. Managing against known risks is easy. We are managing against uncertainties.

> **There Is a Cost**
>
> So, what's the big problem with making the list of risks and chasing each one down? The problem is, the chasing, the mitigation, costs money. Are you sure it's worth it?
>
> We would like to have the comfort of knowing that we've chased down every risk and gained knowledge about it. But that chasing effort costs money and time. Is every risk worth it? Or can we, instead, create resilient teams, processes and relationships that will ward off the risk once it shows up in whatever form?

5.3.9 The Worldview of the New Professional

> The question isn't who is going to let me; it's who is going to stop me.
> Ayn Rand

Being a new professional is a lot different than the professionalism of the past. Since your own perception of professionalism is a big part of what makes up your worldview, it is worth examining and changing what it means to be professional. The buttoned-down, go-with-the-flow, get-it-right-the-first-time, hide-your-dirty-laundry professional of the past must be put to rest. It is asking you to volunteer as a weak stakeholder without voice. We need a new worldview.

> **Test Drive Your Knowledge Again**
> Answer the following questions with the knowledge you have after reading this chapter. Have your answers changed?
>
> 1. What is the best way to handle weak stakeholders?
> 2. What does it mean to be accountable?
> 3. What is an alternative to creating yet another meeting when there is a communication problem between two groups?

> **Try This Next**
>
> **For the executive:** Make a conscious effort to draw out less vocal people in your meetings. Sometimes include a person of a lower rank into meetings where they don't usually attend to provide a unique perspective.
>
> **For the manager:** Introduce the "via negativa" concept to your teams. Ask them to help you to apply it whenever more meetings, roles, handoffs or documents are emerging. Make a list of weak stakeholders and try to find ways to hear their perspectives.
>
> **For the individual contributor:** Set a goal for yourself to speak up in at least one instance per…whatever—week, month, quarter. Do it in a low risk situation at first. See how it feels. Then set another goal to speak up again.

References

Bánáthy B (1997) Designing social systems in a changing world. Springer, New York

Hallowell EM (2006) CrazyBusy: overstretched, overbooked and about to snap! Strategies for coping in a world gone ADD. Ballentine, New York

Scott J (2013) The concise handbook of management – A practitioner's approach. Routledge, London

Solomon RC, Flores F (2001) Building trust in business, politics, relationships and life. Oxford University Press, New York

Taleb NN (2007) The Black Swan: the impact of the highly improbable. Random House, New York

Taleb NN (2012) Antifragile: things that gain from disorder. Random House, New York

Scaling and Sustaining: Avoiding Mechanical Behavior

> *The mechanistic world view, taking the play of physical particles as ultimate reality, found its expression in a civilization which glorifies physical technology that has led eventually to the catastrophes of our time. Possibly the model of the world as a great organization can help to reinforce the sense of reverence for the living which we have almost lost in the last sanguinary decades of human history.*
>
> Karl Ludwig von Bertalanffy

> *The fall of communism can be regarded as a sign that modern thought based on the premise that the world is objectively knowable, and that the knowledge so obtained can be absolutely generalized has come to a final crisis. This era has created the first global, or planetary, technical civilization, but it has reached the limit of its potential, the point beyond which the abyss begins. I think the end of communism is a serious warning to all mankind. It is a signal that the era of arrogant, absolutist reason is drawing to a close, and that it is high time to draw conclusions from that fact.*
>
> Václav Havel, *anti-Soviet activist, political prisoner and first president of the Czech Republic in his speech at Davos, February 4, 1992*

Test Drive Your Knowledge

Answer the following questions with the knowledge you have now. Then answer them again at the end of this chapter.

1. Should you design your organization using the same principles as you design software? Why or why not?

(continued)

2. Is it healthy to question the Agile practices, like "whole team in the room" or "paired programming"?
3. Is it desirable to have a team that operates like a "well-oiled machine?"

6.1 The Burning Question on Robert Rosen's Mind

Robert Rosen (1985, 1991), one of our systems thinking scholars, was a biologist and a mathematician, kind of an amazing combination. Although Rosen died in 1999, he has given the field of biology, and indeed all of science, a lot to think about. Rosen's big question was one of those simple questions with no easy answer. "What is life?" Rosen knew that humans could understand every chemical existing in a living organism and then put exactly those chemicals into a bucket in those same proportions and yet...no life. Life had to be much more than just the right set of chemicals.

Rosen's mathematics background, with direction from his astute mentor, Nicolas Rashevsky, helped him to see biology in a new way. Rosen's research led him to understand that the assortment of chemicals contained in an organism were not the key to life at all. Instead, the way the pieces were organized was the common factor among organisms. Rosen created what he called his "M-R Model" which stands for Modeling-Relation.

As we show in Fig. 6.1, every organism has functions that deal with *metabolism*, the everyday processes of taking in food, pushing out waste and living a life. They

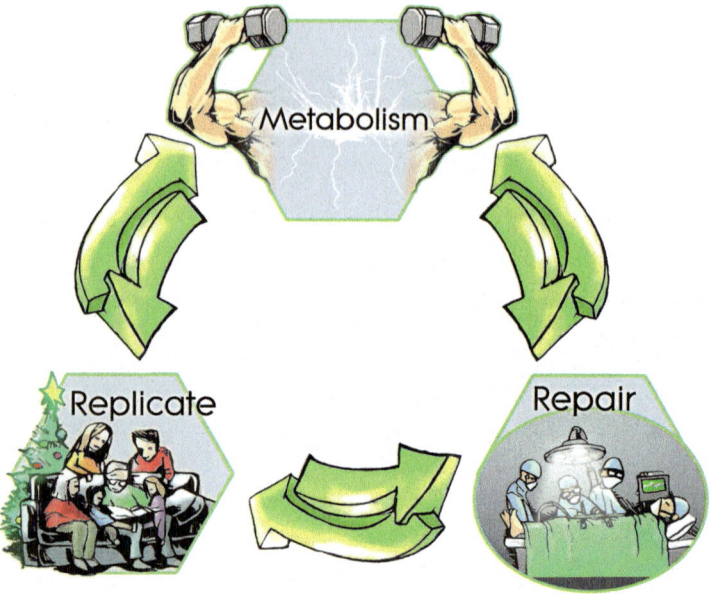

Fig. 6.1 Rosen's M-R Model. © 2017 by Daryl Kulak and Hong Li—reprinted with permission

also have ways to *repair* when things go wrong. Organisms have the ability to heal, which does not come naturally for things that are mechanically constructed.

And organisms can *replicate*, including cellular division as well as producing offspring.

These divisions of work were understandable, but Rosen was especially interested in the relationships between the pieces. Rosen consistently believed that relationships provided the "life" in organisms, so he was most interested how things were organized, rather than the details of each piece.

Rosen realized another aspect of his study of organisms. He saw that his theories applied beyond organisms. His work could be applied to a plant or an animal, true, but it provided a way of understanding any type of organization—a team, a department, a company, a government, a society.

It is this part of Rosen's work that interests us most. Rosen said that organizations of people could either act like something living and breathing (an organism) or they could act like machines. The organisms from within could self-organize, innovate and adapt to new situations. The machines could only do what they were instructed by the machine-creator as an outsider.

Rosen's theory of organizations is what drives the ideas in this chapter. We have more information about Rosen's M-R Model and other theoretical work on the website EnterpriseAgile.biz.

6.2 Allow Me to Work Somewhere Fit for Humans

For many years, poets and philosophers have been mourning the loss of humanity in today's society. Western countries and communists alike have put in place structures that seem to take away what makes us human. Cold, corporate hierarchies just don't seem natural or enjoyable. Silos and layers in large organizations seem to be very effective work prevention systems. Governments often are barely able to function, much less move forward or innovate.

Václav Havel, as shown in the quote at the beginning of the chapter, saw the fall of communism as an important sign that our mechanical view of human society was incorrect and that we needed to move on to something more human. But he could have said the same thing about capitalism, in terms of how people can be viewed simply as machines.

6.3 Are Humans Similar to Software?

Conway's Law was created by Melvin Conway in 1967. It reads as follows:

> Organizations which design systems are constrained to produce designs which are copies of the communication structures of these organizations.

This means that if you have a data group, a business logic group and a user interface group, you will almost certainly create a three-tiered architecture with those layers, mirroring the way you've layered your people. To Conway, the structure of the software is a result of the way you've structured the people.

But more recently, people have discussed what you might call Reverse Conway's Law. James Coplien, of software design patterns fame, has said that you need to structure your people the way you want the software to come out, or else you'll have problems.

Coplien and others have missed an important point, however. People and software are different. Software is, by its very nature, mechanical. People can operate inside mechanical structures, but they will not be very productive or happy doing so.

For software, the engineering practices of Clean Code (see Chap. 9) tell us to add layers of abstraction, to divide and conquer. This makes sense. If each small piece has an identifiable purpose, well-known interfaces, good cohesion and low coupling, then the machinery of software will work well.

But what happens when we add layers to our people organization? More layers means more handoffs, more communication problems, more finger-pointing, more controls, more metrics. More and more important decisions, technical or non-technical, will be made in the layers of management outside project teams where the work is happening. The thing that works so well in software design (more layers) works terribly with people organization design.

And yet, this is what we do. It comes from a misunderstanding that people must be machines. People are not machines. Remember Systems Thinking Principle 6—Treat People Like People, Not Like Machines. Most of today's managers will acknowledge this fact. But their way of coping with this hard reality (people are not machines!) is to build a mechanistic structure and then to throw in a bit of HR puffery—fun picnics, confetti throwing to celebrate birthdays, and other office rituals that so many of us dread. In a way, the HR puffery makes the workplace more mechanical, rather than less. It reinforces the mindset of a prescribed time and place (boundary) for "fun" rather than fun being embedded into day-to-day work.

This chapter, and indeed the entire book, is dedicated to a rethinking of people and machine comparisons. It is one thing to declare that "People are not machines in this company!" but it is quite another to know what to change in order to create a workplace that treats people like people.

There is a class of behavior that people exhibit all the time but machines cannot. One good example of this is highlighted in Malcolm Gladwell's book *Blink* (Gladwell 2007). Gladwell points out that many experienced professionals have a kind of "gut feeling" that relates to their work that far exceeds any kind of rational analysis of a situation. One poignant example is when museum curators are able to look at a painting and instantly tell whether it is a forgery. There is no particular problem they can point to immediately that gives away the fake painting, but instead just a feeling that tells them "something's wrong."

You can see this also with experienced Agile developers and leaders. They can walk into a team room and instantly tell whether that team is going to do well or if they are in trouble. They can see a piece of code and instantly know that "something's not right." This is where the term "code smell" comes from. It refers to a trusted intuition.

People's ability to innovate and creatively solve problems far exceeds any machine and always will. But if we organize our people using a machine structure ("your people structure must match your software architecture") then you will never access their special abilities. In fact, they will be forced to act like a bunch of dumb machines. And then you'll despair because they lack creativity.

It is better to think of an organization as an organism rather than a machine. The organism is not an analogy for an organization. It is what an organization truly is. It's a homology (see Sect. 4.1.3). Rosen's equations that explain metabolism, repair and replicate in an organism apply equally well to Agile teams and programs.

6.4 But Agile Ain't Mechanical, Is It?

Some people see Agile as disorganized, ad hoc or chaotic. Those who have used the Agile processes know that these characterizations are not at all accurate. In truth, Agile, in many of its forms, suffers as much from "mechanical behavior" as any other way of developing software.

Will Agile be just another fad? It's starting to look that way. The biggest reason why software processes become "faddish" is because the proprietors encourage a mechanical adoption of them. They tell their customers "Use my process, do what I tell you and it will fix all your problems."

The proprietors of Agile may tell you that they've moved beyond this problem. But they haven't. Why do we have Scrum certifications? Tests? What are you testing if not mechanical knowledge? More and more, we are seeing a move towards mechanical behavior in the Agile circles.

6.5 Conversations with a Terrible Coach

Below is a fictional discussion between a person wanting to learn Agile and an Agile expert.

Scenario #1

Agile expert: "Today I'd like you to get your whole team working in this conference room. This follows an Agile practice called "whole team in the room."

Person: "Okay. Why do we want to do that?"

Agile expert: "Because it's an Agile practice! Don't you want to be Agile?"

FAIL

Scenario #2

Agile expert: "Because it follows the Agile value of Communication."
Person: "What is that value based on?"
Agile: "It came from the Agile Manifesto. Those guys are wicked smart."

FAIL

Scenario #3

Agile expert: "Communication is an important value because if you don't communicate you will have an unsuccessful project. That's been proven by industry statistics."
Person: "Really, how do you measure the amount of communication?"
Agile expert: "?$%*@@"

FAIL

Just simply asking "Why?" causes our fictional Agile expert great anguish. Without something backing up the Agile values and practices, it is very difficult to explain why you would want to do any of this stuff. It breaks down very easily.

We actually need an underlying reason for doing all this.

It is NOT too much to ask "Why are we doing this?" And the answers "Because it's Agile," or "Because the boss says so," or "Because the Agile experts tell us so," are not valid answers.

Let's return to our beleaguered Agile expert one more time. Maybe he can improve on his fourth try.

Scenario #4

Agile expert: "Today I'd like you to get your whole team into this conference room. This follows an Agile practice called "whole team in the room."
Person: "Okay. Why do we want to do that?"
Agile expert: "Because it is one of several possible practices that will increase communication, trust and appreciation among the team."
Person: "Why do we need communication, trust and appreciation?"
Agile expert: "Because if we don't have those things we are limited to a machine organization, and people can't be productive in a machine organization."

Person:	"Why not?"
Agile expert:	"Because people aren't machines. And if we treat them like machines we won't get their best, most creative work."
Person:	"That is true. We need people's best work. Do we have to bring the whole team into one room or can we achieve communication, trust and appreciation in a different way?"
Agile expert:	"Sure, there are lots of ways that can help us achieve those things. Let's discuss what you have in mind."

WIN!!!

Can you see the mechanical behavior in Scenarios #1, #2 and #3? Many Agile initiatives in corporations are on the path to "mechanical adoption" and are therefore doomed to fail.

6.6 Why? What's the Purpose?

One aspect of "knowing why" is to know the purpose of the work. But why should you have to know the purpose? Why can't I just give you instructions and you follow them? The problem is that no level of instruction can cover every decision, every situation, every judgment call in Extremistan (see Chap. 5). Things that might seem obvious to the experienced person might be a complete mystery to the newcomer. So, in order to guide those moments where the instructions fall short, it helps to know the purpose. Give a man a fish, you feed him for a day. Teach a man to fish, and you feed him for a lifetime. More importantly, to learn how to fish will take a longer time and a different worldview and intention that are not mechanical at all.

W. Edwards Deming (1992) gives the example of cleaning a table. He says it is not enough to give an instruction to a person to clean a table. You must say why you want it to be cleaned, the purpose. For instance, Deming says, if we are cleaning it to place boxes on the table, a quick wipe with a washcloth or perhaps some dusting is sufficient. But if you need the table to perform a medical operation, the table must be thoroughly scrubbed and disinfected. Knowing the "why," the purpose is extremely important, even to the person who has the job of cleaning tables.

6.6.1 Thin Knowledge Versus Thick Knowledge

Thin knowledge (Fig. 6.1) is when you know enough to do the work. Thick knowledge is when you know WHY you are doing what you're doing, as well as how to do it. If the "workers" have low-quality knowledge about their own work, that is always dangerous. You cannot expect the managers (or architects or

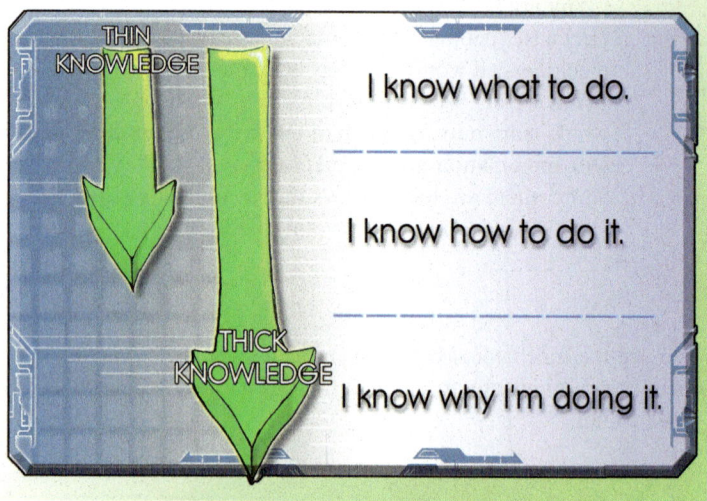

Fig. 6.2 Thin and thick knowledge. © 2017 by Daryl Kulak and Hong Li—reprinted with permission

methodologists) to be the keepers of the high-quality knowledge. Every person on the team must have high-quality knowledge about what they are doing (Fig. 6.2).

If your teams do not have high-quality knowledge, the improvements you make will not be sustainable and will not scale. Think back to the story of Sticky LaGrange from Chap. 1.

6.6.2 Why? Tell Me Your Thought Process

"What was your thought process for this decision?" It might seem strange for an executive to explain their thought process, as though having to justify their actions to their subordinates. But it is necessary to share their worldview and intentions in this process to invite active participations. Although it's not likely to convert everyone into one worldview and one intention, this type of open sharing will build a troop of willing participants from ground up.

If an executive gives the order to move the company into a new market, the employees may not understand. They may think the executive is doing it to burnish their own personal legacy. But the executive may have very good reasons and a good thought process which led him to this conclusion. By revealing that thought process, the executive may help convince his own employees that this is a good idea. Most executives do not do this. Instead, they launch into a "features and benefits" type of sales pitch, rather than showing the steps in their own thinking that brought them to this point.

6.7 What Type of Organization Do You Work In?

Does your organization run top-down or outside-in? A top-down organization is most focused on its organization chart. People in the top-down organization look to their leaders to understand what to do next, whereas an outside-in organization looks to its customers and marketplace for guidance. Here are the comments you hear in a top-down organization:

- How can I get to the next rung of the ladder?
- Why are those guys in those other departments so stupid and our department is so smart?
- The biggest problem in our organization is nobody communicates with one another
- Ed is really high up the chain; he should be able to make that decision
- We need to escalate this issue immediately
- You can't question that one

People in an outside-in organization look to their stakeholders (customers, etc.) to understand what to do next. The comments you might hear in an outside-in organization:

- I think things could run better if...
- The next job I'd like to learn is...
- I wouldn't feed that to my kid. Why are we producing it?
- But is that what the customer wants?

What about "networked" organizations or "flat" organizations? They aren't necessarily better than hierarchical. Most networked or flat organizations are simply top-down organizations that have been downsized.

The top-down organization tends to be organized functionally. In a software team, that means the testers stick to themselves, the developers cluster together, and the business analysts are off by themselves.

Usually the organizational structure has direct impact on people's world views and intention. The Agile team room concept "can" help with this, but we've seen multiple situations where the entire team was physically in the same room, but the functional teams did not talk to one another. They might as well have been in different buildings. In fact, the manager, at one point, even rearranged the seating so testers were sitting beside developers, etc. It still didn't help! There was some other factor preventing them from talking, but the manager could not figure out what it was.

6.8 Agile Practices and the "Why" Behind Them

We need to use our own critical thinking skills on this stuff. Get down to the why stuff works and then build it back up again.

You will often hear Agile experts telling their teams to ask "why" to justify the business reasons to build some software. But conversely, how many Agile experts will tolerate people asking "why should we do this Agile practice?"

With the Agile practice called "whole team in the room," why??? When you think about how a string quartet does their work, do they always stay together, always in the same room? No, they do some practice alone and then they come back together, then alone again, then together again. Maybe there are situations where it helps to be moving back and forth. Can you imagine this might be helpful for your team? Sometimes it helps to be working together in the same room with the business analysts and testers and other developers, but sometimes you need to work alone for a while? This is where blind allegiance to Agile practices gets us into trouble. We don't think "WHY??"

Here's a short example of thinking through how pair programming can add value for a project.

Pair Programming. Why? (Table 6.1)

Let's try it once more with continuous integration (Table 6.2).

While you're going through this, don't try to make every question have an answer. Give a strong answer or nothing at all.

Now try it yourself, and try to think about a specific team situation in each case.

- Frequent releases. Why?
- Burn-down charts. Why?
- Retrospectives. Why?
- Coding standards. Why?
- Sustainable pace. Why?
- Technical debt. Why?

If you cannot figure out why you are doing a practice, you probably should consider dropping it from your toolset, at least for a while. If your world view and intention cannot identify any value out of the practice, how sustainable will the practice be?

Okay, now for extra, extra bonus points, work on this problem:

Open source development works well with people in multiple locations, many of whom never meet each other. Open source teams seem to completely ignore our cherished "whole team in the room" practice. How is it possible that they can succeed?

Table 6.1 The why of pair programming

Pair programming, as opposed to?	Programming by oneself
How does pair programming increase the trust among the team members?	Pair programming increases trust because we get to know each other better by working so closely together.
How does pair programming increase trust between the management and the team?	Not sure that it does.
How does pair programming increase appreciation among the team members?	Once I see your ability to code, and I see things that you do better than I do, I appreciate your skills more. Once I see your willingness to help me with things where I struggle, I appreciate your help.
How does pair programming increase appreciation between the management and the team?	Not sure that it does.
How does pair programming increase ownership among the team members?	More programmers have a feeling of ownership over more of the total code base.
How does pair programming break down people's boundaries?	It breaks down the boundaries between what is "my code" versus "your code."
How does this change your perspective on pair programming?	Seeing that we are using pair programming to increase trust, we should probably avoid long-term pairings. We want everyone on the team to build trust with everyone else, so some form of promiscuous pairing seems like it might be good. Also, the appreciation might be increased if we make sure to implement pair programming and test-driven development together, because I might trust you more if I see that the code we built together works well when tested. Also, I can see how our developers should probably work on as many different parts of the application as possible, to increase their ownership of the total product, not just "their" piece of it.

6.8.1 Be a Skeptical Empiricist

Nassim Nicholas Taleb (2007), one of our systems thinking scholars, tells us to be "skeptical empiricists." That means that we shouldn't believe anything unless we really see it work. It doesn't matter if an Agile expert tells us, or a top-selling Agile book, or our boss. We should always be willing and eager to try new things, but we should, at the same time, be skeptical of the claimed results, no matter if it worked elsewhere, or if it is an "industry best practice." Try things, measure, judge the results, improve the process. Everything is contextual. Each practice must prove itself to you. Just because it worked somewhere doesn't necessarily mean it will work here and now.

This is how you ensure scalability and sustainability.

Table 6.2 The why of continuous integration

Continuous integration, as opposed to?	Big bang integration at the end of coding and compiling
How does continuous integration increase the trust among the team members?	If we use the "break the build" moments to embarrass a team member, that could destroy trust (depending on how we do it). And that is probably different from one team member to another, so we need to figure out what works there.
How does continuous integration increase trust between the management and the team?	It can, especially if we have a way for the team to show that the integrations are working regularly. If a manager can see that integrations are very often happening successfully, and they can see that without even having to ask a team member, that could help to increase the manager's trust of the team. It can also be a trust-breaker, if there are rituals that embarrass people who break the build. Many teams have adopted these tactics, which sometimes work to strengthen the team's relationships (like pledges at a fraternity) but they can also be divisive. Can't see how it increases trust the other way (team's trust of the management).
How does continuous integration increase appreciation among the team members?	Not sure that it does.
How does continuous integration increase appreciate between the management and the team?	Not sure that it does.
How does continuous integration increase ownership among the team members?	Not sure that it does.
How does continuous integration break down people's boundaries?	It can, if we approach the build breaks as a team, fixing it no matter who wrote it originally. But if we maintain the boundaries of "You wrote it, you fix it" we'll have more of a machine model team.
How does this change your perspective on continuous integration?	It seems like we need to make sure our management gets good visibility into the continuous integration results, maybe with a big visible chart. Also, we should carefully plan how we are going to handle it when some code breaks the build. Try not to break trust bonds when that happens, but also do something that people consider to be fun and that is noticeable.

6.8.2 Run a Process Experimentation Lab in Every Team Space

It is good to think of your own team as a process experimentation laboratory. Every "practice" is up for grabs. We measure whether it works or not, if not, we discard it and try something new. We are continually evolving and taking in new practices, trying them, measuring, and throwing stuff out as well.

It's good to take the ownership out of practices. "We are capital-A Agile because we do standups and demos—see?" Instead, we are always improving and we take nothing for granted.

As we said in Sect. 4.1.2, we shouldn't blindly do practices just because some expert told us to do them. Instead, experiment and create your own that fit your organization's culture and the team members' worldviews.

> **Test Drive Your Knowledge Again**
> Answer the following questions with the knowledge you have after reading this chapter. Have your answers changed?
>
> 1. Should you design your organization using the same principles as you design software? Why or why not?
> 2. Is it healthy to question the Agile practices, like "whole team in the room" or "paired programming"?
> 3. Is it desirable to have a team that operates like a "well-oiled machine?"

> **Try This Next**
>
> **For the executive:** Explain your thought process next time you announce a change in direction to your staff. Tell them how you arrived at this idea rather than just trying to sell the idea to them.
>
> **For the manager:** Allow your teams to set themselves up a "process experimentation lab." Maybe choose just one team as a pilot. See how it goes. Allow the team to fix the problems that arise using the PDSA cycle.
>
> **For the individual contributor:** Make a list of 6–8 practices that you currently use and use the "five whys" exercise with each.

References

Deming WE (1992) Out of the crisis. MIT Press, Cambridge, MA
Gladwell M (2007) Blink: the power of thinking without thinking. Back Bay Books
Rosen R (1985) Anticipatory systems: philosophical, mathematical and methodological foundations. Pergamon Press, New York
Rosen R (1991) Life itself: a comprehensive inquiry into the nature, origin and fabrication of life. Columbia University Press, New York
Taleb NN (2007) The black swan: the impact of the highly improbable. Random House, New York

Business Value, Estimation and Metrics 7

> *Life is not long, and too much of it should not be spent in idle deliberation how it shall be spent.*
>
> Samuel Johnson

Test Drive Your Knowledge
Answer the following questions with the knowledge you have now. Then answer them again at the end of this chapter.

1. What's the longest any software release should run before making it into production?
2. How can you ensure that you're delivering the most valuable features first?
3. What's the difference between estimating and sizing? Why is the difference important?

7.1 Do We Really, Honestly Need a PMO?

Program management offices (PMO) have been a big part of software development for at least 15 years. The purpose of a PMO is to manage the initiation of new projects, monitor on-going projects and handle interactions between projects. The PMO accomplishes what is called "portfolio management" in this chapter.

In this chapter, we will introduce several ideas that may seem antithetical to the old PMO world. This may cause you to wonder "Do we still need a PMO?" But we've seen that the PMO is still necessary. Its function and relationships with projects and executive management should change, but there is still a place for a group that connects to all projects and provides summary information to the executive suite. It's the intention of the PMO that matters. If the PMO is a servant to its teams, then it should stay. If the PMO has the intent of controlling the teams, then it is not helping anyone. The PMO must become more of a Servant PMO (see Chap. 11). And the Agile teams must find ways to help the PMO do its job, as we discuss in detail in Chap. 15.

7.2 How an Idea Becomes a Project

Portfolio management is the process of evaluating projects to decide if they are worthwhile (at the beginning as well as on-going). In order to determine worth, we must know how much they will cost and the benefits they are predicted to bring—a cost-benefit analysis. Then we, meaning some group of executives, can decide whether this project should be tackled this year, or whether some other project will be a better investment of the company's money. There is a fixed budget, and we fit as many projects into it as we can, the remaining projects fall off the plate until next year (or never).

Once those decisions are made, the management can begin slotting the projects into the yearly timeframe and estimating the resources we will require from our various software groups, including the number of people, hardware, software package licenses, etc. to accomplish the goals of each project.

Portfolio management also includes monitoring the on-going projects, making sure they are meeting certain success criteria and investigating into those that are not doing well.

It is fair to say that most of today's PMOs use methods from the Project Management Institute (PMI) in North America or PRINCE2 in Europe.

7.3 The Problems with Today's Portfolio Management Processes Are...

In this section, we itemize the problems with the current methods of portfolio management. As we change the processes of software development teams, we also have the opportunity to improve the processes of how an idea becomes a project.

7.3.1 The Annual Portfolio Management Cycle

The idea of portfolio management is to prioritize projects based on the benefits they will bestow on the enterprise and the costs they will incur. Those figures need to be estimated, based on whatever is known at the time.

7.3 The Problems with Today's Portfolio Management Processes Are...

If you've seen a cost-benefit analysis, you will notice that the costs are a heckuva lot more detailed than the benefits.

How well known are these costs and benefits? They are both, honestly, only ever guesses. This process highlights the difference between accuracy and precision. Accuracy is getting a number right. If you guess that 5 inches of snow fell yesterday and we measure the snow and it comes to about 5 inches, then your guess is accurate.

Precision refers to a level of detail. If you guess that exactly 5.15218 inches of snow fell yesterday, you are being very precise. Further, it sounds like you really know what you're talking about. Precision gives the impression of accuracy. However, there is often no correlation between a precise answer and an accurate answer.

With cost-benefit analyses, precision is usually highly valued and accuracy is usually nowhere to be seen.

7.3.2 Projects Incur Unnecessary Costs and Risks

Most likely, a portfolio management process is about evaluating and prioritizing "projects," which have a particular goal, budget and duration. That's the good aspect of projects. The bad aspect happens when we go on to assemble a project team. We pull people together who then have to figure out how to work together, incurring the costs of forming, storming, norming, etc. every time. With this build-up and tear-down of teams for each project, we are incurring unnecessary costs as well as risking that the teams might not work well together and cause the project to have problems.

7.3.3 Early Estimates Are Inaccurate

The portfolio management process doesn't work very well unless the "cost" side of the cost-benefit equation is known. So, often, a person who is knowledgeable about the technology/applications/domain is asked to come up with an estimate for how long this project might take. Inevitably, these estimates are wildly inaccurate, and almost always they are too low. This causes an additional estimation cycle once a team is assigned the work, and usually the cost-benefit is not rigorously re-evaluated to ensure that it is still worth the money. However, the existing portfolio management process will impose its budget control and project plan as if it were operating in the deterministic Mediocristan rather the reality of nondeterministic Extremistan.

7.4 Ideas for Portfolio Management

> Larry Page (Alphabet CEO): Have you ever seen a scheduled plan that the team beat?
> Jonathan Rosenberg (Alphabet executive): No.
> LP: Have your teams ever delivered better products than what was in the plan?
> JR: No.
> LP: Then what's the point of the plan? It's holding us back. There must be a better way. Just go talk to the engineers.

We need a better way to manage our portfolio[1] of what are basically investment opportunities in technology.

7.4.1 The Fleeting Concept of Value

Everyone feels like we know what value is.

Look - we produced a new product. That is value!

I'm doing something that our customers will pay for. See! Value!

Value seems measurable and permanent. But the truth is that value is fleeting. It can appear and disappear just as quickly. This means that all our efforts to "calculate value" in great detail, whether to show some detailed return-on-investment, or "cost of delay" calculations, are really a bit of overkill.

Let's set a scenario. A team of 50 people are working on a software product to be delivered to customers on May 1. They are putting features into the product and taking out defects. Value! Value! Value! The executives of the company are congratulating the team each week and month on the value they are adding.

Suddenly, the company is purchased by a larger company. Two weeks later, the larger entity decides that this product, currently underway, is not part of their strategy. Poof! The value is gone. For those weeks and months, the team was working diligently, they were producing value. That's true. But with the stroke of a pen, or the wave of a hand, that value became worthless. Throw that shit away. No one needs it now.

Don't cry over killed value. It's gone. You can't revive it. Just get refocused on what is valuable NOW. Figure out what the company needs to produce and jump on it. That big pile of something formerly known as value isn't worth your time. Don't sift through the code and try to figure out what you can salvage. Move on.

---

[1] A note about SAFe (Scaled Agile Framework): We support the portfolio processes in SAFe, as created by Dean Leffingwell, including the shared backlog, release trains and program increments. What we discuss in this chapter is compatible with, but beyond, those constructs. We've had direct experience with SAFe with multiple clients, and the mechanics of the framework work well. But SAFe tends to focus on the perfect world—the end game. This chapter, and indeed this book, focuses on the winding, tortuous road that you must navigate to get to that perfect world.

This is a very difficult concept for many of us who have a technical background. "Oh my—look at the wasted work!" But for businesspeople, it is just how things work. We've decided that the old product isn't what we need to work on right now. We'd prefer to take that money and those people and put them to use in the pursuit of something even more valuable.

The disappearance of value can happen in many ways. Corporate mergers. Changing of the guard—a new CIO, CDO, CTO, CFO, CEO. A radical and unexpected move by a competitor. Changes in customer needs. Missing a time window ("we needed that software for the audit in May, it doesn't help us in July!"). Or the validation of a first release that shows that there is no demand for further development. There are lots of ways software can become less valuable. There are also ways software can dramatically increase in value. And those shrinking deadlines that we all hate? You know—"I know I told you we needed it in May, but now I'm telling you we need it by April." Those often come from a value perspective. A competitor is creeping up on us and so we must change our game. Lots of overtime? Not needed. We just figure out a smarter way to slice the work. (See further in this chapter.)

This is a hard message we are giving you about value. Sorry to be jerks about it. We just need you to realize that those fancy value calculations, or cost-of-delay or whatever, are mostly crap. Yes, calculate the value. But do it on the back of a napkin, don't put days of work into it. Because tomorrow it could be gone. Poof!

7.4.2 Value Stories

> My dad used to have an expression: "Don't tell me what you value. Show me your budget, and I'll tell you what you value."
> Joseph Biden, former U.S. vice president

Colleagues[2] of ours developed the concept of the "value story." You can use value stories to help connect the lofty return-on-investment (ROI) calculation done before the project starts to the work done later by the team.

You can think of a value story like a group of user stories. (No, it is not an epic. More on that later.) Here is the template for a value story:

As <the enterprise> I want to <create something> so that I can <achieve something>.

---

[2] A group of individuals working at Pillar Technology created the value story idea around 2007–2008. The people we know who were at the center of it (although we may miss someone) were Matt VanVleet, Bob Myers and Chris Beale.

Here are some examples of good value stories:

As Global Manufacturing Inc. I want to provide up-to-the-minute order and inventory information to my customers so that I can increase customer satisfaction by 10–15%.
As Customer Service Inc. I want to have a product catalog system so that I can reallocate $400K–$800K in the yearly labor cost by decreasing the time taken to enter a new product from 4 h down to 15 min.
As Software Company Inc. I want to include a calendar feature in my software product so that I can close an additional $5M to $10M new sales in the next year.
As Legacy Company Inc. I want to have a new order fulfillment system so that I can retire the old system for a savings of $500K to $900K per year.

You can see that value stories sort of resemble return-on-investment statements; however, the "investment" part is missing here (intentionally).

Here are some aspects of value stories that are important to know:

1. You create value stories at the beginning of the release cycle and you organize your backlog with them throughout the release cycle (unlike ROI).
2. There is often more than one value story for a single product release, sometimes as many as five or ten value stories for one release.
3. Value stories can represent monetary gains as well as the achievement of other corporate objectives (increase in customer satisfaction, increase speed of new factory setup, etc.).
4. Monetary value stories can represent cost saved or revenue gained.
5. Value story gains are often shown as ranges to avoid implying false precision.
6. Value stories can change during a release cycle as the team and their stakeholders learn more about the business problem and the technology involved.
7. One user story can be part of more than one value story (unlike epics).
8. It is possible that once a team finishes value stories #1, #2 and #3, value story #4 requires no additional user stories (again, unlike epics).

Teams use value stories to prioritize their user stories. With a large release, the number of user stories can multiple into the hundreds or even thousands. If this is the case, prioritization of user stories becomes a real challenge.

With an epic approach, you are asking **"What are the major functions of this application?"** But with value stories, you are asking **"What are the ways this application is valuable to the business?"**

The difference in the questions can be stark. Some of the functions might be individually valuable, but maybe not. Maybe a group of functions have to be delivered together to have any value. Also, there could be releasable chunks that cut across functions that have value. For instance, if a new application is to replace a legacy app, then the point where the new app does everything the old one did, so we

7.4 Ideas for Portfolio Management

can shut off the old one, has value. We will no longer have to pay to maintain the old app. That's valuable. That's probably one of several value stories.

Another example is that it may be valuable to implement the features that relate only to one region, let's say Scandinavia. This might be a grab bag of features, and also it might include only portions of other features. But the Scandinavia rollout is where the value is.

Scrum will tell teams to prioritize epics instead of individual value stories. But epics are not associated with business value. They are groupings of user stories, usually by subsystem or other technical category. This will cause the team to build the application one subsystem at a time, which means they will not be able to offer any end-to-end functionality until the release date is upon them.

Value stories, in contrast, must provide end-to-end functionality. For instance, with an inventory system, you might have the following epics:

- Receive inventory items
- Check inventory
- Pick item
- Ship item
- Automatic restocking
- Reconcile inventory

If the team uses epics to create their priorities, then "Receive Inventory Items" might be done first, then "Check Inventory," etc. The problem with this approach is that you do not have a working application until the very end of the release cycle. You cannot ship an inventory system that does not have a capability to reconcile inventory. So you need to get through all the epics before you can release. And therefore, any tiny problem during your release cycle will cause you to miss your deadline. In a way, you are stuck in waterfall thinking, even though you are producing working software in short sprints! How disappointing!!

Instead, by using a value story approach, you can slice the release a different way. The team should look for ways to produce an end-to-end solution—receive/check/pick/ship/restock/reconcile—as quickly as possible. How can we do this? By removing the complications.

Let's do an end-to-end for only simple items, where there are no sub-components or bills-of-material. That will simplify things greatly. Let's also not worry about items that are perishable. Let's also focus just on one particular warehouse, ignoring the others for now, with all their attendant complexities.

We can simplify the end-to-end inventory process down to such a degree that the team might create the solution in just a few weeks. This is important because most of the risk of any application lies in the integration between the steps (receive/check/pick/ship etc.). So we should expose those risks as early as we can. Let's solve those risky areas now with a simple set of variables and then layer on the complexity bit by bit.

This is a very different approach from the way work is allocated in a typical Scrum team. But it is a necessary change, because the team is able to showcase business value very quickly, and the stakeholders are able to see the progress and offer input much earlier in the release cycle.

7.4.3 The Cisco Rule

Cisco is generally known as a company that sells routers, but they do lots of other work too. Cisco has solutions for phone systems, video conferencing, network and server management, cloud computing and security. They sell hardware but they are also a giant software company.

At Cisco, to our limited understanding, there is a particular rule. No team can proceed with a release of a product that goes longer than 90 days. No excuses. No exceptions.

They probably don't call it this, but we have taken to calling this "The Cisco Rule."

No release cycle is ever allowed to take more than 3 months.

Why would a large company like Cisco make such a confining rule as this? The reason is simple. Cisco is a publicly-held company. They must report their financial results to Wall Street once every 3 months. That means that the Cisco executives must look at each software release underway and make some determinations. Is this going well? Is it worth the money? Should I cut it and put that money elsewhere? If I need to cut my spending, where should I cut?

These questions come up at least once every 3 months at Cisco (and almost every other company). So, they set up a rule that teams must release software to production every 3 months or even faster than that.

Your company or nonprofit or government agency should adopt The Cisco Rule too. The IT world has too many projects that go on for months or years without providing any value. Software metrics have told us year after year that large projects fail and small project succeed. This tells us that we need to turn those giant projects into a sequence of smaller projects.

Oh, but we have this big project that absolutely cannot be broken down into 3 month projects!

We have heard this from every one of our clients. "Some big projects just cannot be broken down; they must be approached as one large unit." But it is seldom true.

7.4 Ideas for Portfolio Management   103

We've worked with clients to break down every manner of "indivisible large project," including package implementations, enterprise systems and highly-regulated applications.

The key is to use value story breakdowns instead of epic breakdowns. Divide the large effort into end-to-end chunks that are valuable to the business, rather than technically-based subsystems or business process steps.

7.4.4 Prioritizing Value Stories

Now that you have value stories as collections of user stories, you can prioritize at the value story level instead of trying to prioritize individual user stories. For large releases, there can be hundreds or even thousands of user stories, so prioritization of user stories is not wise.

Think of moving the value stories up and down in the backlog with all their requisite user stories following them.

Since there will be some revenue value stories (increase sales by $5M), some expense cutting (decrease expense by $500K), some percentages (increase efficiency by 5–10%) and some intangible (increase customer satisfaction) you will need one scale that applies to them all. We suggest using a t-shirt sizing system to signify value among value stories. Value stories can have a value of small, medium or large. This is a simple system and can help the product owner prioritize value stories in the release backlog.

The small, medium and large buckets also keep us from being too focused on the false precision of the dollar values inside the value stories. These dollar values are just guesses. So many factors can cause them to go up or down when the software goes into production and reality hits. SML categories can help you abstract from false precision.

7.4.5 Slicing Value Stories

Value stories are a useful way to group user stories. But they are often too big for release planning and certainly for sprint planning. We need something smaller than a value story but larger than a single user story. We need to "slice" our value stories.

To accomplish this, we will use a technique that we've called "boundary critique," borrowing from systems thinking.

Boundary critique is a way to look at the various dimensions of a value story and begin to break it up into tiny pieces that can be addressed one by one. Here's an example of a mobile application that we worked on. The mobile app needed to read bar codes on devices on shelves in a storeroom and be able to pass the information to a central database as part of an inventory reconciliation. The deadline was tight.

Initial discussions occurred in the middle of December and the inventory event had to be conducted in the first week of February. Only a few weeks to build it! Ahhhh!

So, we came into the situation knowing that we would have to find a tiny slice and get that done with high quality. There wasn't much time. We held a couple of meetings with the right stakeholders and listed a set of items that were potential slicing dimensions:

Purpose of the app
Data upload method
Mobile platform
Validation method
Authentication method
Input method
Location awareness

Then we listed the slices for each of the dimensions (Table 7.1):

The highlighting showed the slices that we would try to accomplish in the short few weeks we had to work with. If things started to look bad, we would go back to the list and try to cut back even further. The team had the deadline firmly in mind and managed each decision based on whether it would put the deadline in jeopardy or not. The approach worked wonderfully and we've used it ever since. Even on very large projects, the boundary critique has worked to corral the various dimensions of a project into clear focus.

Notice that the dimensions can be feature-based (purpose) or they can also be nonfunctional requirements (platform). In fact, you can use any of the following as dimensions on your list:

- Features
- Nonfunctional requirements
- Customer segment (by location, type, persona, task, situation, etc.)
- Interfaces to other applications
- Fidelity (increasing levels of quality, error handling, beauty of UX, etc.)
- Classes of data

7.4.6 The Real Day-to-Day Magic of Value Stories

In our experience, the amazing part of using value stories is a shift in intention and worldview for the enterprise. Instead of an ROI being calculated by some wise financial types at the beginning of a release, we now have value stories that are meaningful for any person at any level.

If the culture shifts enough, you can see an even larger impact. Developers and other team members start to feel ownership of the value stories, to the point where they feel free to question the product owner, or any executive, on exactly

7.4 Ideas for Portfolio Management

Table 7.1 Slicing a mobile app

Dimensions	Slice 1	Slice 2	Slice 3	Slice 4
Purpose of the app	Conduct the physical inventory	Receive	Transfer	Retire
Data upload methods	e-mail (existing)	still do uploads batch	do uploads real-time (is wi-fi available?)	MQ-Series with WebMethods reverse proxy service (individual uploads)
Device platform	iOS (corporate standard)	Android (not supported in MobileIron)	Windows Mobile	BlackBerry
Validation method	No validation	Alphanumeric positional verification (manufacturer ID, device code)	Manual override	
Authentication method	Assume user ID is typed in right	Reuse what Check In/Out is using	Build an authentication system	Proxy approach to user IDs
Input method	Device camera as active scanner	Manual input	RFID	Voice
Location awareness	None	List	Search	Geolocation

why a new feature has value. The conversations, at their very best, go something like this:

Product Owner: *I'm going to add this new user story to the backlog.*
Developer: *Hmmm. I don't see how that gets you to any of our value stories?*
Product Owner: *Yeah, but it's super important. I know people want it.*
Developer: *Should we create a new value story that gets prioritized above our current ones?*
Product Owner: *Well, umm, no. Dang it, I guess I can't really connect it to any business value. You're right, it doesn't belong in the backlog.*

We have seen this behavior many times in our team rooms. It is healthy. It helps protect the team from including work that doesn't connect to the value story, and it helps each person to think like an executive. In fact, we'd go so far as to say that if these conversations are not occurring, the team must improve its own intentions and worldviews to help change its culture.

Each team member, no matter their role, should have the right to say to the product owner who is adding something new "Prove to me that what you're adding is valuable."

7.4.7 "Get Me a Black Truck!"

But why should every person in every role care about the business value? Isn't just important that the executives know the value and everyone else can just play their part?

Maybe a movie example would help. Let's imagine a movie director shares our philosophy, that each person on the movie set should understand the depth of the characters, not just the actors but every person involved with the movie. The director asks each person to read the script and to think about how the characters are feeling and thinking. He answers their questions rather than giving them a mechanical "You don't need to know that" response.

Now the director notifies one of the prop hands that his protagonist will need a black truck.

With an ordinary director, the prop hand will just get the nearest, cheapest black truck and bring it to the set. But with our director who cares that each person knows the characters, the prop hand will think about the particular character of the protagonist, and will realize that he will be proven to be a bit evil later in the script, and therefore the design of the truck should be a bit evil too (Fig. 7.1). Maybe some

Fig. 7.1 A black truck that is a bit evil. © 2017 by Daryl Kulak and Hong Li—reprinted with permission

subtle evil touches that would only be obvious in retrospect once the audience realizes he is really a bad guy.

Can you see that every so-called "bit player" in a movie crew, or a software team, can add their unique skill to the project resulting in more and more value at every turn?

7.4.8 Three Levels of ROI: Thin, Thick and "Thurmanator"

As we've said, value stories are different than the typical ROI (return-on-investment) calculation for project work. First, ROI is created at the beginning and then ignored during software development. Second, value stories help to organize the work so that chunks of value can be delivered one after another and perhaps moved into production sooner than originally expected.

Many people think that ROI calculations are useless unless the team follows through all the way to measuring whether or not the software delivered the value or not. We do not think this way.

7.4.8.1 Thin ROI
Thin ROI is when we create an ROI calculation at the beginning of a project and then let it sit on the shelf during the software development lifecycle. We fulfill a "check mark" to evaluate whether this project is worth starting, then we build a plan and execute without looking back to the value understanding.

7.4.8.2 Thick ROI
Thick ROI is when we use value stories. Now we take that original ROI calculation and break it down into value stories and slices that give us a picture of valuable progress every step of the way.

Value stories can be extremely effective ways to convey information between businesspeople and technologists. By stating that a certain chunk of software is expected to give the company a certain chunk of value (revenue, reduced expense, increase customer satisfaction, PR moment, etc.), the businessperson is able to show a technologist the connection between writing a few lines of code and a genuine benefit for the company and its customers. Making this connection helps the technologist understand the purpose of the work they are doing. And purposeful work is a whole lot more motivating, energizing and interesting than work where the purpose is unclear. "Now I know why I am doing what I'm doing."

But Thick ROI stops short of trying to measure the benefit after the software goes live. The entire purpose of Thick ROI is to provide the team with a tangible vocabulary to tie all activities back to a statement of business value and to prioritize initiatives amongst the pool of what we could possibly work on.

Fig. 7.2 The "Thurmanator"—Tastes great, but too much for a meal. © 2017 by Daryl Kulak and Hong Li—reprinted with permission

7.4.8.3 Thurmanator ROI

The highest level of ROI management is to calculate ROI upfront and then measure the ROI post-production to ensure we receive the return we were expecting. This allows us, in theory, to make adjustments and calculate a better ROI next time.

We call this Thurmanator ROI, in homage to the extremely large hamburger sandwich served at the Columbus, Ohio restaurant "Thurman Cafe"[3] in German Village. The burger (Fig. 7.2) is so large that it is impossible to get your mouth around it, and it is, in fact, a bit of overkill in terms of a dinner for one human being.

Here's why.

Let's say you had a software release that you expected would gain $3M for your corporation. That was the expected return. But when we practiced "Thurmanator ROI" we found out that we only gained $500,000 in the year or two since it went live. What happened? Obviously, the software wasn't as valuable as they thought, right?

---

[3] It is a great restaurant. A tiny little dive bar that serves good food and is almost always crowded with happy customers.

7.4 Ideas for Portfolio Management

No, probably not right.

As it turned out, the sales force was going through a leadership power vacuum just as our software hit the market, and they did a poor job of getting it into customers' hands. Plus, there was another product that our company released at the same time that was perceived to do the same thing that our package did, so we found we were competing with each other for market share and mindshare. Not to mention that a recession happened, which caused us and all our competitors to drag for 14 months right at the time our software was released.

You can see that the success of the software, whether a package released by a software company or an internal app done by an IT shop, comes into an uncertain world, where its own level of quality is only one small factor in a barrage of swirling complexity that can lift the software to great heights or crush it on impact.

All we can do is to create the best quality software we can, in close partnership with the business stakeholders and eventual users, and hope that we can win our chance at the slot machine.

Does this mean we should abandon ROI altogether? No. We still need ROI calculations and value stories as our elegant communication method between businesspeople and technologists, but it also means that Thurmanator ROI, trying to ensure that we get every last penny of ROI in real life, is probably not worth the time and money it will take, since we all live full-time in the land known as Extremistan. Feel free to use Thick ROI, but stop short of going full-on Thurmanator.

7.4.9 Metrics

> The most important things cannot be measured.
> W. Edwards Deming (1992)

> Managers who don't know how to measure what they want settle for wanting what they can measure.
> Russell L. Ackoff et al. (2007)

Why do we measure? As Douglas Hubbard says in his seminal book *How to Measure Anything* (Hubbard 2014), we measure to inform our decisions. First we need to figure out what decision we are trying to inform, then we decide what to measure.

But there are good reasons to gather metrics and bad reasons. For this, we must go back to our on-going dialogue about worldview and intent. Here are some good reasons to measure:

- To understand one's own progress
- To solve a problem using data

Here are some bad reasons to measure:

- To facilitate competition between teams or groups
- To "motivate" a team to do better
- To increase control over a group

In general, measurements must belong to the people being measured. We think of metrics as a mirror. Other groups or managers may collect metrics about a team, but then their goal must be to use those metrics like a mirror to give to the team and allow them to make their own decisions based on those metrics. An outsider using metrics as a way to exert control over a team is an inappropriate use of metrics.

7.4.9.1 Metrics About Progress

Given a compatible intent, metrics can help a team in two ways: to illustrate progress or to diagnose problems.

A good principle for any team room is that metrics should be "big and visible." This can mean printing a chart showing the metric and taping it to the wall of the team room.

In order to have metrics that are big and visible, they usually need to show trends. Deming calls these types of charts "behavior over time graphs." Figure 7.3 is an example (an explanation of which situation we'll offer later in this chapter).

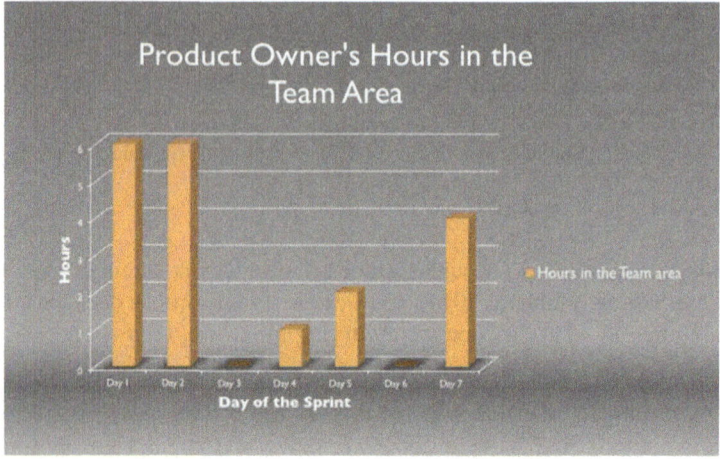

Fig. 7.3 Example of a behavior-over-time graph (we'll explain the details later). © 2017 by Daryl Kulak and Hong Li—reprinted with permission

7.4 Ideas for Portfolio Management

If a trend like this is done well, it should "set a mood," meaning, it should evoke some emotion. "Hmmm, it looks like we are getting slower. That's not good," or "I love seeing code coverage increase like this!"

The principle for big and visible metrics is as follows:

A metric should set a mood at a glance from across the room[4].

If your chart does this, you've done well.

It is important to keep your charts up-to-date. If any team member sees a chart that is outdated, they should write "STALE" on the chart in big letters and someone should take the task of reprinting a new copy. This means that a plotter is a very important tool for any team room. We usually see one plotter being shared by four or five teams without any problem. Taking a trip to the print shop down the street is not usually a good recipe for keeping charts up-to-date.

Burndown Charts

We said earlier that metrics should illustrate progress or diagnose problems, so let's start with the progress metrics.

The burndown[5] chart should be familiar to any Agile enthusiast. Here is a metric that really sets a mood if it's done right. Burndown charts should not be too complicated, otherwise they'll be hard to understand from across the room. Figure 7.4 is an example of a simple burndown chart.

Figure 7.5 is a bit busier, but it comes from a project we worked on where there were thousands of small conversion and validation tasks to be done during a year and no one was really sure what it would take (it was only partially an IT project). After 8 weeks into the project, our burndown showed that the current team operating at the current rate would go far, far past the necessary "Go Live" deadline, which occurred around the 50th week. The standard burndown, looking at the tops of many columns, came out to at least 100 weeks. One standard deviation below came to 79 weeks (shown as SDB on Fig. 7.5), far above what was needed. This certainly "set the mood" for the executives once they saw the chart. The message was "At the pace we are going, we will miss our deadline by at least 30 weeks!" To their credit, they put several improvements quickly into motion and the project got back on track soon after.

Velocity Charts

Velocity charts are sometimes confused with burndown charts but they are quite different. Each column of the velocity chart registers the velocity for that particular

---

[4]Thanks to Chris Beale for this nugget.

[5]We'll leave the debates about burndowns, burnups, sideburns and other variations for the other Agile books that focus on these types of topics.

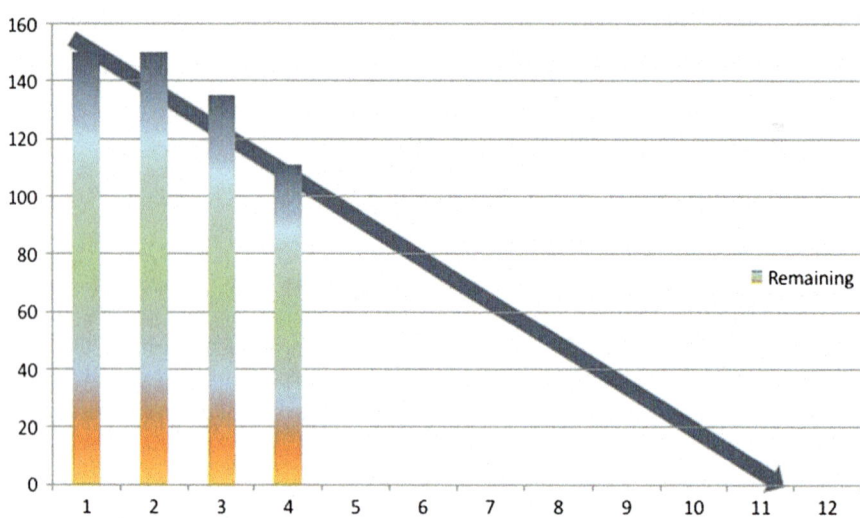

Fig. 7.4 Simple burndown chart. © 2017 by Daryl Kulak and Hong Li—reprinted with permission

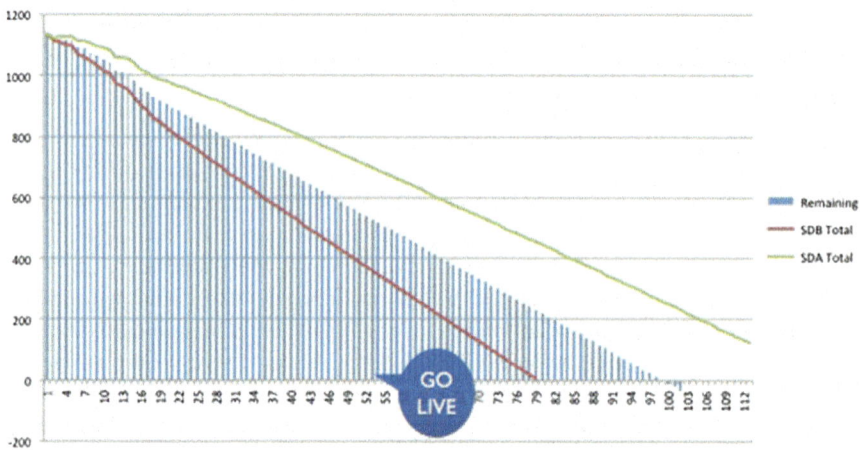

Fig. 7.5 Burndown chart with a message. © 2017 by Daryl Kulak and Hong Li—reprinted with permission

sprint, not the backlog. The trend shows whether the team is speeding up or slowing down much more clearly than a burndown would.

Figure 7.6 shows velocity figures as the blue line and a four-period moving average as the black line. Looking only at the velocity, it is difficult to determine whether the team is improving or degrading, because the volatility of the velocity is so great. (The product owner had limited availability, which caused severe

7.4 Ideas for Portfolio Management

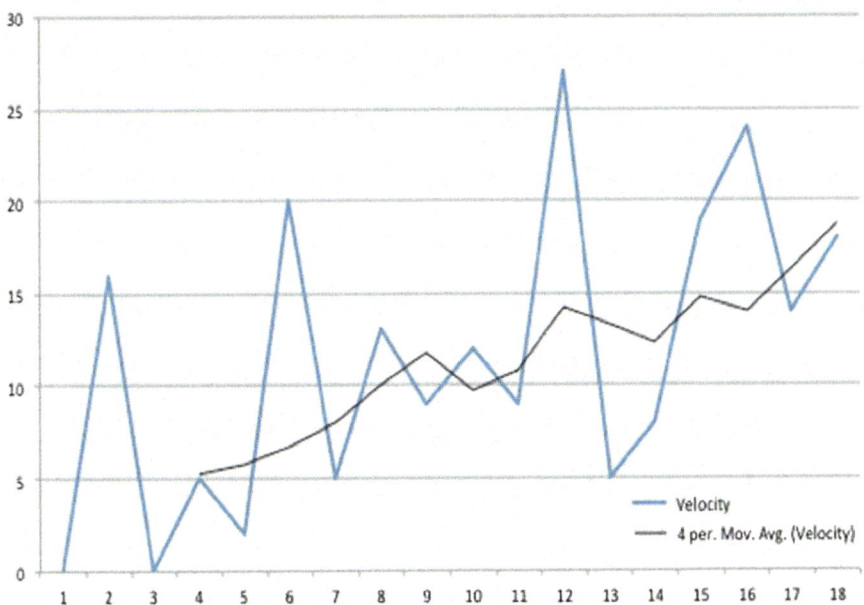

Fig. 7.6 Velocity chart with four period moving average. © 2017 by Daryl Kulak and Hong Li—reprinted with permission

oscillation of velocity.) For this reason, we added a four-period moving average, which makes it very clear that the team is, in fact, improving.

Code Coverage Charts

Most code analysis tools offer a way to print the code coverage as a graphic. Seeing the code coverage change from red to green as more lines of code are covered with automated unit tests is a thing to behold. Sometimes just posting the chart is enough to get people motivated to improve code coverage.

There is one corporate habit regarding code coverage that we'd like to warn against. There is no reason to set a "goal" for code coverage. For instance, an IT department might state that the goal is for code coverage to reach 90% in all modules by a certain date. This seems like a good idea but it isn't.

It's not a good idea because developers could write lots of poor tests just to reach the goal of code coverage, rather than focusing on great tests that might take more time to create. This is another situation where setting a well-meaning goal will usually create mechanical behavior and result in a worse situation than expected.

Other Types of Progress Charts

We enjoy using various types of oddball progress charts. In one team room, we were developing a query system that allowed customers to access a much more up-

Fig. 7.7 The famous piece of twine chart. © 2017 by Daryl Kulak and Hong Li—reprinted with permission

to-date version of their data. To show progress, we tacked up a long piece of twine (Fig. 7.7) and moved a piece of paper along it to show when we had achieved an improvement over the 24-h lag time in data freshness down to 1 min or, eventually, sub-second.

In another case, we built a web service that did formatting of inputs into an industry-standard publishing citation format. There were so many permutations that it was hard to keep track of what was done or not done. We created a chart with a small box for each formatting rule to be completed (author's name for magazine articles, author's name for scholarly journals, etc.) and then put happy face stickers into each box as they were addressed by the team. You could see, at a glance, the progress the team was making by looking for the colorful happy face stickers.

7.4.9.2 Metrics About Problems

It's not possible for us to pinpoint the problems you face in your team room because every team is different. However, we can point out the process of identifying problems and creating metrics that help solve the problems.

The retrospectives are the obvious place to identify problems. But problems can come up anywhere, anytime. The team just needs to create a way of logging the problems and then systematically solving them one by one.

Our method follows the Shewhart cycle, which was popularized by W. Edwards Deming when he worked with Toyota and other manufacturers. It is a simple process but it is seldom followed or even defined correctly in most "lean" literature.

The Shewhart cycle is shown in Fig. 7.8 (refer to Chap. 12 for more details on the Shewhart cycle).

7.4 Ideas for Portfolio Management

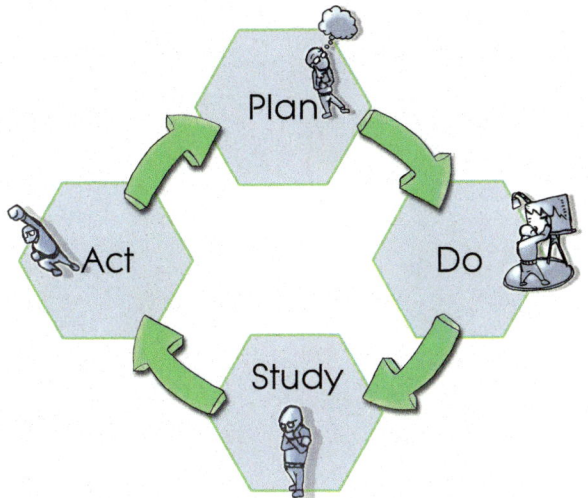

Fig. 7.8 Shewhart cycle.
© 2017 by Daryl Kulak and Hong Li—reprinted with permission

PLAN Here is where you identify the problem you want to work on (perhaps coming from a retrospective) and you create a plan for how to solve it. To solve any problem, you have to know when things are getting better, and that means you need a measurement. Define the measurement that would definitely tell you that the problem is getting better and create the behavior-over-time graph that will show the trend.

DO Collect measurements for a while as work is getting done. Put the measurements onto the chart and watch the trend.

STUDY At a specific point, set time aside to study the trend that has occurred. Are things getting better? Getting worse? Staying the same? Or maybe completely uncorrelated to the original problem? In any case, figure out what is happening based on the metrics.

ACT Based on what you learned during your study, do what you need to do. Either continuing measuring, if that seems right, or change things if the first cycle didn't do what you needed. If the improvement happened and everything is fine, stop measuring. Metrics that have overstayed their usefulness need to be stopped.

Using the Shewhart cycle, decide on some small number of problems to solve and take a shot.

Here's an example (from the chart we showed earlier). We had one team room where the product owner was absent a lot of the time. The product owner knew this was a problem but they didn't feel like they had the power to neglect their other duties. The team (including the product owner) created a chart like Fig. 7.9.

The product owner filled in the number of hours they were present in the team room each day. At one point, the product owner's boss visited the team room.

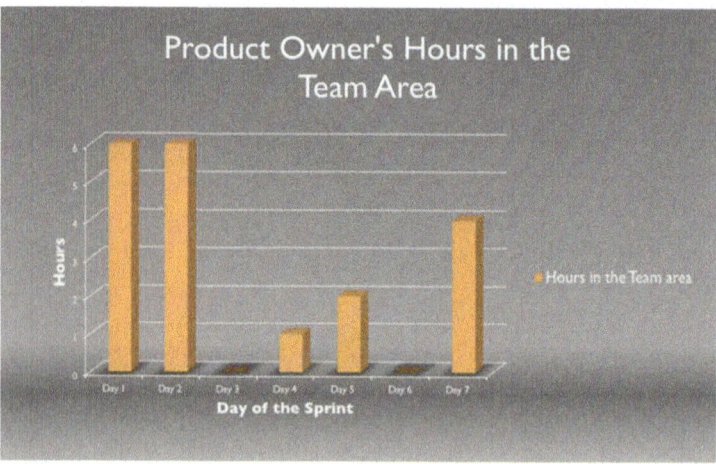

Fig. 7.9 Product owner isn't available. © 2017 by Daryl Kulak and Hong Li—reprinted with permission

"What's that chart?" she asked. When she found out, she was quite motivated to solve the problem. By posing problems in terms of data, the team takes themselves out of the position of seeming to be complaining or whining. Presenting people with data is much more persuasive than talking about general problems.

Think of the various problems you might solve with a data-based approach:

- Too many defects in the weekly demos
- Too much staff turnover
- People are too time-sliced
- Number of interruptions during a sprint
- Wait time for requests from DBA group
- Using a time-wasting timesheet tool

How Symbol Technologies Innovated Past Their Keyboard Problems
Symbol Technologies was a company (now part of Motorola) that produced rugged computing devices. If you're not familiar with this class of computers, the term "rugged" means that these devices can handle situations that would fry most other computers, like extreme hot or cold temperatures, dust in the air, bouncing around in a truck bed—that sort of thing. Symbol was proud of their technology, but they saw one weak link in their devices—keyboards. Predictably, the most likely first failure of the devices was the keyboard. It was easy for dust to enter beneath the keys and the contact between the buttons and the circuit board below was always having problems for at least one of the keys. It's a little tough to type in that e-mail when you've got no "t" key.

For several years, they worked on improving their keyboards. "How can we make them more durable?" But year after year, their keyboards continued to fail, rendering the devices useless and decreasing the life of these rugged devices. Sure, the same thing was happening to their competitors' devices, but that was cold comfort. Symbol was dedicated to innovating past this problem.

What did they come up with? Symbol eventually came to a realization. Keyboards are always going to be the weak point of our devices. By their very nature, they will always be the first to break. So how do we make this weakness less damaging to the device? Their conclusion was simple. Replaceable keyboards. Yes, we know that the keyboard will be the first thing to fail. But you can easily pop out the old keyboard and purchase a new one for far less than the cost of a new device. Did Symbol give up? Not really. They recognized a problem and innovated right past it.

7.4.10 Estimation

How have your estimates been for the last few projects? Good? Not too bad? If you're like most enterprises, your estimates are terrible. The industry is sitting at around a 12% success rate for software projects. Twelve percent of all projects come in on-time, within budget and meeting customer expectations. That's it. The other 88% were poorly estimated.

And, as an industry, we don't seem to be improving. Perhaps as we take on more and more complex projects, including mobile devices and other new technology, our success rate is dropping. A decade ago we were at 17%. So we are getting worse and worse at estimating.

What's our solution? Practically any project manager you talk to will give you one answer "We need to improve our estimation skills." Maybe more classes, more practice, get more senior people involved who have seen it all.

What's your confidence about that? You should have zero confidence that we will increase our skill in estimating. We will not. We will continue to be bad at it.

One of our scholars, Nassim Nicholas Taleb, has a good explanation for why we are bad at estimation. He calls the problem by its true name: randomness. On any project of any considerable size, there is a whole bunch of randomness just waiting to pounce on your lovely estimates. And, as Taleb notes, randomness on projects (any kind of projects) only goes in one direction. More money. More time. Bigger than we thought.

The same is true for airports. Randomness hits all the airlines in all the countries. But which direction does randomness push the flights? Will the flight leave sooner than we thought? Will our travel time be shorter than expected? Almost never. The randomness pushes in one direction only. Longer delays. Missed connections. More frustration for travelers.

So, now that we know that randomness will eat our estimates for lunch, what can we do? We should act like Symbol Technologies. We should innovate past our weakness of being terrible estimators. We should limit the damage of our bad estimates.

How do you limit the damage of bad estimates? Here are some important steps:

- Don't estimate in detail. It's going to be wrong anyway, so don't bother taking so much time.
- Don't try to be precise. Use ballpark figures and ranges rather than hours or days. We shouldn't spend any time arguing over the details of hours, we should abstract our discussions. (Lots more about storypoints later in this chapter.)
- Bite off small chunks, estimate them, and get them done quickly. Small projects have fewer randomness monsters than large projects. Breaking up large projects into a series of smaller projects (sprints) is worthwhile to limit the damage of randomness.

Once we've done all this, it might seem like we'll have an estimate that is so abstract and untethered that it won't even be worth communicating to anyone. But that is not the reality for most Agile teams. In fact, using these abstracted methods, we can actually get much more accurate, plus we can know sooner if we are in danger of missing a deadline or skipping a major feature. The dialog with the business stakeholders can begin sooner and we can come to a calm, measured resolution rather than a rushed, frustrated decision.

7.4.10.1 Estimating Versus Sizing

Let's talk a bit about terms here. As we've discussed, words matter. The word estimating brings along with it a bunch of baggage. We've all been held accountable to estimates that we've regretted. We all hesitate to offer more estimates, in the certainty that it will happen again. Let's stop "estimating." Instead, let's "size" the work. Using storypoints (explained below), we can figure out some abstracted buckets in a conversation that can move very quickly, and then look back later to see how we did. Sizing is a better word that describes what we need to do. RIP estimating.

7.4.10.2 And Now, Here Are Storypoints, the Abstracted Buckets You've Been Waiting For

Storypoints[6] are a much-maligned part of the Agile process. In this section, we'd like to present our view of storypoints and hopefully help teams use them in a way that is productive.

---

[6]There are Agile consultants discussing whether storypoints are really "out of style" now or not. Should we move on from storypoints? Are they getting stale? This is exactly the kind of discussion that we are referring to when we talk about getting too wrapped up in "best practices." This entire

7.4 Ideas for Portfolio Management

Storypoints are meant to offer a way to size user stories. For instance, a user story might be marked as small, medium or large. Another way to size stories is to use a numerical sequence, perhaps 1, 3, or 5.

There are many variations beyond these two simple ones. Some teams use the Fibonacci sequence, which provides sizes 0, ½, 1, 2, 3, 5, 8, 13, 20, 40 and 100. (This isn't the real Fibonacci sequence from the original Italian guy, it is a bit simplified.)

Many, many corporate teams tend to equate storypoints to hours of effort. This is a big mistake, but it requires explanation.

Storypoints should signify the "size" of a user story. Effort is one aspect, but the team should also think about the level of uncertainty (more uncertain, bigger size) and complexity (interfaces to other applications, complex coding required, new tools, etc.).

If storypoints equate to some number of hours[7], then there is no point in using storypoints. For instance, if each storypoint is equivalent to 40 h, then why are you using storypoints? Probably just so you can call yourself Agile.

Storypoints exist to simplify the process of prioritizing cards and to cut down on time spent in sprint planning.

Here's a sample dialogue for a team doing standard estimation:

"I could write this module in 12 hours."

"Well, I'm not as fast as you, so I'd say it would take me 24 hours."

"Did you realize the interface to the accounting system is already written? This module shouldn't take anyone more than 5 hours."

"Are you guys including system testing in this or not?"

"I think the test data for this module isn't available yet. You'll have to create your own. Have you taken that into account?"

Trying to estimate tasks has many variables. Different developers operate at different speeds. People have specialties. Some people take certain factors into account, others don't. We might come up with a very precise estimate for a release, but it will almost certainly not be accurate, because of many of these problems.

---

discussion is a time waster. If teams are able to focus on the principles, going back to the Agile Manifesto as well as the principles we outline in this book, they can use storypoints or not as it suits them. They do not need Agile consultants to tell them "Oh dear, storypoints are so 2015!" This type of advice is worse than worthless for teams trying to get work done, yet it often dominates the dialog in blogs and conferences.

[7]There is a relationship between storypoints and hours effort, but we will get to that later in this chapter.

With storypoints, we don't even pretend to be precise. We know it's impossible. So we just create wide buckets into which the user stories can fall. At best, we have three buckets—small, medium or large. (1, 3, 5 is fine too.) The amount of debate between developers ("I think it's 5.5 h!" "I think it's 7.25 h!") is dramatically reduced.

Mohs Scale of Mineral Hardness

Mohs scale of mineral hardness allows geologists and mineralogists to rate the level of hardness each type of mineral possesses.

For instance, calcite can scratch gypsum, therefore calcite is harder than gypsum. But topaz can scratch calcite, so topaz is harder than calcite. And, of course, a diamond can scratch anything, so it is the hardest mineral of all.

Mohs scale is a relative scale. Gypsum is a hardness of 2. Calcite is 3. Topaz is 8 (there are others in between). And a diamond is 10. If you find a new mineral, you try to scratch it with other minerals and you figure out where it lands in the hierarchy. There is no definitive chemical analysis of the mineral that can tell you the precise number on the Mohs scale. It's just relative.

Storypoints are also a relative scale. You can pick one story that you think is somewhere in the middle regarding size (effort, complexity, uncertainty) and then you look at other stories, one by one, and rate them relative to the first one. No one needs to figure out how many hours are involved, because everything is relative. The long estimation debates are gone.

Storypoint can be a great timesaver or they can be a complete waste of time as "Agile window dressing.". Be careful using them and try to keep in mind their central purpose: to create a layer of abstraction beyond the usual hours estimations. Your goal is not to "do" or "be" Agile.

Storypoints and Executives Do Not Mix

Storypoints are a tool for team rooms, not really for executives. Executives need dollars and hours figures. Storypoints don't help them at all.

Avoid publishing documents with storypoints anywhere beyond the bounds of your team space.

The Relationship Between Storypoints and Hours

Yes, there is a relationship between storypoints and hours, but it's not what you might have thought. Storypoints should never be related to hours (or days or ideal days, etc.) during planning. They should be disconnected and only relative from one user story to another.

However, storypoints can be converted to hours/days looking backwards at sprints that have already been completed.

The way the team can provide reports to executives about their ability to meet a particular deadline or budget is to use the historical cost of their sprints (team cost multiplied by the length of the sprint) and divide it by the average storypoints accomplished per sprint. Here again, a four-period moving average might work best.

7.4.10.3 Sprint Commitments

Many of the current Scrum processes encourage commitments from teams as to what they plan to accomplish in the upcoming sprint. In our experience, there is no purpose to this practice.

Here's the theory. When a team "commits" to do 30 points of work in a sprint, they then have a goal that they'd like to reach. They try to reach that goal, but things get in the way, so maybe they reach it, maybe they don't. Then they retrospect and figure out whether the commitment was too high or their productivity was too low. They commit again, and the cycle continues.

What is the goal of commitments? As far as we can tell, the goal is to get better at commitments, for the sake of commitments. That's it.

Commitments easily shift the focus of the team away from creating values, are an unnecessary waste of time and are potentially demoralizing for the team. Instead, the team can simply use a four-period moving average of their previous four sprints and use that to forecast their burndown chart. It's much simpler, requires less time and does not put the team in the position of "missing your commitment."

7.5 Meanwhile...Back in the Team Space

To understand what we're proposing for portfolio management more holistically, it might help to look at what changes further downstream, after the portfolio of initiatives has been prioritized and funded and the projects have begun.

The Agile teams will need to accommodate the requests from portfolio management to estimate various initiatives that might or might not become projects. These sizing requests should be work that gets prioritized into the sprints along with the rest of the work coming to the team.

Also, the teams should begin with some setup time for their iterative process. Often, we have teams execute a Sprint Zero, which allows them to do the following:

- Creating a user story backlog (using the value stories and end-to-ends as input)
- Size the backlog
- Spike (or research) initial technical challenges that are causing concern

7.6 Portfolio Management Does Not Have to Be a Dinosaur

There is no reason for portfolio management, as an organizational construct, to go extinct. It is useful. Small and large companies need a way for an idea to become a product in an organized way. The ideas need to be prioritized and assigned with some assumed value. These are all good concepts. It is only the way that portfolio management is currently structured that is a problem. We can change portfolio management so that it does not cause us to lose market opportunities by taking too long to bring work to the Agile teams.

> **Test Drive Your Knowledge Again**
> Answer the following questions with the knowledge you have after reading this chapter. Have your answers changed?
> 1. What's the longest any software release should run before making it into production?
> 2. How can you ensure that you're delivering the most valuable features first?
> 3. What's the difference between estimating and sizing? Why is that difference important?

> **Try This Next**
> **For the executive:** Use the ideas in this chapter to redesign your portfolio management process to be (a) shorter cycle to be more responsive, (b) more business value oriented and (c) contain less waste.
>
> **For the manager:** Encourage product owners and teams to prioritize their work using value stories.
>
> **For the individual contributor:** Examine your usage of storypoints and look for ways to make them more abstract, thereby reducing the waste of estimation time.

References

Ackoff RL, Addison HJ, Bibb S (2007) Management f-LAWS: how organizations really work. Triarchy Press, Axminster

Deming WE (1992) Out of the crisis. MIT Press, Cambridge, MA

Hubbard D (2014) How to measure anything: finding the value of intangibles in business. Wiley, Hoboken, NJ

Missing Deadlines Means Missing Market Opportunities

> *It's easy to spot a purist. They're the one without any skin in the game.*
>
> Hugh MacLeod (2009)

Test Drive Your Knowledge
Answer the following questions with the knowledge you have now. Then answer them again at the end of this chapter.

1. Is it possible to have a firm deadline and still be Agile?
2. Is the "iron triangle" still applicable to Agile projects?
3. Is there anything dangerous about the word "requirements?"

8.1 How to Miss a Deadline

There are a bunch of ways we can miss deadlines:

- Our stakeholders may have added scope which caused us to have too much work to complete by the deadline
- The project might have been estimated incorrectly, not taking into account certain details that were fuzzy at the time of estimation but are obvious now that we are in deep
- There might have been political considerations that caused the project to have an unrealistic deadline

- Changes may have happened to the team (someone got sick, timeslicing, etc.) that caused the team to be unable to finish the work by the deadline
- Interactions with other groups (upstream apps, downstream apps, etc.) may have proven problematic and caused a missed deadline

Is it a problem that we so often miss deadlines in software development? Some would say no. Some would say that the deadlines are often arbitrary and unrealistic, so it is only natural that we miss these deadlines that others have set for us.

Let us make a bold statement. Deadlines are never arbitrary. If, as IT people, we just make this assertion, that deadlines are never arbitrary, we can change our behavior and, hopefully, start hitting deadlines more consistently.

Deadlines are most often business driven. "We need to get this piece of software into production before our competitors wake up to this opportunity." "We need this application finished before the legislation goes into effect." There are usually lots of good business reasons for deadlines.

But even when there aren't, deadlines are still hugely important. That is because software is usually only one component of a business strategy. "We need to coordinate the release of the software along with the social media push, the documentation, training and policy changes; they all must happen simultaneously." Because of this, if a software team misses their deadline, the whole dependency chain comes crashing down and the business goal becomes more difficult to reach.

Agile processes are meant to address some of the challenges of meeting deadlines. But it is horrifying to listen to some Agile team members complain about deadlines.

"Business people set deadlines without even thinking about how much work is involved!"

"How can we already know the budget before we've even estimated anything?"

If you hear yourself (or others on your team) say these things, it means you are thinking backwards about deadlines and budgets. It means that businesspeople think you're weird and a nerd and that you don't understand business. Because you don't.

Missing deadlines means missing market opportunities. We must take deadlines deadly seriously.

8.2 Why Requirements Is a Bad Word

The idea of "requirements" is actually the root of our problem.

The "requirements" word is a holdover from the waterfall era. We figure out what is required for this application and then we jump in and do our analysis, design, construction and testing of those requirements. It doesn't help at all if our business stakeholders change their mind after the requirements phase, because we've already done work assuming the complete set of requirements. We do analysis and design of ALL the requirements, then we construct and test ALL the requirements at once, then we go live.

Agile lifecycles are supposed to take a different twist on the requirements game. It is true that you need to analyze and design before you can construct and test. However, you can do this one chunk at a time, rather than all at once. So, you can pick just one user story, a very fine-grained chunk of functionality, and you can analyze and design, construct and test and then move on to the next user story. This is powerful. It may look like we are still doing waterfall for each user story, but we have removed the silos between the roles. The worldview, intention, speech and practices are all different from waterfall.

In a typical waterfall cycle, we don't like change; in fact, we try to make it difficult to change. It doesn't matter if the business stakeholders are adding new requirements, taking stuff out or exchanging new for old. None of those changes are welcomed in waterfall.

But in Agile, we can welcome those changes. Taking requirements out, for instance, can actually reduce the scope of the release and make things easier. If you are most familiar with waterfall, or if you still insist "requirement changes" be under your control, you might not believe this, but most of the Agile projects the coauthors have worked on actually reduce scope along the way. Product owners actively remove requirements that are no longer valuable, and that makes the job easier and the deadline more realistic.

Ah! There's the problem. In Agile, product owners are removing requirements. How can you remove something that is required? How can you remove a "requirement?"

Here's where that word "requirement" gets us into trouble. A chunk of functionality may seem like it is required at the beginning of the cycle but then it becomes obvious that it is no longer required once you are in the details of the thing. With waterfall, that is not helpful, because a special group of people have already done a bunch of work that includes that piece that's no longer required, then another group has to anyway take over the whole thing and follow it through with little change, so you're really not saving much. But in Agile, it is helpful. But we need another word.

Here is where your genius coauthors give you the magical replacement word for "requirements" that solves the problem. Oops! We don't have one. Sorry. Our best solution is to stick with "user stories" to describe the finer-grained chunks of functionality and to refer to "value stories" at the higher level when describing what the team is trying to accomplish holistically. But we certainly have to get away from the thinking that we can establish a set of "requirements" at the beginning of a release cycle and then never allow ourselves to rethink when the picture changes.

8.2.1 Shotgun or Rifle Approach?

From a waterfall worldview, our statements in the previous paragraphs of "reducing scope" may sound quite horrendous. "How could you conscientiously reduce scope? Why don't you do everything the customer asked you to do?"

This is truly a change in worldview. We'll try an analogy here of a shotgun versus a rifle. With a waterfall worldview, we take a shotgun approach. We want the widest spray of pellets coming from the shotgun and hope that some of those pellets hit the target. The target is small and far away, but if we have more and more pellets and a wider scattershot, we have a good chance of hitting it with at least a few. In this analogy, each shotgun pellet is a single, granular user story. We don't know if this requirement is really needed, but if we have enough of them, we're bound to hit the target with some of them!

But there is another worldview that we can use. Let's say we have a rifle but we aren't sure if the sights are accurate or not. What should we do? Let's take a few shots towards the target and then notice what we need to adjust. If we take a few shots, and we can see that we are consistently hitting above and to the left of the target, we know we can adjust the sights or scope, then take a few more shots and measure our accuracy again. Yes, we are firing fewer bullets, compared to the shotgun approach, but we are able to adjust as we go. The rifle bullets are user stories, and we are shooting them only a few at a time in short sprints. Adjustments, in the software world, are demos and frequent conversations between business and the technical team members, using the real coded, tested software as the basis for our conversations.

The big problem is that each pellet in the shot gun shell costs the same as one rifle bullet (in our by-now tortured analogy world). So, with waterfall, we are paying for a bunch of pellets that came nowhere near the target, but we had to make lots of guesses because we only had one big shot. With our rifle, we could make several, cheaper shots and adjust each time until we could reliably, accurately hit the target time after time. The worldview could not be more different.

8.2.2 Adding a Sponge to the Iron Triangle

> We advise startups to release something as soon as you possibly can, because the point of releasing is to start learning from your users what you should have actually been building. Release something that has anything good enough that even ten people would care, then watch really carefully what those ten people do. That's when you start building your product.
> Paul Graham, programmer and venture capitalist

Probably most people are familiar with the "iron triangle" (Fig. 8.1) of software development. We have three factors to setting a release cycle—scope, cost and schedule. If you want to include more scope, then you better increase the cost or

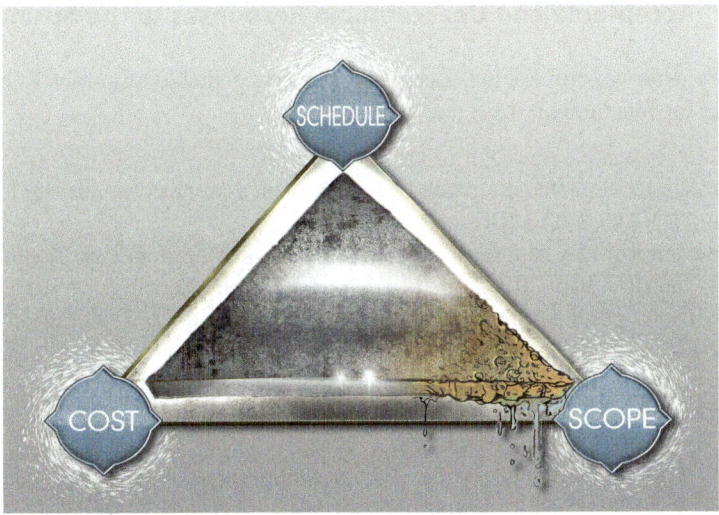

Fig. 8.1 The "iron triangle" should be spongy when it comes to scope. © 2017 by Daryl Kulak and Hong Li—reprinted with permission

schedule or both. If you want to set an earlier release date (schedule), then you must increase the cost or decrease the scope or both. You get the idea.

Most people often say "You cannot fix all three aspects of the iron triangle." This means that you need flexibility, you need to be able to take out scope if things get rough, or you can add team members (cost) or get to push the due date out a bit.

Many things about the iron triangle make sense. It is a good common sense tool to help convince business stakeholders that "something's gotta give."

We'd like to take a slightly different slant on the iron triangle. The "scope" corner is kind of a problem. By saying that you have a scope, this means that you've figured out, early in the release cycle, what the requirements are (there's that word again) and you can balance that against the other two factors. But if we are using an Agile lifecycle, then we admit that we don't really, truly know the scope at the beginning of the release cycle. We know the budget, we know the schedule, as dictated by business needs, but we would be lying if we said we knew every aspect of the scope.

Here's a quandary. As an IT team, we are good Agilists and we admit that we cannot possibly know the scope at the beginning of a release cycle. But our business stakeholders want to know what they are going to get for their money and time (cost and schedule).

But there is a solution. Using the value story concept from Chap. 7, we can specify the value that the team will work towards instead of specifying a detailed list of requirements that will definitely be coded and tested by the due date. This simplifies the world tremendously.

8.2.3 Acceptable and Unacceptable Responses to the Business

Here are what we propose are acceptable and unacceptable responses to business requests for functionality by a date within a budget:

1. "We can deliver software to you by the date you asked for, we just can't tell you what." **UNACCEPTABLE**
2. "We cannot give you a fixed date. We'll keep iterating until we're done. This ain't waterfall, baby. It's Agile!!" **UNACCEPTABLE**
3. "We can commit to higher-level requirements and a fixed date and budget." **ACCEPTABLE**
4. "We can commit to fulfilling a set of value stories without specifying detailed requirements, by a fixed date and budget." **ACCEPTABLE/BEST ANSWER**

High-level requirements—or, even better, value stories—give the product owner the flexibility to decide how to fulfill those higher-level requests and don't tie them down to a (likely) flawed initial design guess. Value stories are the best way to negotiate a commitment by a date/budget, because they allow a lot of flexibility for the product owner without jeopardizing the needs of the executive suite for fulfillment of that value by the date.

8.2.4 The Steel Query Application

Here's an example from one of our projects. Our client, a steel company, had created a very detailed list of requirements for a Web application that allowed the steel customers to look at their pending orders and see shipment dates and quantities. There were two types of customers. One type, called tolling customers, was supplying the input steel and had lots of data they wanted to see as the steel was moving through the fabrication plant. The second type, called direct customers, just wanted to receive fabricated steel and didn't care where it came from, as long as the chemical composition matched their needs. There was also a requirement for customers being able to input orders themselves, rather than calling orders into a call center.

We, as consultants, asked at the very beginning of the project whether we could disregard the requirements document. Our client was kind of shocked, but trusted us to take them through the process. Instead of using the existing requirements document, which was already over a year old and had become somewhat obsolete, we created a set of value stories as follows:

1. As Steel Company I want to supply our direct customers with an order and inventory query system so that I can increase share-of-wallet with those customers by ___%.

8.2 Why Requirements Is a Bad Word

2. As Steel Company I want to supply our tolling customers with an order and inventory query system so that I can increase share-of-wallet with those customers by ___%.
3. As Steel Company I want an order entry system so that I can decrease customer service costs by $_____.

Our team, along with the product owner and his boss, prioritized the value stories in the above order. The more we found out about direct versus tolling customers, the more interesting things became. The value of getting new business from direct customers was tremendous. However, the possibility of getting new business from tolling customers was almost nil, because we were already the sole supplier for most tolling customers.

Further, the data entry functionality came into question the more we built and the more we demo'd. In our demos[1] we often invited customer service reps to see the query system that their customers would soon be using (for direct customers only). The reps saw huge value in this. However, once we started to explain the data entry function, they went into shock. "Please don't build that," many of the reps said. They saw that the customers would usually be ordering the wrong quantities and would be making all kinds of mistakes that the reps would then have to fix. Most reps said that it would be faster if customers continued to call their orders in to the call center than trying to build a data entry system. Soon we confirmed this viewpoint with managers and executives in the company that the data entry function would add new cost, rather than reduce cost. Everyone agreed that the order process needed to be consultative and was probably too complex to simplify into an online order form.

So here we were with three value stories. The first value story was hugely valuable. The second value story was marginally valuable, perhaps at 10% of the first. And the third value story was a cost, providing negative value.

All these things we found out by simply prioritizing the value stories and then starting to build the first one, talking all the while about what work remained. An additional part of the story is that the second and third value stories represented probably 80% of the cost, as compared to the first one.

With the value story approach, the steel company saved 80% of the cost but gained over 80% of the value. This is probably not something you could say about most IT projects.

What is the lesson from this story? All those "requirements" at the beginning should not have been treated like fixed contractual requirements. With this new

---
[1]This type of demo is so different from what occurs in a waterfall project. The customers are present in the demo and are able to adjust, in this case significantly adjust, the course of the team's future progress. This demo is not the same as a waterfall "sign off." It's less "Ta da!" and more "Hey, what do you think?"

worldview, they needed to be a bit spongy, a bit fluid, until the team and the business stakeholders really understand all the perspectives at once (the sales reps, managers, executives, etc.) and the true value and costs.

8.3 "How Much Will It Cost?" Is the Wrong Question

So now let's question the question we ask about all our projects. "How much will it cost?" It seems like we obviously need to ask this question if we're going to figure out the details of the project, right? If you were going to build a bridge across the river, you'd have to figure out how much it would cost, right?

Trouble is, software and bridges aren't the same thing. We can have multiple solutions that solve the problem in different ways, for different costs. There could be a software-as-a-service option that only costs a few hundred dollars a month. Then there are open source tools that do an "okay" job that you could implement for a few thousand dollars of development cost. Or you could go with a full-blown custom development perhaps costing millions.

There's another problem. If we're at the beginning of a project, we can't know what the whole thing entails yet. We admit that. So what are we doing estimating a thing that we don't understand yet? We will understand it when we are in the middle of coding it, but then it's too late. Budgets and schedules are already assigned.

Value stories are very helpful here. Can the IT team commit to fulfilling a value story at the beginning of a release cycle for an exact dollar amount on an exact release date? Yes we can.

Let's say the value story is that we want to monetize our scrap steel. We have lots of choices on how we can do that. We can use the auction-as-a-service guys or we can build our own branded site, and perhaps we can connect it to the messy ERP system. The development cost of this value story might be more than $5000 (third-party auction site) but less than $10M dollars (messy ERP integration). So let's stop asking "How much will it cost?" It's a terrible question.

Instead, let's ask "What can we do for $900K?" and/or "What can we do by February 1?" These are relevant questions. These are questions that our business stakeholders can relate to.

We once talked to a business analyst in a software product company who said "My businesspeople don't know exactly what they want but they've given me a hard date and an exact budget! Can you believe it?"

He saw his task as getting detailed requirements from his stakeholders (which they were hesitant to provide) to figure out if the work was possible given the hard date and budget. But he had it backwards.

What our beleaguered business analyst didn't realize is that he was in the best possible world. He had an exact date and budget to work with, no ambiguity. And he also was able to play with the details of the features all the way through the release cycle as the team and the product owner learned things and started to truly understand the solution. He had the ability to pick between the auction-as-a-service cheapo solution or the Cadillac, depending on how things went.

8.3.1 Thinking in Buckets

It's good to think of the fixed budgets and deadlines as "buckets." It allows the team to think in terms of what amount of stuff can fit in the bucket.

With a bucket mentality, first you need to know the size of the bucket, then you can decide what you will put into it. It is the opposite of our current "We have to figure out how big the application is" type of thinking. But it is much more productive.

With "bucket thinking," several IT organizations we've worked with have made the transition to where teams simply do not miss deadlines. Putting applications into production are nonevents. No one is surprised that a team met its deadline and did not exceed its budget.

Another interesting thing happens with these organizations. The phrase "scope creep" disappears. In fact, on many of the teams we've worked with, the scope is actually decreased over the course of a release cycle. How can this be? What we've observed time after time is that the people in the team room operate as a team, including the product owner. And everyone is focused on meeting the deadline and staying within the budget, including the product owner. Business and IT team members have a "we're in this together" attitude. Because of this, we often see that the product owner will remove items from the backlog once she realizes that they don't contribute enough to the value story. It becomes a timing effort among the whole team, trying to judge exactly the right amount of user stories that will provide the maximum amount of functionality within the time and budget bucket size.

Why do we put so much emphasis on never missing deadlines or overrunning budgets? We do this because it is so important for IT groups to build up trust with their business stakeholders. In the past decades, IT groups around the world were contractually committed to the initial "requirements," and at the same time, did everything possible to diminish the trust placed in them by business groups. We missed deadline after deadline, blew budget after budget. As an industry, we have to start from scratch. We have to build trust with our business stakeholders, one kept promise at a time.

The iron triangle has a flaw in it. Our business stakeholders do care about the iron triangle, but they only care[2] about two of the sides of the triangle—cost and schedule. The scope side is a different story.

Here's what your business stakeholders really care about. Not what they say they care about, but what they really care about. They care about achieving the value of the application. That's it. Features be damned. Just solve my damn business problem.

With this knowledge, it seems counterproductive to spend so much time locking down features early in our process. Let's lock down the two important sides of the triangle and figure out the third side as we go.

There is opportunity for feature switching at every point in the release cycle. At the beginning, you can make decisions about the platform, vendor solution, open source, etc. You can decide among different solutions with different price tags.

Further on, when you are building the solution, you can make decisions for certain modules. Should we build this UI component from scratch or is there an open source unit that does almost what we want?

Even at the user story level, each team member can be looking for ways to decrease the cost. Over time, we've known some amazing developers who are really good at this. They see a user story card and they start thinking about the fastest way they can get it into production. Not short-cutting; not reducing quality. They think of ways to build that tiny chunk of software in a way that might cut 10% or 30% of the time spent. This happens over and over until you realize that the team has reduced the effort of the release by a large amount, just by keeping the question in their minds "How can we get this value for less cost?"

Maybe the word "value" has a bad connotation in your mind. Lots of retailers have used the word to entice customers who want to spend less but then have to deal with the hassle of product issues or poor service. The "value customer" often means someone who is willing to shop in a dingy store or buy products that won't last a year. That's not the type of value we're talking about.

Real value comes from software that's implemented well. Money gets generated. People's jobs get easier. Customers and employees become happier. The world is a better place in some small way. That's value as we're defining it.

In the "iron triangle," it is much more helpful to think of a "value" dimension rather than a "scope" dimension. The business stakeholders really don't care a whole lot about particular features, particular scope. They need to achieve the value. When IT people needle the businesspeople saying "We need to lock down the scope," businesspeople are, legitimately, squeamish. But, instead, if everyone,

---

[2]If your mind is wailing right now "Oh, but our business stakeholders do indeed demand the entire scope be completed!" then we'll graciously refer you to Sect. 11.3.5.

business and IT, is focused on achieving the value for the business, the scope can vary up, down and sideways without any bother.

8.3.2 Short Sprints Really Help

It helps to think of sprints the same way we're describing release deadlines. Never miss a sprint deadline. If your sprints are set at one per week, then your team holds a demo, sprint planning meeting and retrospective every week. It's predictable and reassuring.

Orderly sprint ceremonies are important for several reasons. First, it helps to establish trust with the business stakeholders. For them, the demos are status reports. So if a team cancels or postpones a demo, something might be wrong, or the team is afraid to share the status with the stakeholders. But if teams hold demos showing their progress in working, tested code every week, stakeholders get a comfort feeling with the team and trust inevitably builds.

Orderly sprints also give the team confidence. There's something special about showing what you've just accomplished to people who care about it. It builds pride in the work. The demos also allow tangential stakeholders to get a picture of what the team is working on. Upstream and downstream software teams can understand the software they need to pass data to or from. Architects, database administrators, security analysts and other technical stakeholders can see the demos and get an understanding of the team's approach and the need for conversations about potential shortfalls and issues.

With Agile teams, the idea is that the direction can change. The team, with the guidance of their product owner, can zigzag through its feature set, finding better and better ways to achieve the value stories. But if the team is doing this in isolation, that could be a problem. The demos are the times when the evolving direction can come into the light. Stakeholders other than the product owner can see what's going on, and correct any misconceptions the product owner might have had. "Sometimes you just need to see the thing." It helps for people who are loosely connected to the work see what's happening and offer ideas and critiques.

8.4 Stop Thinking Like an IT Person: Think Like a Businessperson

This whole chapter is about IT people thinking more like businesspeople. Businesspeople have always had to live within the constraints of budget and deadlines. Somehow, with the additional complexity and mystery of technology, we in IT have had a different view of these constraints. But we shouldn't.

8.5 Things Move So Dang Fast

A few decades ago, it was okay to have software projects where we defined the requirements in 1981 and the production software rolled out in 1983. The business world didn't move as quickly as it does now.

Imagine being an executive at Yellow Cab. For years, you were transporting people around cities, happily raking in money and paying the drivers. You didn't bother upgrading the consumer-facing technology (what consumer-facing technology?) because everything seemed to be going along fine. Sure, other industries were getting crushed by Silicon Valley, but those were information-based businesses. You can't use a computer to replace a driver and a car, right?

Then came Uber. Suddenly, customers had a wonderful user interface and a much more efficient way of getting a ride. Boom! The taxi companies were absolutely screwed. It is true that Uber rides generally cost less than taxi rides, but if the taxi companies had continuously innovated with technology, they wouldn't be left so far in the dust by technology companies like Uber and Lyft and they would at least be able to attempt to compete on price. But now their only hope is to convince state legislatures to outlaw their new competitors. That's embarrassing.

In another situation, the music industry snoozed while Apple ate its lunch with digital music. The music industry could have built its own iTunes, but they missed their opportunity.

A few years later, incredibly, Apple (after the death of Steve Jobs) snoozed while Google and Samsung ate their lunch with smartphone and tablet market share. In the late 2000s, Apple dominated smartphone and tablet market share, owning over 80% in both categories. But by 2017, Apple's worldwide market share for smartphones had dropped to under 20%, with Google's Android operating system and Samsung's hardware stealing almost the entire market. To make things worse, Apple is consistently 18–24 months behind every innovation in the smartphone category, trailing Samsung and many of the other manufacturers. The moral of the story is: Every company is susceptible to getting complacent and blind to market opportunities and threats.

Business landscapes change quickly. Every company, no matter how safe they think they are from competitors, must be pushing themselves to become more and more friendly to customers using technology. As IT professionals, we must always be ready to switch direction and be responsive to new business ideas. And when businesspeople need a new technology by July, we have to figure out a way to give it to them. Not by working a bunch of overtime, but by giving our business stakeholders choices, given their timelines. We don't answer "Here's the date it can be done." We answer "Here's what we can build by the time you need it."

That is true responsiveness to the business. Hopefully this chapter has helped you to see deadlines, budgets and scope in a new context.

Test Drive Your Knowledge Again

Answer the following questions with the knowledge you have after reading this chapter. Have your answers changed?

1. Is it possible to have a firm deadline and still be Agile?
2. Is the "iron triangle" still applicable to Agile projects?
3. Is there anything dangerous about the word "requirements?"

Try This Next

For the executive: Create a set of buckets to represent t-shirt sizing for project efforts (small, medium, large, etc.) or use example sizing ("bigger than Project X was, but smaller than Project Y was last year"). Help business and technology participants to set goals for achieving value stories rather than feature sets and screenshots. Raise the discussion to the value needed by the organization rather than a prescription of exactly how the application should look and behave.

For the manager: Counter business requests with "Here is what we could achieve by that date" rather than "Here is the date when we could be done."

For the individual contributor: Look for ways to achieve a value story with less code, less effort, less time. Make these suggestions to the product owners and business stakeholders. Calmly welcome changing requirements coming from the product owner, using a "What shall we swap out?" mindset and intention.

Reference

MacLeod H (2009) Ignore everybody: and 39 other keys to creativity. Portfolio, New York

9. Flipping the Run/Build Ratio: The Business Case for Software Craftsmanship

> **Test Drive Your Knowledge**
> Answer the following questions with the knowledge you have now. Then answer them again at the end of this chapter.
>
> 1. What business value does software craftsmanship bring?
> 2. Is software craftsmanship applicable to package implementations? If so, how?
> 3. What is the right intention for a software craftsman?

9.1 Just Keeping the Lights On

To say software development in large enterprises is bogged down is an understatement. We have processes and policies that slow us down. We have meetings scheduled throughout each day that keep us from doing our work. We have career bureaucrats who get in our way. But, most of all, we have legacy applications that need care and feeding and absorb tremendous budget and time.

Why do our legacy systems take so much of our effort? Most internal IT shops allocate 60–80% of their budget to "keeping the lights on." Does this seem excessive? The worst part is what doesn't happen as a result. What doesn't happen is new software, new ideas, and new competitive advantages. That 60–80% of every IT budget sinks into the assets we've already paid for, and we pay and pay and pay again.

The single largest payoff of any IT productivity improvement would be to reduce that 60–80% down to something more manageable. What if you could take your investment in RUN (maintaining the status quo) down to 20% and ramp up BUILD (creating new capabilities through technology) to 80%? The overall IT budget does not increase, but the productivity goes up fourfold? Would that be worthwhile?

There is another advantage to flipping the run/build ratio. After all, the "run" function is nondiscretionary spend. You have to pay it if you hope to keep the lights on. But new development, or "build," is discretionary (to a point). You can decide to do more or fewer projects in a given year, depending on the economic conditions and outlook. Now, we're not saying it's a great idea to hire a bunch of developers and then lay them off when times get tough. But if a CIO is planning smartly and is conservative with budget and staffing levels, that switch from mostly mandatory to mostly discretionary spending can be a huge help when times get tough.

Flipping the run/build ratio is not necessarily a pipe dream. As consultants, we've seen the run/build ratio flipped at several of our clients. Each of them made the conscious effort to find ways to reduce their run expenses and divert those same dollars into creating new software. This is not about blind cost-cutting, but instead about changing how software gets built.

So, what's the alternative? Proponents of the waterfall lifecycle would say that we should just put more effort into the initial development, do more analysis, do more testing and everything would be fine. Get it right the first time. But that is not the truth. Elongating the development cycle will not bring in the desired quality but only exacerbate the problems of long projects—complexity, missed deadlines, bloated budgets. Making long projects longer is not our answer.

Instead, we need to look towards a mindset called "software craftsmanship[1]." This is nothing short of a "movement" that began in the American Midwest and has spread around the USA as well as the world.

Let's examine the business implications of software craftsmanship:

- **Craftsmanship Advantage #1**—Lower total cost of ownership. Software craftsmanship reduces the cost of maintaining existing "legacy" applications often by a factor of five or ten. It allows us to flip the run/build ratio from 80/20 to 20/80.
- **Craftsmanship Advantage #2**—Increased speed of development. The counterintuitive sounding practices of craftsmanship actually increase the speed at which software is created quite dramatically. This may seem in conflict with advantage #1, but it isn't. Both can (and do) happen simultaneously.
- **Craftsmanship Advantage #3**—Faster ramp-up time for new team members. Junior team members come up to speed quickly, even in complex environments.

---

[1]We mention the "Scrum and Done" approach later in Chap. 13. This is where companies (and coaches) focus on the Scrum visibility practices (card walls, short sprints, etc.) but ignore other Agile practices. The biggest problem with Scrum and Done is that the software craftsmanship practices, what we're describing in this chapter, are deprioritized or ignored in favor of the Scrum practices. However, the craftsmanship practices are often far more valuable than all the Scrum visibility practices.

- **Craftsmanship Advantage #4**—Lower cost of development tools. Almost all the tools used by software craftsmen are open source, meaning no cost (or a small support cost) to the corporation. (As a bonus, you get to tell IBM and Oracle where they can shove their high-priced development tools.)
- **Craftsmanship Advantage #5**—Reduced developer turnover. We have found that once developers make the leap into a software craftsmanship mindset, they don't want to go back to the old ways. They enjoy their work more and they form deeper personal bonds with their coworkers.

You might think that you can get these advantages simply by instructing your developers to "build more maintainable code." But it isn't that simple. It isn't always obvious how to create code that will be easy to interpret by another person down the line.

Detailed design documentation certainly isn't the solution. We worked on a project that was meant to replace an existing enterprise service bus (ESB). Our goal was to create a new bus that did everything exactly as the old one had done but just performed better. The old bus had significant speed problems that could not be fixed.

We first turned to the documentation of the existing software. It was immaculate. Beautifully written, extremely detailed, well organized, focused on the exact structure of every XML SOAP transaction that we had to deal with. Wonderful! We created new test data that matched the documentation of the old bus, thinking that this would ensure that we were writing tests that would tell us if the new bus was working like the old bus did. But the tests failed. So we diligently checked our new code. No, everything was as it should be. We asked around about the documentation. "Oh sorry, that documentation is out-of-date. Someone must have changed the code but forgot to update the documentation." Darn it! After several of these situations, we began to distrust the documentation and simply ran our new test scripts against the old bus at the same time as we tested the new bus. If the results came out the same, we were satisfied. The documentation, the beautiful, detailed, voluminous documentation—was worthless to us.

9.2 Software Craftsmanship: How a Movement Among Developers Is Good for Business

> Open the door!
> I will not open it.
> Wherefore not?
> The knife is in the meat, and the drink is in the horn, and there is revelry in Arthur's Hall; and none may enter therein but the son of a King of a privileged country, or a craftsman bringing his craft.
> The Red Book of Hergest, a fourteenth-century Welsh Bardic manuscript

Fig. 9.1 There's a craftsman at the door, let's see what he's got for us. © 2017 by Daryl Kulak and Hong Li—reprinted with permission

With these advantages, you might be excited to find out what software craftsmanship[2] actually is. As with the quote above, you might relate the word "craftsman" to the Middle Ages, when people learned crafts such as carpentry, swordsmithing (Fig. 9.1) and beer making without the benefit of classrooms, consultants or online tutorials.

And that's a great perspective. That's what we're talking about with software craftsmanship.

Why were craftsmen held in such high regard? Really? No one other than a prince or a craftsman may interrupt the banquet?

We're not fourteenth-century mind readers, but we think it is because being a good craftsman represented years of learning and hard work. Before the industrial age with its factories and mass-produced products, craftsmen were the only producers of goods. And, sometimes, having a really good product could be a great advantage. Think about swordsmiths. After a few days of training, anyone could put together something that looked like a sword. But how good would it be? Would it shatter on the first impact? Would it be too heavy or out of balance? There are so many factors to a hunk of metal being a great sword; it probably took decades to master the various

---

[2]We apologize for the obvious gender bias in the words craftsman and journeyman. We decided that changing these terms to be gender-neutral (craftsperson, journeyperson, etc.) would be too clumsy and would disconnect our book from the craftsmanship movement already underway. We personally know many software craftsmen who are women and they are every bit as talented as the men. There seem to be some efforts in the industry to fix this gender bias problem.

processes to get it truly right. So once a swordsmith had learned how to do it well, they were in high demand and valuable to everyone, even to the royalty. So much so that they'd let you in the door even though there is a party going on.

What's the benefit of having a nicely balanced sword that is not too heavy and won't break easily? Life and death, obviously, in a battle. We've even seen swords treated as mystical objects throughout history, like the swords of Japanese samurai or King Arthur's sword Excalibur. The respect given the products, though, leads directly back to the craftsmen who created them.

You may have heard that these medieval craftsmen used an apprenticeship system to bring younger people into the guild. The young person would spend years learning the craft, watching every move of the older master, taking in every word of advice. What the younger person was learning was not just the "right action." The learning included the right view, right intention, right speech and right action. The craftsmen understood that this would take years of working together; learning, watching, participating, failing and climbing into the worldview of the master.

Okay, what's this got to do with software? Well, software craftsmanship is an attempt to bring those medieval ideas into the twenty-first century to help us build software. Sounds crazy? Yes, it probably does. Thinking about a software developer worrying about making some eight lines of code just right isn't the picture of business productivity to most managers, right? Do we really want to encourage a detailed, perfectionist attitude with our developers when we actually just need to get the work done quickly?

The short answer is "yes."

Software craftsmanship isn't about making small bits of code perfect. It is about solving business problems. But the end result, as we pointed out earlier, with lower cost of ownership and faster time-to-market so that we could cut down significantly on high-maintenance legacy code, is exactly what we need right now.

Let's walk through a few of the software craftsmanship practices to provide a flavor of this way of working. We cannot do this topic justice. There are great books written about software craftsmanship, which we will point out throughout this chapter. Just consider this a 30-min tour around the village of Software Craftsmanship.

9.2.1 Software Craftsmanship Practices

It is not really correct for us to call these "practices." They represent a different view, intention, speech and action. With software craftsmanship, it's not enough just to use the new practices. That's only changing your actions. Each developer also must have a new worldview and intention when using those practices to flip the run/build ratio on its head.

9.2.1.1 Clean Code

The concept of Clean Code doesn't sound new. Every software person throughout history has been told to write code that's maintainable and easy to understand, because someone else will have to figure it out someday. But the Clean Code concept is quite unique. It states a specific set of principles that developers must follow and helps to ensure that code gets written where errors are easy to spot, things are named properly and learning curves are shortened.

The best book about Clean Code is, appropriately, *Clean Code* by Bob Martin (2008). "Uncle Bob," as he is known throughout the industry, provides his wisdom in this easy-to-read, well-organized book that has become the go-to tutorial and reference for writing maintainable code. The downside is that Martin's book has examples that relate to object-oriented programming, and so his book does not address older (structured) or newer (functional) languages nor does he talk about package implementations (but we will in Chap. 17).

Developers who live by the Clean Code principles (view, intention, speech and action) write code that requires less time to maintain and is much easier for someone else to change when the business needs change. Clean Code is the first tool to help your organization flip the run/build ratio from 80/20 to 20/80.

9.2.1.2 Pair Programming

Here is an odd-sounding practice used extensively by software craftsmen. It involves pairing two developers together and them working on the same piece of code. Two developers, one computer, two monitors. They operate as a tiny team, with one person, the "driver," writing the code and the second, the "navigator," watching and helping.

Most managers are initially horrified with this idea. "Won't everything be twice as slow? How can this be productive?" But, in fact, our observations have been that pairing speeds up everything. Here's why.

Software development is usually pretty complex. You need to write some code to create some business functionality. You have to connect your code to everybody else's code. Most likely, the architecture involves a framework or platform like an application server, which are always complex. If you are by yourself, it's easy to beat your head against a wall for minutes or hours without being able to get past a particular problem. But with pairing, you've got two people, with two perspectives, who can help each other and make creative leaps that take much longer (if they happen at all) with a solitary person.

In short, typing speed is not the bottleneck. A programmer's productivity has no relationship to her ability to type fast. Learning is the real bottleneck. The programmer has to learn the details of the business problem she is trying to solve, and then learn the best way to implement that with software. And a group of two people learn faster than one person.

There is another aspect of pair programming that is quite astonishing. It banishes the vast majority of bugs before they are even written. We fondly refer to pair programming as "instant quality assurance." The navigator is watching the code being written and offering instant advice on how this might go wrong. A discussion ensues and the code is better for it.

Pair programming provides the fastest on-ramp for new team members that we've ever seen. Junior or senior people joining the team can become acclimated and knowledgeable blindingly fast with this process. It is the closest modern equivalent to the apprentice system back in the Middle Ages. And it seems to work very well. *New developers merge into the team's worldview because they pair.*

Finally, developers really seem to enjoy pairing. In our experience, seeing hundreds of developers enter into this strange world of pairing, we've been surprised at how much they like it. You might think that your horde of antisocial, awkward developers would never make the leap to such a collaborative process. But they usually do quite well. Pairing makes a software development team more social and more interesting. People get to know each other better, and that helps to break down cultural or generational barriers that might damage the team later on. Pairing can help team members share a common intention and worldview, which is very beneficial. The teams can become a kind of "hive mind" where it becomes difficult to spot one person's coding style from the others.

Pair programming is a fundamental pillar of Extreme Programming (XP) and the best advice on pairing is in the books in the Extreme Programming series written by Kent Beck, Ward Cunningham and others (Beck and Andres 2004).

9.2.1.3 Test-Driven Development (TDD)

Here's another strange-sounding development idea that sends productivity through the roof. Test-driven development (TDD[3]) involves writing an automated unit test before writing the code to make the test pass. It's as simple as that. Of all the software craftsmanship practices, this one is the hardest for people to get used to. It is like trying to use a pencil with your toes—completely unnatural at first.

However, the productivity improvements we've seen when developers use TDD are almost beyond description.

The most important benefit of TDD is actually the least described in the literature. TDD forces a developer (or a developer pair) to truly understand the business function she is building in every detail. If the developer has close contact with the

---

[3]Test-driving code on mobile platforms is a bit harder. We've been involved with a large number of mobile development projects and there are certain adaptations that need to occur to get the TDD approach to work in mobile, particularly Apple's iOS, which powers the iPhone and iPad. We are not able to delve into these details here in this book, but suffice to say that TDD is possible on mobile platforms, including iOS, and it is extremely helpful, providing the same benefits noted in the above paragraphs.

business person (often called the "product owner"), she needs to ask all the right questions in order to create good automated tests, even before she thinks about the code itself. This is such a healthy practice. It almost creates an express route between the businessperson's mind and the developer where all the details can quickly travel. Simply by switching the order of code and test, we change the way a developer thinks. Rather than creating a solution and then figuring out how to test that solution, she creates a test based on conversations with the businessperson and then writes the minimal amount of code to make the test pass. It is genius.

TDD changes the intention of a developer. Instead of having the intention of writing code that meets the minimum requirements of a specification given to them, the developer is now thinking of how they can truly realize the business value in the mind of the product owner. TDD works best when product owners are always available in the team space for questions about the right tests to write.

But there are many other benefits to TDD. Writing a suite of automated tests allows developers to easily pinpoint where things have gone wrong. Make a change, run all the tests, and see what you've broken. It helps to take the angst out of working on a complex code base when you have a set of automated tests helping you find problems you've introduced.

Another benefit is that the team can prove that their application is always working. They can run the automated tests continuously (using something called a continuous integration server) and build more and more parts of the application, secure in the knowledge that everything built so far continues to work fine. This is kind of an amazing feeling for a developer or even a manager. And it facilitates a new kind of confidence—the confidence that the application can be put into production at a moment's notice without having to worry about a lengthy "testing phase" to validate that the application really does work.

TDD reduces the learning curve of new team members, because they are not as worried to change things with the security of the tests telling them what went wrong. TDD increases the speed of development because we are not spending hours trying to figure out why some random error just popped up. And TDD allows us to reschedule production deadlines to be even earlier than expected, because we have a codebase that is always running.

9.2.1.4 Continuous Integration
Now that we've got this inventory of hundreds or thousands (or tens of thousands) of unit tests done with TDD, what shall we do with them? Let's run them!

In fact, let's run them all the time, multiple times every day. A continuous integration stack, as it's called, is just a script running program that often executes the following types of scripts:

- Pull the code from the version control system
- A build script (compiling, linking, etc.)

- A dependency manager (making sure the modules that you depend on exist and are the right versions)
- Unit tests (those produced by TDD practices)
- Story tests (those produced by BDD practices)
- Static code analysis tools (like Sonar Qube, etc.)
- Code coverage tools (like Clover, etc.)

Software teams set up a separate server they call the "CI Server" and then ensure that the CI stack continuously runs and ensures that the application is always working.

Most teams we've worked with create a visual build indicator (Fig. 9.2), like a light, to show if the CI Server encounters any problems. If a test fails or the build script runs into issues, the light turns red and the team knows to quickly fix the problem and get back to a running state.

The level to which this simplifies teamwork in software development cannot be overstated. If you know that the application was working before you checked in your code, and an error results, you can be sure it's something that you added.

In our minds, having a CI Server and good test coverage can "take the legacy out of legacy applications." If we define a legacy application as one that "people are afraid to touch," then the assurance that a set of tests are constantly running against the codebase and you can make some questionable changes to the code, run the tests and find out what you did, is quite an incredible confidence booster.

Fig. 9.2 A build indicator shows the status of the continuous integration process. © 2017 by Daryl Kulak and Hong Li—reprinted with permission

Changing the intention of a developer from "I need to check in a bunch of code" to "I need to avoid breaking the build" is a very big step. It helps the team's ability to create an application that is always "runnable" even in the first few weeks. It isn't quite this simple, but the team should have the intention that the executable code could be whisked off to production at any time and it would work fine. There are lots of other considerations, of course, like performance, other nonfunctionals and exploratory testing, but it is good for the team to have that intention that "Our code is production ready at any moment," which is possible with the continuous integration practices and tools.

9.2.1.5 Behavior-Driven Development (BDD)

Behavior-driven development (BDD[4]) is another type of automated testing that helps a team maintain a fully-functional application all the way through a release cycle. BDD is at a higher level than TDD. If you think of TDD being at the unit level, then BDD exists at the user story level.

Each BDD automated test shows that a particular path through a user story is working and producing expected results.

But if our TDD tests are ensuring expected results, why do we also need BDD? The fact is that every single TDD test might pass, and yet the application might be producing the wrong results for an entire user story. TDD is looking at microlevel results, but we also need to test the macrolevel.

BDD tools include JBehave, Robot Framework and Cucumber. These tools offer an English language interface where you can create readable tests and then connect those to the code to automate them.

BDD tests are written in the style of GIVEN-WHEN-THEN:

GIVEN   the system is in a particular state
WHEN   a trigger occurs
THEN   we expect the following response from the application

With BDD testing, we are looking to reduce the distance between the vision of a user story in the product owner's mind and the representation of that user story in the code.

---

[4]There is currently significant controversy over the BDD tools and the English language interface. A number of developers we know do not feel there is an advantage to this because they don't see that the end users are really writing or even seeing these tests; it ends up being developers who interact with the tests. And developers don't need the English language interface; they can work perfectly well with Java, Ruby, Scala, Rust or whatever. This is a valid concern and should be considered as your organization moves to BDD. As for us, the authors, we've seen sufficient benefit from BDD to continue to advocate for its usage with our clients, despite the controversy.

9.2.1.6 Legacy Rescue
"Oh, but all this stuff you're saying applies to green-field development. We are a legacy application team; we can't possibly make use of any of these software craftsmanship practices."

Not so.

There is a "bible" for all of us who are maintaining big, crufty legacy applications and trying to make things better bit by bit. It is called *Working Effectively with Legacy Code* by Michael Feathers (2004).

With his years of consulting experience, Feathers has created 24 tools to help developers who are dealing with legacy applications. In our experience, these tools are extremely powerful and can take the monstrous job of improving a legacy application down to daily, measurable steps.

We've seen teams use these techniques to slowly improve the code under test, adding small unit tests each time a defect is discovered and fixed.

9.2.1.7 Screaming Architecture
We address enterprise architecture in another chapter, but it is worth including Robert Martin's "screaming architecture" as part of the software craftsmanship mindset.

Martin, who we mentioned earlier in the Clean Code section, tells us that the practice of creating an architecture for an application that is not yet developed or maybe even not yet known is a bad idea. In his words, each architecture should "scream" the type[5] of application it supports. For instance, if architects are creating an architecture for an inventory system, then the architectural components (the code, integrations, etc.) should be very obvious about the fact that they are supporting an inventory system. No architecture should be "generic" for many types of applications; they should be deeply connected to the application for which they provide a foundation.

We'll revisit this approach to architecture in the future chapters, but suffice to say that application architecture and enterprise architecture must fundamentally change to support the new ways teams are creating software.

9.2.2 Software Craftsmanship with Commercial Packaged Software

"Software craftsmanship is great for custom code, but it couldn't possibly apply to package implementation!"

Our experience has shown differently.

---

[5]bit.ly/BobScream

We've had the opportunity to observe multiple package implementations at companies after the fact. It is the same sad story, time after time.

"Sure, the vendor[6] knew the package very well, and implemented it quickly. But when it came to connecting the package to our legacy applications, they stumbled badly. Their estimates came nowhere near the real effort it required, and they pawned as much as possible back onto our people with misleading status reports and craftily-written contracts."

Sound familiar? It is true that the software craftsmanship practices have limited value when developers are configuring package elements or writing "customer exits" within the package. However, that's not where the risk is. On the projects where we've been involved peripherally, 80% of the risk of a package implementation is in connecting to legacy applications. Do software craftsmanship practices apply there? You bet they do.

There are two main aspects to integrating a package to existing legacy applications. One aspect is data migration. If you have lots of data in your old applications, you may need to migrate it to the new package. You need to make sure the data is good quality as it exists and then reformat it so the package can accept it.

Data migration involves writing lots of batch programs and jobstreams that will only be useful to the point where the data exists in the new package. The software craftsmanship practices can really help here. If those data migration jobs are written using TDD, BDD and CI, the team knows that the whole process is working and tested 100% of the time during development. The originating data is known and can be used to power the TDD and BDD tests. The panic of data migration jobs that suddenly stop working for no apparent reason goes away. We can follow the failing test to where the problem is.

The second aspect of package implementations is a set of integrations. The new package will have to talk to existing applications and there will be lots of mismatches between what the package is expecting and what the legacy applications can supply. These are similar jobstreams like data migration, except that they will continue to run after the package is live. Software craftsmanship provides the same value here. Jobstreams can be complicated, rickety and confusing. TDD, BDD and CI take the confusion out of these monsters and allow developers to make changes with reduced threat of weird errors popping up months later. Having a jobstream that is known to be working at all times is quite a nice feeling for any development team, just like any application.

Software craftsmanship applies only marginally to package configuration and customization. However, that's where perhaps 20% of the risk lies. The other

---

[6]For more details on package implementations done by vendors, see Chap. 10.

80% most risky areas, data migration and integrations, is where software craftsmanship is extremely helpful.

9.3 DevOps

The basic idea of DevOps is that we should treat environment changes the way we treat application code. "Configuration as code" is another name for this type of thinking.

Many, many times, we've worked with software teams who are able to deliver gobs of working, tested software in a few weeks or months, only to find out that the release management group has no capability of moving that software to production nearly as fast as it can be produced.

DevOps is meant to fix that. What about release management can we automate? The answer, thanks to a set of new tools and a new worldview, is "most of it." We've worked with a number of clients who are pushing this idea to the limits, automating lots of tasks formerly considered hands-on manual tasks:

- Workstation configuration
- Server configuration
- Network configuration
- Environment configuration (setting up a new DEV, TEST, or PROD environment)
- Virtual environment creation and configuration
- Migrating software from one environment to another (from TEST to PROD, for example)
- Making performance improvements to an environment

Creative use of a new breed of tools, with names like Puppet, Chef, Docker, Salt and Vagrant, is making mincemeat out of these formerly manual-intensive activities and turning them into a set of scripts that can be run "push-button" style whenever needed. The productivity improvements here are massive, and it is only a matter of time before all large organizations move to these amazing practices.

The DevOps tools and practices use many of the practices from the software development world, including TDD, BDD and CI, most commonly. And DevOps is a new worldview, like the rest of software craftsmanship.

We predict that the next decade will see a mass migration of companies to DevOps and all the productivity enhancement it promises. Cloud technology only makes DevOps more powerful, with its virtual servers and networks.

DevOps, when combined with the other software craftsmanship practices, has the greatest potential to flip the run/build ratio from 80/20 to 20/80.

9.4 The Intention of Software Craftsmanship

So far, we've described the practices of software craftsmanship. But, once again, the practices are just the tip of the iceberg. The speech, intention and worldview of software craftsmanship are where most of the value really exists.

We won't go into much on the "right speech" for craftsmen, but there is plenty of it described in the books we've recommended above.

But it is worth examining the intention and worldview of the craftsman. The entire landscape of software development changes when a person adopts the worldview that you are creating something to be proud of, something that you'd want associated with your good name. It goes back to the swordsmith who wants to maintain a good reputation with his craft. Compare this to a person who is contractually building software to gain a paycheck from a faceless corporation. The work output quality is day versus night.

As a manager, it is tough when confronted by developers who see themselves as craftsmen. They will make demands about the quality they expect to be able to put into their work that will make you uncomfortable. Their demands may not fit nicely into your workplan. But you cannot crush these demands nor dismiss them. If you do, you'll lose the benefits of the craftsman mindset that we've described in this chapter. Better to negotiate a way to give the craftsmen what they need to take pride in their work, and also to be able to meet your deadlines and budgets. It won't be easy but it will be worth it.

> **Test Drive Your Knowledge Again**
> Answer the following questions with the knowledge you have after reading this chapter. Have your answers changed?
>
> 1. What business value does software craftsmanship bring?
> 2. Is software craftsmanship applicable to package implementations? If so, how?
> 3. What is the right intention for a software craftsman?

> **Try This Next**
> **For the executive:** Ask your IT staff to find ways to reduce the cost of "keeping the lights on." Ask them to consider the potential of software craftsmanship practices. Treat the fact that it costs 80%+ of your budget to maintain legacy applications as an urgent problem to be addressed.
>
> **For the manager:** Look for opportunities to increase your investment in DevOps, automating repetitive and error-ridden tasks for developers.
>
> (continued)

> **For the individual contributor:** Start a book club to read Bob Martin's book *Clean Code* (Martin 2008). Join (or start) a local Code Retreat to hone your skills in test-driven development and other practices. Learn about BDD.

References

Beck K, Andres C (2004) eXtreme programming explained: embrace change, 2nd edn. Addison Wesley, Boston
Feathers M (2004) Working effectively with legacy code. Prentice Hall, Upper Saddle River, NJ
Martin R (2008) Clean code: a handbook of agile software craftsmanship. Prentice Hall, Upper Saddle River, NJ

Better Vendor RFPs and Contracts 10

> **Test Drive Your Knowledge**
> Answer the following questions with the knowledge you have now. Then answer them again at the end of this chapter.
>
> 1. What are the general problems with the RFP process?
> 2. What is a good first step for a vendor and customer who do not have an established relationship yet?
> 3. Which is more helpful, to create detailed RFPs or to keep them more general?

10.1 Let's Put It Out to Bid!

Most large companies and government agencies have policies that dictate projects over a certain dollar limit must be "put out to bid." This means following a process where the customer creates a list of what they want, publishes it to a variety of vendors, the vendors respond with their prices, and the customer picks the best choice. The customer's wish list is called an RFP—request for proposal. The vendors responses are called proposals.

This sounds like a highly efficient process. But it's really not. Most people involved, the people generating the wish list, the vendors and certainly the team who does the work later, are not very happy with the RFP process. Throughout our careers as consultants, we've often been team members having to implement the promises of a newly-won proposal, and our experiences have seldom been positive.

10.2 The Alan Shepard Principle

When asked what was on his mind as he awaited the *Freedom 7* mission to become the first American to travel into space, Alan Shepard answered "I'm thinking about the fact that every part of this ship was built by the lowest bidder." Shepard speaks for all of us when it comes to the RFP process that deliberately creates a competitive scheme for the lowest prices. There are many, many problems embedded in the RFP process itself:

1. **Silent periods.** The communication process between customer and potential vendors is regulated to "make things fair" so it is difficult for the vendors to really understand what the customer is asking for. The RFP is truly a low-bandwidth way to communicate, so misunderstandings and confusion happen a lot. Vendors may get frustrated by the lack of access to knowledgeable customer employees who could quickly answer questions, but are not allowed to. Most RFP cycles include a question-and-answer period, where questions are collected from the vendors, then the answers are published back to all vendors. The usual clarification and restatement that any two human beings would engage in is missing here in an effort, again to "be fair." It is a product of a mechanical worldview. Plus, vendors are worried about asking questions that might tip off their competitors, so they might hold back on important topics and guess instead.
2. **Vendors may underbid.** A frequent trick used by vendors is to offer an extremely low price to the customer, win the business, and then begin an elaborate game of "change control," charging extra for anything that they can point to that might be outside the bounds of the contract. Given the confusion and ambiguity that any RFP will undoubtedly contain, this turns out to be a pretty easy way for a vendor to work their way back up to a profitable bid.
3. **Lack of flexibility.** Once the project is underway, the team is held to success as defined by the original contract. That means that the flexibility that helps to make Agile teams successful is not possible. Once the team identifies that certain functions are not really necessary, they are not able to remove them from the backlog because those items were specified in the RFP cycle. To remove the now unnecessary items would be "unfair" to the vendors who lost the bid, because maybe they could have produced a lower price had they known that piece was not needed.
4. **Tendency towards waterfall and traditional project management.** The RFP process lends itself to traditional project management and the waterfall process. "Hey vendor, make a plan and then we'll hold you to that plan." If the vendor deviates from the plan, even with the best of intentions, they put their payments into jeopardy. Anyone who has dealt with the "change request" process in a waterfall project knows that it can overtake the entire project with its bureaucratic, bickering, nickel-and-diming mentality. Assuming that things will go according to plan and "we'll just do change requests when it doesn't" is a horribly bad assumption.

These problems lead some Agile advocates to declare "You can't do Agile projects using the RFP process. It's impossible."

And yet...

10.3 A Better Way to Write RFPs

We've seen RFPs and proposals done well. An Agile team needs flexibility when they are implementing the solution. The product owner needs the ability to throw out features that seemed like a good idea at RFP time but have proven to be silly as the team proceeded. The vendors need the ability to provide a price for a solution that they don't completely understand yet, and be comfortable with that. And the RFP authors need a way to say the problem they want to solve without setting themselves up for "change request hell" with the winning vendor later on.

The changes in practice are relatively minor. What is needed is more a change in worldview and intention. Systems Thinking Principle #1 Trust = Speed applies here. The more the client and the prospective vendor can learn to trust one another instead of relying on contract language to save them, the better chance of success. Trust is always a gamble, but humankind had been finding ways to trust each other thousands of years before the contract was invented.

To summarize:

1. Specify value stories instead of requirements. (For a definition of value stories, see Chap. 7.)
2. Evaluate the vendors in terms of their expertise in solving business problems and managing organizational change, rather than their specific technical expertise.
3. Give the vendor team the freedom to solve the value stories without pinning them down to specific requirements or screenshots in the RFP whenever possible (with big integration firms it may not be possible).

10.3.1 RFPs with Value Stories

It is possible to write an RFP in terms of value stories instead of detailed requirements. In fact, just using an approach of more general requirements in the RFP, you can improve the RFP significantly. This sounds counter-intuitive, of course. But if general requirements are paired with a statement of the business problem to be solved, the RFP can be surprisingly powerful.

Here is an example:

Value Story

As ABC Utility Company I want to create a mobile inventory scanning application so that I can save $500,000 in labor costs during mandated inventory reconciliation events.

General Features Needed

- Scan meters located in storerooms
- Work on Apple iPhones and the iOS platform
- Mobile app should be able to work when there is no Internet or WiFi connection
- Solution must be completed by February 3

Now view this RFP from the vendor's perspective. All the sweat and fear associated with complying with dozens of pages of requirements is gone. The question from the customer to the potential vendors is simple "Do you think you can build this mobile app for something less than the value we expect it will generate?"

So yes, it is an easier RFP to write and to comply with, but then how can we evaluate the responses? Here, the highly labor-intensive process of walking through line-by-line to ensure the vendors have complied with each feature is reduced, so the focus becomes the oral presentations, which involve each vendor showing up at the customer's office and presenting the reasons they should be chosen to win the bid. Here the customer staff and vendor team can begin to get to know one another and the likelihood of a fit can be evaluated. The customer can decide whether this vendor will be easy to work with and whether they've solved problems like this before.

In our experience, this process, while it still technically fits the RFP guidelines, reduces the headaches of the usual way of soliciting bids for work.

We know the boundaries of what this thing is worth to the company, we know the realities of when it must be done, and we have the flexibility[1] of tweaking the features to make it fit! It is the best of all worlds!

RFP authors need to provide information about exactly how the product is valuable to the customer company. They need to specify when it is needed. But the features should be general, allowing refinement and learning to occur as the engagement progresses.

---

[1] See Chap. 8 for more about changing the question from "When will it be done?" to "How much can we do by this date?"

How will the vendors price their bids, given such general feature lists? They can look at the value in the value story and think about similar projects they've done for other clients. If the customer is asking for something that will likely cost more than the value, the vendor shouldn't bid. But if the vendor thinks they can deliver something for, perhaps 1/3 or 1/4 of the value, it may make sense to bid.

The seemingly sensible practice of ultradetailed requirements in an RFP is actually the source of problems during project execution. Taking an approach of more general feature lists is a more practical approach, allowing the implementation team to learn and adapt as they fulfill the contract.

This is about bringing decision-making as close to the work as possible, as we mention in Chap. 11. Why make decisions during the creation of the RFP when we can leave those decisions to the team that does the work? Let's make only those decisions necessary (what value do we want to achieve?) during the creation of the RFP and leave the rest to the team if we can.

10.3.2 Sprint Zero Contract with Follow-On

For projects that have a high level of uniqueness or where the vendor and customer do not have an established relationship, there is another safety measure we've used that can be helpful.

The RFP is written to specify a 2- or 3-week Sprint Zero that allows the team to create value stories and a user story backlog, as well as executing some initial technical spikes. This is a fixed-price, fixed-time engagement with the winning vendor. Immediately after the Sprint Zero is complete, the vendor provides a revised bid to the customer, now that they've learned more about the problem domain and technical hurdles. That bid must be within a certain range specified in the RFP, and as long as it is, the customer and winning vendor proceed with the next set of sprints after Sprint Zero and work towards the first release.

This can be helpful when the level of uncertainty is too great to proceed on day one with a full release cycle. Frankly, we use this safety measure on most of our engagements.

10.3.3 Connecting Non-Agile Vendors to Your Agile Process

Many enterprises who have made the transition to an Agile enterprise discover it becomes very difficult to work with large IT integrators, most of whom are far behind the curve in adopting Agile (even as we write this in 2017). If your own IT shop has transformed to Agile, you will be facing an impedance mismatch with the non-Agile vendor (Fig. 10.1).

Fig. 10.1 Dealing with a non-Agile vendor can be a frustrating mismatch. © 2017 by Daryl Kulak and Hong Li—reprinted with permission

Although the coauthors have never worked inside the giant consulting firms, we've worked with enough ex-employees to hazard a guess at what's going on. We think that there are certain aspects of the Agile lifecycle that are antithetical to the cultures of these companies that keep them from being able to understand and adopt it. Most larger integrators are highly competitive, command-and-control systems that thrive on a kind of dog-eat-dog mentality, with respect to their competitors but, even more so, with tight control of projects and teams. The egalitarian aspects of Agile are very foreign to these consulting firms and their internal cultures. Instead, it is still considered to be a norm that all important decisions about schedule, requirements, technical architectures, client communication, etc., will have to be controlled by management. The strong culture of the large consulting company feeds their views on software process and vice versa.

However, this may place the large integrators at a disadvantage in today's marketplace, as more and more customers are asking for Agile expertise and hope to gain the advantages offered by the Agile practices and worldview.

The reaction from the large integrators has been to place "Agile labels" on their existing waterfall processes in hopes of fooling prospective customers. To a large extent, this can be a successful strategy, if only in the sales cycle. "Look! They do sprints too! They're just a bit longer..."

Three Times Must Be a Charm!
We encountered a mid-size regional insurance company that was complaining about problems with their large integrator. The integrator had won a contract to

10.3 A Better Way to Write RFPs

install a large package several years previously and had claimed that they would use an Agile process. Once the project was underway, however, the integrator used their standard waterfall process and ignored the customer's calls for increased agility. One particular problem was that the integrator installed the package and configured it in the first set of sprints (lengthy months-long phases, really), but left all the legacy integrations until the end. Once the package was fully installed and configured, the money had run out and the vendor went back to the customer asking for "change requests." At that point, the vendor estimated that it would cost double the originally negotiated price to finish the legacy integrations. The expected hand-wringing and frustration ensued, with threats of lawsuits, but the customer and integrator finally settled on the extension price and continued working. The entire project was over budget by much more than double (there was a second extension) and was more than a year late.

Surprisingly, once the next part of the package needed to be implemented, the customer again chose this same large integrator. The integrator took the same approach and the same contractual issues surfaced. Again, they were resolved, at a steep cost to the customer. Again, the project was more than double the cost, double the schedule.

Now comes the part where you might not believe us at all. Guess what happened when the third part of the package needed to be completed? The customer chose the same integrator. When we asked the CIO about his logic he replied "We decided to go with the devil we know."

Once a client organization has made a successful transition to Agile, there is still the question of how to work with outside vendors who have not made that transition. Should you simply avoid them? Usually, that is not possible. Most large integrators have excellent networks in all large companies, so they can ensure a winning bid no matter who the "logical choice" might be. Additionally, the large integrators are often considered a "safe bet" when implementing big applications, especially with packages like SAP, Oracle Applications, Salesforce.com, or similar ERP (enterprise resource planning) and CRM (customer relationship management) solutions.

No, it isn't an option to rule out the non-Agile vendors. You have to figure out a way to work with them. But there are ways of assuring quality. We will provide several guideposts below.

An Agile RFP Won't Work in This Case
Unfortunately, the big integrators and offshore firms will not be able to deal with an Agile RFP, as we described in the earlier part of this chapter. Or rather, they will respond in a way to look like they are dealing with it, but will cause problems during execution of the contract.

If you are issuing an RFP that you know will only be able to be fulfilled by a large integrator, an SAP implementation, for instance, you will need to write a standard RFP with detailed requirements, but you can create a few good additions to it to nudge the engagement towards a possible success.

Your RFP can specify the following:

- **Package configurations and legacy integrations must be executed together from the start.**
  - Most large integrators start with the package configurations, which is nothing more than "knob-twiddling." This is the easy part. Once they've been on-site for several months doing this work, the customer begins to get comfortable with them and is able to see progress being made. Once the package is in place, the vendor will start doing integrations to the customer's legacy applications. The vendor knows that this is where 80% of the complexity lies. (This is especially true for ERP systems that must integrate with the factory floor equipment.) Once the vendor begins this work, it is easy to point fingers back at the customer "Your legacy systems are a mess," or "Your legacy staff isn't giving us the data we need," etc. This is the point where the vendor can ask for a contract extension, because they had "no idea" your legacy systems were in such bad shape. It sounds kind of logical, actually, so sometimes customers go along with it. However, there is no reason why the legacy integrations should wait until the end. Since these integrations easily represent 80% of the complexity of the project, they should actually happen at the beginning, along with the package configuration. Now the problems become apparent more quickly, and the customer has time to react and move staff around to accommodate the needs of the vendor package team. This provides a much better chance for success.

- **Data migration must happen at the beginning too.**
  - Data migration is another task that integrators like to leave until later. It's a big job to get the data from the legacy systems into the package, and it should begin early in the lifecycle. Specify in your RFP that this activity will begin at the start and the vendor must establish certain early milestones that are meaningful and show whether things are going off track.

- **Watch for long "sprints."**
  - Since the integrators are simply placing Agile labels onto their waterfall process, they will want to create very long pseudo-sprints. You can't turn the vendor into an Agile shop, but you can demand to see real business functionality at regular points in the lifecycle, after, let's say every two months. Most likely, the vendor will create several-month-long sprints where nothing can be demonstrated at the end of the early sprints, except for certain documentation or diagrams. They are placing a sprint framework on top of their regular requirements, design, development, testing lifecycle, so the first "sprints" will really just be a bunch of requirements activity. You

can short-circuit this somewhat by asking for demonstrable software after each 2-month period, which will force the vendor to write at least a little bit of code and even integrate with legacy systems earlier than they intended. This also helps to keep them from offering you a "big whammy" a few weeks before you thought the project should be almost done.

- **Consider contracting the legacy integrations and data migration separately.**
  - Most large integrators are interested in doing the package configuration work and actually fear the integration and data migration work. It may be possible for you to contract the package work to the large integrator and then use a more Agile vendor to do the integrations and data migration, both of which benefit greatly from the engineering practices we described in Chap. 8—Flipping the Run/Build Ratio.
- **Use BDD specifications to manage offshore work.**
  - We've heard very common complaints from customers about working done by offshore vendors. "The quality of code is terrible!" Our solution to this is to use a BDD cycle of testing to ensure the quality of offshore code is continuously up to par. Here are the steps. The customer meets with the offshore vendor at the beginning of a sprint (1-month sprint or less, hopefully) and creates a BDD specification. The offshore vendor uses this BDD spec to test their code during the sprint until all the BDD specs run flawlessly. The offshore vendor returns the BDD specs and working code to the customer as one package. The customer can examine the tests, the integrations between the tests and the code, as well as the code itself. This cycle helps to ensure that the customer is not saddled with an overwhelming amount of low-quality code at the end of the development phase and is now in an unenviable position of having to test the pile of garbage. The BDD cycle should be specified in the contract and the consequences of failing BDD specs can be clear from the beginning.

These are some strategies for you to manage contracts with vendors who are not able to produce working software in an Agile way. It is certainly not ideal to work with vendors who are able to fit into your own Agile lifecycle, but it is possible and can even be successful. Just don't let anyone tell you it will be easy.

10.4 Working with Vendors Is Not Always Easy

Most corporations have a policy to use software vendors in some capacity, either for cost savings, to smooth out ups-and-downs of demand or perhaps to increase the capabilities of the staff through training and coaching. But working with vendors who don't operate the same way as your internal staff does can make things chaotic. We hope this chapter has brought a few tools to bear that will lessen the chaos.

Test Drive Your Knowledge Again

Answer the following questions with the knowledge you have after reading this chapter. Have your answers changed?

1. What are the problems with the RFP process?
2. What is a good first step for a vendor and customer who do not have an established relationship yet?
3. Which is more helpful, to create detailed RFPs or to keep them more general?

Try This Next

For the executive: Change your next software RFP to be more value-oriented, allowing more innovation during the development process.

For the manager: Get involved in writing an RFP and use your influence to push it a big higher level rather than detailed requirements and screenshots.

For the individual contributor: When starting on an RFP-driven project, ask if the RFP was specified in great detail or written at a value story level. Use this to decide whether you will join the project team or find something better.

Servant Leadership 11

> *He who seeks truth shall find beauty. He who seeks beauty shall find vanity. He who seeks order shall find gratification. He who seeks gratification shall be disappointed. He who considers himself the servant of his fellow beings shall find the joy of self-expression. He who seeks self-expression shall fall into the pit of arrogance.*
>
> Moshe Safdie, *architect of Habitat 67 in Montreal, among many other buildings*

Test Drive Your Knowledge
Answer the following questions with the knowledge you have now. Then answer them again at the end of this chapter.

1. How does the level where a decision is made relate to servant leadership?
2. What is the servant leadership approach to measurement?
3. How would you describe your company's corporate culture?

11.1 The Basis of Servant Leadership

Let's look at the typical large corporation (Fig. 11.1).

Corporations are structured in a pyramid. The highest-level executive stands at the very top, then the managers and finally the employees at the bottom. One may wonder where this idea came from? It came from the ancient military. Remember, there were military organizations hundreds of years before there were corporate organizations. In ancient militaries, there was a general or warlord at the very top,

Fig. 11.1 Typical corporate structure. © 2017 by Daryl Kulak and Hong Li—reprinted with permission

who had his top people, who had their top people, who managed the soldiers. Who did the soldiers interact with? They interacted with their direct supervisors, with each other and with the enemy.

Of everyone, the soldiers had the most direct contact with the enemy. This was reasonable, because you could lose a few good soldiers to the battles and still survive, but if you lost a higher level strategist, you might be in trouble.

Okay, so in the corporation, the CEO replaces the general or warlord. Seems reasonable. There are middle managers, just like the military. Then you have the employees or workers, who are like the soldiers in the battle.

And who are we battling? Who do the employees have contact with day to day? We are battling...the Customer. **The Customer is the Enemy.** This is where the analogy starts to break down in a very bad way. (We will come back to this later in this chapter. Remember Principle #3—Beware the immense power of analogies!)

If you've ever been on the phone trying to cancel your cable television service, you know what it's like to be treated like the Enemy. By structuring our corporations like the military, we are able to maintain control over things, but we are also in a position where we are treating our customers like our enemies.

If ever there was a holistic explanation for why corporate customer service is so terrible, this might be it.

11.1 The Basis of Servant Leadership

Which direction do people in the hierarchy look for their guidance? They look upwards to their own manager. That person has control over their livelihood, their salary, perhaps their incentive pay and their work environment (they can make your life hell). So you want to make sure they are pleased with you.

What's the problem with this? Well, we now have a hierarchy where everyone is facing away from the customer. The employees are more concerned what their bosses think than what the customer thinks. And first-level managers are more concerned with the opinion the second-level managers have than what their subordinates think. And so on, up the hierarchy.

Wondering why you have a customer service crisis?

What's the fix? The true fix is called "servant leadership." Servant leadership turns the pyramid upside down. We still need the employees to interact with our customers, but we need the focus to be different. Instead of the employees serving their leaders, the leaders need to have the mindset of serving their employees. Those are servant leaders.

There is a great book on this topic called *The Servant* by James C. Hunter (Hunter 1998). You should read it to get the full picture of servant leadership in any industry, not just technology.

11.1.1 Needs Not Wants

Here are a few key points about servant leadership. First, servant leadership isn't about satisfying your employees' wants. "I want a faster computer." "I want to get a pay raise." No. Instead, it is about finding out what your employees need and then satisfying those needs. Needs aren't quite as easy. You can't just ask an employee, because they'll probably tell you their wants. Asking questions is a good start, but you, as the leader, have to apply your own intelligence to the situation and figure out what they really need. Maybe they really do need a computer, but maybe that's a symptom of something else that you need to go solve. You probably have a bigger picture view, so you need to use that to give your people what they need.

Servant leadership flips the pyramid to help corporations serve the customer and serve the employees who directly serve the customer. It takes a very difficult mind shift, but it's worth it in terms of customer satisfaction and loyalty.

The same servant leadership approach works for any IT department. The department is there to serve business stakeholders. The IT employees work with those businesspeople day to day and try to help them. The IT managers need to have a servant leadership approach to ensure that the "frontline" employees have everything they need to give the customers the best service possible.

11.1.2 Management and Leadership

Having skills in management and leadership are necessary. Here we will try to provide a few new perspectives on this age-old question of the difference between management and leadership.

No one should say that management is bad and leadership is good. Both are required. However, management has been emphasized for many more years and is more entrenched in most corporations. We even have global certifications for "being a good manager" with the Project Management Institute (PMI) in North America and PRINCE2 in Europe. But no equivalent certification exists for leadership. Certifications are bunk anyways, but it is telling that there is so much focus on management and leadership is pretty much left out in the cold.

> A leader is best when people barely know he exists. When his work is done, his aim fulfilled, they will say "We did it ourselves."
> Lao Tsu

One of our systems thinking scholars, Peter Checkland, said the following at the Fourth International Conference of the United Kingdom Systems Society:

> *Anyone who has been a professional manager in an organization knows that it is a complex role, one that engages the whole person. It requires not only the ability to analyze problems and work out rational responses, but also, if the mysterious quality of leadership is to be provided, the ability to respond to situations on the basis of feelings and emotion.*

Certainly, leadership is more mysterious and emotional, perhaps leading to a more difficult widespread understanding in the hard, cold world of business.

11.1.2.1 Management and Leadership at the Movies

In an attempt to (gingerly) use an analogy, let's look at how organizations are built to create motion pictures.

Movies have at least one director and one producer. The director has the artistic vision for the movie. She will be looking at the lighting in a particular scene to ensure that it sets the right mood. She will think for hours about whether to place a potted plant in the background of a scene or not, worrying about if it will give the right artistic message.

The producer, on the other hand, makes sure that the movie gets funded. The producer is meeting with the investors and studio executives to make sure things are proceeding according to their expectations. Budget overruns and drastic theme changes are a big problem for the producer, who must convince the "money men" to go along with the changes as they occur.

The director is the creative leader of the film. The producer is the manager. You need both. In software, we often expect the same person to provide both, but that is a rare individual who has great skills in both.

11.1.2.2 Battling Hunger in Sub-Saharan Africa

In a meeting of the ISSS (International Society of Systems Science), we met a man named Dennis Finlayson who had worked all his life on international aid projects. If the Swiss government decided to spend some money to reduce hunger in Sub-Saharan Africa, my friend Dennis would be the point person they would call to work locally in the country to make sure it happened.

He would regularly move to remote locations and set up camp, figuring out logistics and watching for disasters around every corner. Dennis is, to say the very least, a very interesting person to have a drink with (or, if Dennis gets his way, nine or ten drinks).

Dennis told us that he structured his leadership teams a certain way. He felt that there was one type of person who excelled at working with the funders, understanding logistics and filling out all the right forms. He also felt that the person who was providing leadership on the ground—working with the volunteers and aid workers, helping families, negotiating with warlords—was a completely different kind of person. Dennis said he was not sure that he'd ever be able to find one person who could do both. You could say Dennis was looking for a manager-type (funding, logistics, bureaucracy navigation, etc.) as well as a leader-type (helping families, negotiating, etc.).

11.2 A Leadership Culture

In giving leadership advice, we offer it to people at all levels of the organization. A CEO should offer lots of leadership, but so should a vice-president, a middle manager, a team lead, a developer, a data scientist, a business analyst or a DBA. Leadership comes from everyone. We all have our own perspectives, our own unique intelligence that we can bring to bear in any situation. Part of the key is to "trust your gut" and have the courage to offer your advice about whatever is happening with the team at the moment.

So leadership is more of a culture than a trait of an individual. It make sense, then, to identify the principles of a culture that shows strong leadership. We've identified nine principles from our work with clients and our research in systems thinking.

11.3 The Nine Leadership Principles

1. Bring decision-making as close to the work as possible
2. A leader is anxious when the team is calm, calm when they are anxious
3. A leader is a systems scientist
4. A leader understands the benefits and dangers of measurement
5. A leader negotiates
6. A leader leads across team boundaries using scouts and ambassadors
7. A leader organizes field trips
8. A leader is a student of corporate culture
9. A leader respects the psychological contract

11.3.1 Leadership Principle 1: Bring Decision-Making as Close to the Work as Possible

Decision-making should happen as close to the work as possible. We've learned this from W. Edwards Deming, one of our most important scholars. When he worked with the manufacturing lines at Toyota and other companies, he discouraged decision-making at-a-distance and instead tried to help managers move decision-making to the people working on the line. In current parlance, this is often called "empowerment." Decision-making should exist at the level of the developer, tester, even the lowest-level worker, unless you can prove that it must exist elsewhere.

Unless you are doing the work right now, you really don't understand it.

Even if you were a software developer last year, and now you're a manager, you don't really "get" what the developers are dealing with at this exact moment. You think you do, but you don't. Uncle Bob (Robert Martin) in his Clean Coder blog[1] presented an interesting discussion to explain why the most important decisions on architectures should be made much later in development cycle by developers themselves when more information is available, instead of upfront by managers/ architects.

Moral Hazard and the 2008 Financial Crisis
There is a phrase called "moral hazard." It refers to a situation where one group makes a decision but another group has to live with the consequences. The Financial Crisis of 2008 was an example of moral hazard. The Wall Street bankers made very poor decisions about their investments but they did not have to live with the consequences. They did not go to jail and, crazily, many of them continued to receive large bonuses (remember AIG?).

---

[1] bit.ly/UncleBobClean.

But the US taxpayers did have to live with the consequences. The large bailout of the firms came from government money, funded by the taxpayers. The crisis created the largest federal budget deficit in the history of the country and a recession that lasted several years. It also created a ripple effect in many other countries who had counted on the Wall Street bankers to operate smartly, including Iceland, Ireland and Brazil, who all descended into a years-long decline.

The problem of moral hazard is that it does not allow the decision-maker to learn from their own mistakes. The Wall Street bankers went immediately back to the same risky behavior once the crisis was over. They continue to use the credit default swaps and other complicated financial instruments that caused the original problems. But why should they care? They didn't lose a job, or a paycheck, or even a bonus check. What's the big deal?

Moral Hazard in the IT Department

The methodologist who decrees a new standard for data diagrams doesn't have to live with that decision. The data analysts and DBAs have to live with it. They can complain or resist, but there is some risk to their careers if they do. "Oh, they're just resistant to change," says the methodologist. But how does he know? He isn't in the trenches doing the work.

Another example is a software development team who passes their work onto a maintenance team. The developers can make decisions that they don't have to live with because the maintenance programmers will be the ones stuck with those decisions. Here we have decision-making removed from the work, in this case maintaining the application.

You can see the same perspective when architects make rules and structures that developers have to live with, often causing slowdowns and problems that the architects could not have predicted.

It isn't enough for the decision-maker to just observe the work either. The person making the decision has to be actively doing the work, involved in it day in and day out. There are many subtleties in every decision and they might be hard to explain and might not arise until after a few weeks or months. But the people doing the work will often have a gut feeling that the new decision is wrong, they just cannot express it until it's too late.

History has many lessons about the problems of decision-making being too far removed from the work.

Moral Hazard and the Great Wall of China

The Great Wall of China is considered one of the world's greatest engineering feats. It was begun in seventh century BC and construction continued for 1700 years. But did you know it was built by slaves?

Multiple Chinese Emperors saw their chance to continue to extend or fortify the wall as part of their own legacy. To gain the labor for the construction effort, they "recruited" peasants from the countryside, as well as taking people from the jails—enemies of the state, prisoners of war, political enemies, petty criminals and even scholars who dared to disagree with the Emperor.

These people were fed barely enough to stay alive and were not paid. They were, in every sense of the word, slaves in their own country. Many of them died in the construction process. Often the people who died were not given a proper burial but were instead cemented into the Wall itself.

There is the well-known Chinese legend of a peasant couple who were newly married when the Emperor's soldiers came to their home and removed the husband. They took him to work on the Great Wall for several years. Finally one year when the wife inquired as to where her husband was, the Emperor's soldiers told her that he had died. The legend says that she cried and cried for many days until her tears formed a giant river that rushed toward the Great Wall and broke it. In the place where the Wall was broken lay her husband's cement grave and his bones.

How could the Emperor and his soldiers be so cruel? Easy. They weren't involved in the work. They did not know what it was like to work on the Wall or lose a husband or to have a loved one buried without a ceremony. They were conveniently disconnected from the reality.

Removing decision-making from the work is dangerous in the workplace too. When you hear terms like "methodologist," "wise ones" or "decision-makers," think of the Chinese widow and her husband. People can make terrible decisions if they are not the ones who have to live with them.

The Alternative to Separated Decision-Making
So, are we advocating a "Wild West" where there are no standards and no inter-team communications and decisions? No. The question itself is rooted in the worldview of hierarchy that assumes without the hierarchy, any organization will inevitably fall into anarchy since most of the individuals are not capable of managing their own accountability.

How can we bring the decision-making as close to the work as possible? If we allow each team to make their own decisions, we might get a proliferation of different techniques and tools used which could be costly to the organization.

We've seen a solution to this with several of our clients. Let's say there are nine software development teams. It is possible to create a group that contains one full-time team member from each team who can act as a spokesperson for that team. This group meets regularly to decide on standards for the teams. You probably need to start with some existing set of standards (architecture, toolset, approaches, etc.). Then this team has the full power to decide to make changes to the standards. When the group agrees to a standard, each team member must agree to follow it.

When a new tool or technique is discovered, one of the teams may decide to try it out. They get permission from the group to try it, and then they proceed for a while using the new tool or technique. The team reports back to the group on whether they think the new thing works or not. It may be that it works for that particular team, but not for the others. That's okay, we just document the reason for the difference and move on.

Here the decisions are coming straight from the team members. They are the ones on the "committee" and they're the ones who have to live with the decisions. We've effectively melded the decision-makers into the teams. This approach has worked with several of our client organizations and we haven't seen serious breakdowns in the approach after teams have been following it for multiple years.

11.3.2 Leadership Principle 2: A Leader Is Anxious When the Team Is Calm and Calm When the Team Is Anxious

We've noticed that certain people at all levels have a special quality. You could call it "calm in the eye of the storm," but it is actually more than that.

A great leader, at any level of the organization, is a person who feels and exudes calm when things get heated in a team room. They don't necessarily play the "Calm down everybody!" role (which is seldom helpful), but they are a beacon of calmness when other people are feeling panicked. The effect is usually immediate. "If she is calm, then I could be too!" a frantic person starts to think, and quickly the room temperature comes down a notch. This is helpful when there are personality conflicts, but it is extremely advantageous when the team is faced with a giant roadblock that has no apparent quick fix. Remaining calm when these events happen is a great personality attribute.

The second part is just as important. The great leader also injects anxiety into the team space when it's needed. When the team is feeling comfortable or even complacent, the leader (again, a leader can be at any level) is looking for the problems. She is thinking about what could go wrong, what problems we are not seeing and what kind of goblins are around the next corner.

The combination of these traits is something that any person can learn. It becomes reflexive. You notice that the team room is feeling very comfortable—hmmm, time for me to look for problems. You can see that people are frantic—I'll radiate calm.

11.3.3 Leadership Principle 3: A Leader Is a Systems Scientist

Each leader should endeavor to be a systems scientist. Systems thinking requires some deep investigation, some modeling, fixing and measuring. The easiest model to use is the Shewhart cycle,[2] advocated by W. Edwards Deming, which goes Plan-Do-Study-Action (PDSA).

The leader looks for problems, finds related measurements and then feeds that information back to the team so they can make a decision on how to proceed. We think of leadership as systems science where the leader is taking measurements and holding those back to the team like a mirror to show the team what is occurring from different perspectives.

Taking this "systems scientist" approach to problems helps leaders to take a "Blame the system, not the person" mindset to problem solving, which also lowers the tension in a team space.

11.3.4 Leadership Principle 4: A Leader Understands the Benefits and Dangers of Measurement

> People with targets and jobs dependent upon meeting them will probably meet the targets—even if they have to destroy the enterprise to do it.
> W. Edwards Deming

You read in Chap. 7—Business Value, Estimation and Metrics—how our approach in this book revolves around measuring progress and problems and learning from those measurements.

However, measurements can be a danger as well. When we try to measure performance without a knowledge of the problems we could cause, we can run into big trouble.

Cowboy Accountability
Team accountability is infinitely more useful a concept than individual accountability. But we must define what we mean by "a team."

Individual accountability[3] (one person) means that we are setting up measurements that will show us whether that single person is doing good work or not, and perhaps allow us to compare him to his peers to see which one is better than another. We call this "cowboy accountability."

---

[2]There is more detail on the Shewhart cycle in Chap. 12—How Teams Keep Learning and Improving.

[3]Even aspects of personal success are drawn into doubt with Malcolm Gladwell's book *Outliers* (Gladwell 2008). Gladwell shows how, even for the biggest individual successes of our era, most people owe much of their success to the people around them and the coincidental events of their lives, in addition to their own tenaciousness and intellect. Both the environment and the individual attributes must be present for success to happen. Our Agile measurements should take this into account. If one of your 12 Agile teams is doing exponentially better than the others, it probably has something to do with their own talents and hard work, as well as the environment around them and the coincidences they've benefitted from.

11.3 The Nine Leadership Principles

The big problem with cowboy accountability is that it pits one team member against the other. Tremendous waste enters the system as soon as individual accountability is set up, because each individual is looking for ways to push problems onto others and take credit for themselves. The more devious the person, the better they will be at this game. The more honest the person, the more certain you are to drive them off any team where individual accountability is used. This is certainly worse if the cowboy accountability measurements are published for all to see, as with a big, visible chart (BVC).

This seems so simple and yet we continue to have teams and companies who enforce cowboy accountability in many instances.

Now, what about team accountability? Yes, it is better than at the individual level. But wouldn't the same thing happen among teams as does among individuals in a team? Wouldn't Team A try to push off their problems to Teams B and C, while taking credit whenever possible?

Bravo! We've just described corporate life in a nutshell.

The concept of accountability needs to change. We cannot be accountable to a set of measurements and targets. Instead, we need to be held accountable to work with each other. That is the major form of accountability.

> *I, as the delivery lead, am accountable to work with my businesspeople to ensure that we are meeting their needs, and sacrifice my own project plan if necessary.*
>
> *I, as a business analyst, am accountable to work closely with my designers, developers and testers to ensure that they have everything they need to do their best quality work. And I don't care if what they're doing messes up my grand traceability matrix, because my main accountability is to work with them.*

What we are describing here is true professionalism (see Chap. 5—Redefining Professionalism). Professionalism is severely damaged when individual or team accountability is set up incorrectly. In a way, it is creating an environment where it is not possible (or at least not individually profitable) to be professional.

What you do when you set up accountability standards, either at the individual or team-against-team, is you make it so that what is best for the individual (or team) is NOT what is best for your whole organization. The whole organization does not benefit from arguments over who broke the build or who miscommunicated requirements, and yet with individual accountability you ensure that those costs will exist and you are ENCOURAGING them, even locking them into place.

Accountability, fortunately or unfortunately, is not a measurable activity. You cannot measure the extent to which people work together. You can only build an environment where it is encouraged. Managers know that their number one job is to break down barriers and encourage communication, shared ownership and trust.

Individual contributors know that it is their job to work closely with people on their own team and to build bridges to other teams whenever possible, building trust in the process.

Keep a focus on accountability. Just don't try to measure it.

When a manager is set up as the liaison to the business stakeholders, that puts tremendous pressure on that individual. That manager has to incorporate all the worldviews that his team members would be able to bring to each decision, as he interprets the needs of the clients into tasks for the team. It's too much for one person.

As a matter of fact, when the individual accountability is reinforced as such, it will break up the team accountability. A positive worldview, "All for one and one for all, united we stand divided we fall" will be replaced. Everyone will be encouraged to work only for himself and his manager, and no one will focus on the needs of customers.

11.3.5 Leadership Principle 5: A Leader Negotiates

What is it about IT people that makes us such terrible negotiators?

Often, in our experience, the failure of projects to maintain a sustainable pace happens simply because the IT leaders have poor negotiation skills.

Let's look at a typical example. The businessperson and the IT manager meet to discuss a particular feature being included into the next release. The businessperson demands that the feature be included. The IT manager calmly asserts that the businessperson can add the feature but has to take something out of equivalent effort. The businessperson becomes red-faced and bangs his fist on the table. The IT manager backs down, wanting to avoid a scene.

Then the IT manager sheepishly goes back to his team and tells them they will need to work weekends to incorporate this new feature by the unchanged deadline.

The businessperson, on the other hand, goes back to his department and says "Wow, that was an easy negotiation. I got everything I wanted and the other guy got nothing. All I had to do was get red-faced and bang on the table with my fist! Huh. Weird."

People who have a technical mindset get into a pattern where "Well, if the businessperson asked for it, we have to do it." They do not understand that there is a negotiation that takes place. We need better skills in negotiation. Practice negotiation wherever you go.

You must know the negotiation techniques. You must know the gambits and the trickery. Not necessarily because you're going to use it all, but because you need to know when it is being used against you. The best source we've found for good negotiation skills is the book *The Secrets of Power Negotiating* (Dawson 2012). It's a breezy, fun quick read filled with personal stories that is also available on audiobook.

11.3.6 Leadership Principle 6: A Leader Leads Across Team Boundaries Using Scouts and Ambassadors

Software teams, and particularly Agile teams, can tend to get very self-focused and inward looking. Every leader at every leadership position needs to watch for this tendency and create ways to avoid it.

We discussed technical groups meeting regularly cross-team to set standards and make decisions in a previous section. This is a manifestation of an approach called "scouts and ambassadors" from the book *X-Teams* (Ancona and Bresman 2007).

Scouts are people who venture outside of their own team room to find out what is happening elsewhere and bring those observations back to the team. Ambassadors act as public relations agents for the team, helping to smooth negative perceptions that exist elsewhere and start to create a positive message with other groups. These are not full-time roles, but rather just a responsibility that an existing team member will take on. Even in a large organization, this will only be something that occupies 2-3 hours a week for a particular scout or ambassador.

In Chap. 1—Today's Problems with Business Software, we examined the concept of "Agile illth." Most Agile software teams face some amount of backlash from the existing entities in a large organization. The PMO, enterprise architects, DBAs and corporate methodologists are not likely to be in your camp from the beginning. It takes work. It takes attention. It takes diplomacy.

Our experience has been that it makes sense to use the scout and ambassador ideas when working in a team space (Agile or not).

The *X-Teams* book lists the following scouting activities for any team:

Scouting

- Investigate the organizational terrain
- Investigate customers, competitors and current trends
- Investigate yourselves (figure out if team members are on-board and, if not, how to get them included)

Ambassadorship

- Link to strategic initiatives and get buy-in
- Lobby for the team's interests
- Cultivate allies and protect against adversaries

When it comes to investigating customer needs and the competitive landscape, a software team may say "That's not our job, that's why we have product managers." It is true that product managers spend more time on these activities, but it still helps if software team members are conversant in how their software product fits into the competitive landscape and what customers might think of it. Ask the product manager, ask other business people what they think. "How do you think this product our team is building will be valuable?" Most times you will hear people's doubts and cautions, which will serve you very well as part of the team creating the product. You are not trying to double-cross the product manager, but instead to support them and provide them with additional perspectives. With every line of code you write, or test or analyze, you can keep those doubts and cautions in mind. As with any organizational boundary, the wall between software developers and product/marketing people should be porous and well traveled.

The scout has to be curious as to what other groups might need from the team. The lists can be endless:

- Teams who might need our test data
- Teams who need to see our requirements
- Teams who need to know our Web service definitions
- Testing groups who need to have our exact user interfaces, to allow them to map their automated tests
- Performance testers who need the functioning code to run performance tests against in a special environment
- Network analysts who need to know our transaction loads across certain bottlenecks
- Production deployment groups who need to know which slot we will fit into and which servers we intend to use, what services (load balancing, security, etc.) we will want or not want

The ambassador's list can be similarly endless:

- Check on PMO's needs for the team
- Check with the enterprise architect assigned to our team
- Understand the length of time needed for architectural approval of a new tool
- Find out what was said at the last CEO roundtable regarding our team

The scout is looking for information and ways to be helpful to, and get help from, other groups. Being an ambassador is more about politics.

We've found it can be helpful to have a "Scout and Ambassador" wall with its own cards and columns for completion.

11.3.7 Leadership Principle 7: A Leader Organizes Field Trips

As a leader, you are responsible to help your team get connected to the business domain that you are serving. The best way we've found to do this is with a field trip. Now you might say, "With such short sprints, I'd be hesitant to take my whole team out on a field trip and potentially waste a whole day." That's true, and a good caution. But our experience is that the time your team spends on the field trip is paid back doubly or triply with what you learn.

We worked on a project where a mobile app had to be created in only 5 weeks. The app was to be used to conduct inventory of electrical devices in storerooms around the country. Even though we only had 5 weeks, we decided to conduct a half-day field trip to see one of the storerooms that was nearby. The developers on the team were positively shocked by what they learned. The field trip changed the entire trajectory of the project.

While the storeroom workers were showing how they were currently doing inventory, they picked up a small device no bigger than a thumb drive and started to scan the barcodes on the devices. We could see that the barcode reader was using a red laser to read the barcodes, while our mobile phone app would be using digital photography. The laser was lightning fast. Beep Beep Beep Beep—before we knew it he had scanned an entire shelf of devices. Our current scanning app, after the first two or three sprints of development, was much, much slower. Panic crept across the faces of the developers.

Secondly, we saw that the storeroom worker had to reach far back under long shelves, which meant that there wasn't much light. Our technique of taking pictures with the mobile phone camera would need some extra help.

Once we got back to the team room, one of the developers wrote two columns on a whiteboard labeled "How the New App is Better" and "How the New App is Worse." Speed and low light conditions were definitely in the second list. From then on, the team was truly focused on making sure the new app would be as fast as the old laser method, and they also quickly added a feature that turned on the flash on the phone camera to make sure it worked in low lighting. And they did it. They found ways to speed up the photo process and added a flash to handle the backs of shelves.

We've taken teams on field trips to everywhere from sulfur plants (stinky) to steel fabrication factories (loud) to solid waste facilities (also stinky). It is true that industries that produce tangible products, like manufacturers, lend themselves to a field trip, while service industries, like insurance companies and banks, less so. But give it a try. If you are building an application intended to be used by independent agents of a large insurance companies, go visit one of the agent's offices. You'll probably be surprised. Our team once visited an insurance agent only to find out that he had three computers on his desk, one connected to each insurance company he worked with. He would run a quote on each computer to see who would come back with the cheapest price. Our new app would be competing head-to-head with these other companies' apps. What we realized was that even the smallest problem in ease of use would be smack-your-forehead obvious in this "insurance application cage match" situation.

The field trips are important for reasons beyond "seeing the work." It is important for the team members to meet the people who will use their apps. Just personalizing the "end user" can help immeasurably when the team has to make decisions about the app. And, in the best cases, those field workers are invited and come to the occasional sprint demo, providing real-life input into the progression of the features being built.

11.3.8 Leadership Principle 8: A Leader Is a Student of Corporate Culture

What culture do you work in? Usually, software people might respond with vague notions of culture "Command and control," "Like a startup," or similar. But there is a lot of research behind cultures that we can make use of. We should each be students of what makes cultures different from one another and how we can adapt to them in a healthy way. For us, as consultants, this is doubly true.

David Livermore (Livermore 2013) of the Cultural Intelligence Center has spent a great deal of time working to understand the cultures of the world, what makes them different, and how travelers can adapt to them. He has created a set of ten cultural dimensions to map the various world cultures (Table 11.1).

What Livermore discovered is that while these cultural dimensions apply very well to cultures of countries, there is also excellent applicability to corporate cultures. Certainly, a corporation in a certain country, say Denmark, will take on some aspects of that country's culture. But even within Denmark, corporations will vary on each cultural dimension and be different from other corporations. Given this, we've taken to using Livermore's ideas to evaluate corporate cultures and help us, as consultants, understand corporate cultures and how to navigate them.

Each team should spend time thinking about the culture surrounding them, whether it's a team of consultants coming into a company for the first time, or a team of employees who are embarking on something new in their own company. Many more projects fail from misunderstanding corporate culture than from poor technology.

Corporate cultures are not right or wrong, good or bad. But each of us who work in the culture must have examined the culture itself, understood aspects of it and learned how to prosper inside it.

Table 11.1 Cultural dimensions

Cultural dimension	Description	Examples
Individualism versus collectivism	Decisions are made quickly by individuals versus a slower, consensus-basis	USA—individualist China—collectivist
Power distance	How comfortable the society is with differences in equality, influence and wealth. Status consciousness	India—high power distance Denmark—low power distance
Uncertainty avoidance	How comfortable a society is with ambiguity and vagueness; how much people follow the dominant norms	Germany—high uncertainty avoidance Denmark—low uncertainty avoidance
Cooperative versus competitive	Nurturing supporting relationships or achievement, success and results	Thailand—cooperative Russia—competitive
Time orientation	View of time as exact and punctual or as approximate and flexible	Norway—clock time Mexico—event time
Direct versus indirect	Communication styles of low-context, open communication versus subtle and high-context	USA—direct Most of Asia—indirect
Being versus doing	Taking life as it comes versus being busy and focused on accomplishment	China—being Japan—doing
Particularism versus universalism	Approach to "the rules" of society—every situation is different based on my loyalty and relationships (particularism) or "the rules apply to everyone (universalism)	Venezuela—particularism Swiss—universalism
Neutral versus affective	Approach to display of emotions—neutral, unemotional or highly expressive and emotional	Japan—neutral Italy—affective
Tight versus loose	Approach to social norms—tight control or left to personal preferences and diversity	Saudi Arabia—tight The Netherlands—loose

There is good research on how to change corporate cultures.[4] It is not easy, to be sure. For more information about this, examine *Lead with a Story* (Smith 2012) and Marshall Ganz's "public narrative," which is best explained in a simple, easy-to-use workbook.[5]

11.3.9 Leadership Principle 9: A Leader Respects the Psychological Contract

A servant leader knows that the employer/employee relationship goes beyond just the contract that was signed when the employee joined the company. There is also an "unwritten contract." There are certain expectations that the employee has of the employer that weren't specified in the written contract but that are real nevertheless.

---

[4]We have a few articles on storytelling and public narrative on the EnterpriseAgile.biz website.
[5]bit.ly/PublicNarrative.

The same goes for the expectations of the employer. This is known as the "psychological contract."

We worked with one client organization that had always treated its employees well with few layoffs and good benefits for over many years. Suddenly, a newly appointed executive decided to force his IT workers to work overtime in order to meet one of his goals for a production software release. There was not anything in the written employment contract that said an employee could expect to work a certain percentage of overtime (or not), but the employees certainly had an expectation in mind. The new executive had rewritten that part of the psychological contract without warning.

As a leader, do your best to understand the expectations employees have of the psychological contract. Then be careful not to break it, or to at least show that you understand when you are breaking it and provide an explanation of what measures you've taken to rebalance the contract.

Psychological contracts are much harder to deal with than written contracts, because many aspects of them are subjective in each person's minds. But they are still necessary to understand and part of the corporate culture, and violating them or rewriting them without warning can cause the same reaction as breaching a written employment contract.

11.4 The Desolate Wasteland of Management Training

Jim Hertzfeld, a colleague of ours in the software field, likes to draw a picture that shows the nature of management training and certification today.

He shows four areas that make a good manager/leader:

1. Managing tasks, schedules, risks and issues
2. Managing budgets
3. Managing client relationships (business stakeholders, executives, users, investors, etc.)
4. Leading the people on the team

Project management training and certification focuses primarily on #1 and #2 with only lip service given to #3 and #4. Not coincidentally, the third and fourth areas are less mechanical and more fraught with emotions, human frailty and unpredictability. However, they are as important as the first two areas.

This approach to project management education has created a class of managers who are quite good at managing numbers but fail consistently when it comes to the messy people issues of team and stakeholder politics (Fig. 11.2).

Fig. 11.2 Management and leadership training often misses important topics. © 2017 by Daryl Kulak and Hong Li—reprinted with permission

11.5 Getting Started with Servant Leadership

Taking this very different approach to leadership can be daunting. Feel free to print the poster of the leadership principles, available on the website EnterpriseAgile.biz.

Begin to talk to your fellow leaders about ways to embody these principles. Approach the principles one at a time. Look for small, simple opportunities where you can practice them without much risk. Ask people how they view you with regard to these principles.

> **Test Drive Your Knowledge Again**
> Answer the following questions with the knowledge you have after reading this chapter. Have your answers changed?
>
> 1. How does the level where a decision is made relate to servant leadership?
> 2. What is the servant leadership approach to measurement?
> 3. How would you describe your company's corporate culture?

> **Try This Next**
>
> **For the executive:** Mentor your managers to become better negotiators. Evaluate managers based, at least partially, on how helpful they are to their peers. Ask your direct reports how they view you with regard to the various principles.
>
> **For the manager:** Teach your teams the PDSA cycle and ask them to use it on a small problem. Use Marshall Ganz's public narrative process to explain a change to your team.
>
> **For the individual contributor:** Arrange a field trip to help your team better engage with the "real life" of your potential application users. Map the corporate culture of your company using the cultural dimensions. Compare your results to your coworkers. Involve your manager.

References

Ancona D, Bresman H (2007) X-teams: how to build teams that lead, innovate and succeed. Harvard Business School Press, Boston, MA

Dawson R (2012) The secrets of power negotiating. Nightingale-Conant, Wheeling, IL

Gladwell M (2008) Outliers: the story of success. Little, Brown and Company, New York

Hunter J (1998) The servant: a simple story about the true essence of leadership. Prima, Roseville, CA

Livermore D (2013) Customs of the world: using cultural intelligence to adapt, wherever you are. The Great Courses, Chantilly, VA

Smith P (2012) Lead with a story: a guide to crafting business narratives that captivate, convince and inspire. AMACOM, New York

How Teams Keep Learning and Improving 12

> *He who occupies himself with things other than improvement of his own self becomes perplexed in darkness and entangled in ruin. His evil spirits immerse him deep in vices and make his bad actions seem handsome.*
>
> Ali ibn Abi Talib, cousin of the Islamic prophet Muhammad

> **Test Drive Your Learning**
> Answer the following questions with the knowledge you have now. Then answer them again at the end of this chapter.
>
> 1. Once you've identified an action item in a retrospective, how do you go about fixing it, and making sure it is really fixed?
> 2. What's the best length for a sprint? Why?
> 3. What are some examples of "systems" in terms of systems thinking as it applies to your software team?

12.1 Continuous Improvement with W. Edwards Deming

For many years, W. Edwards Deming (one of our systems thinking scholars) has been referred to as the thought leader of continuous improvement. Ever since he worked with Toyota and other Japanese companies after World War II, his practices, intention and worldview have helped companies around the globe to think of improvement in new ways. We borrow heavily from Deming, but, for the most part, we ignore the derivative[1] works that came later, particularly the "lean manufacturing" movement (Womack et al. 1990) and "total quality management" (Juran 1988).

Ask any Agile expert how teams can improve continuously and they will undoubtedly say "retrospectives." Retrospectives are where the team looks back on their previous sprint and tries to understand how they could improve. It's pretty simple. The fact that there are multiple books in our industries dedicated to this simple team activity is quite puzzling. It is a symptom of our industry's obsession with ever fine-tuning "best practices."

But retrospectives are just a small part of the picture. What do you do once you've identified a problem to fix in your team room? There are problems in your team's control and problems outside of your control. In either case, you can use the same process, which we've borrowed from Deming.

12.1.1 The Shewhart Cycle

We've already mentioned the Shewhart cycle several times in this book, but now we will dive into it in earnest.

Part of Deming's advice to the Japanese companies was to use the Shewhart cycle to continuously improve their processes. Walter Shewhart was a Deming collaborator who created this easy-to-use cycle.

The Shewhart cycle has the structure shown in Fig. 12.1.

Plan—understanding what is going on in your system, modeling it, discussing it, picking a problem to fix

Do—executing the fix

Study—setting up measurements (not targets) to understand whether your fix is working or not

Action—based on your measurements, take action to fix the fix, or continue to make improvements (if it actually worked)

For certain problems that you discover in a retrospective, you can begin the PDSA cycle to try to solve it. In most retrospectives in which we've participated, there are too many problems pointed out to run the PDSA cycle on them all. As you'll see, there is a bit of work involved in solving each individual issue. Instead, pick the most important one or two.

---

[1]Womack and Jones' book *The Machine That Changed the World* (Womack et al. 1990) badly misapplied Deming's original work. They see teams of people as machines. They see success as the output of a mechanism. This was the opposite of Deming's intentions. John Seddon provides a very good critique of the mismatches between Deming and the derivatives. (Seddon 2005). Deming's own rants about derivative works are also quite legendary.

12.1 Continuous Improvement with W. Edwards Deming

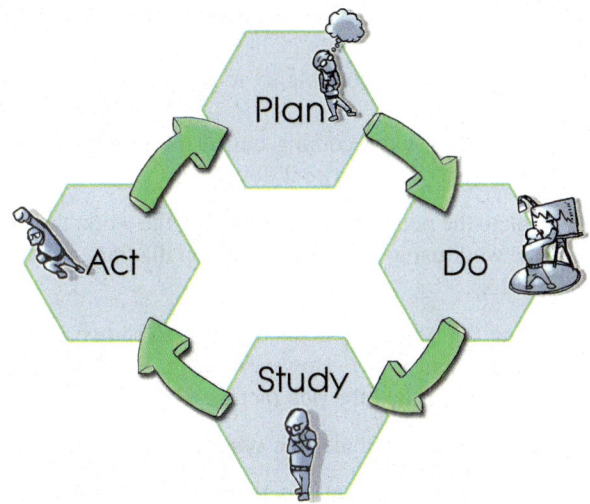

Fig. 12.1 Shewhart cycle.
© 2017 by Daryl Kulak and Hong Li—reprinted with permission

We enjoy using the Shewhart cycle for several reasons:

- **It is humble.** The Shewhart cycle assumes that we are going to have to take multiple runs at solving the problem. We probably won't do it right the first time.
- **It provides measurable improvement.** It's one thing to solve a problem. It's quite another to know that you've solved it. The way you know you've solved it is to measure the improvement.
- **It is looking for continuous improvement, not a target.** Deming did not focus the Japanese teams on specific targets. Instead, he always coached them to a cycle of continuous improvement. (See Chap. 15—HR Agility—Goal-Setting and Specific Targets.)
- **It is low maintenance.** Some of the Scrum "best practices experts" scoff at the PDSA cycle as being "big planning up front." This is a naive view. PDSA is all about making lots of improvements continuously, not creating a "big plan." A tiny amount of planning, a little doing, a little checking, a little action. This was Deming's intention at the beginning and it what PDSA continues to represent today.

Here's a bit more detail on each of the PDSA steps in the Shewhart cycle.

12.1.1.1 Plan
When you "Plan" you are:

- Identifying the problem you want to solve
- Investigating the problem situation

- Figuring out a measurement that would show whether the problem is getting better or worse
- Deciding on one possible fix to the problem that is worth trying

Take the problem coming out of the retrospective (or coming from any other source, actually) and write it down.

Talk to the people involved in doing the work, the people inside the system. Map out the work using a quick causal loop diagram, also known as a systems diagram. (Fig. 12.2).

Using the type of systems diagram as shown in Fig. 12.2 is one way to map a system (Senge 1994). However, there is an alternative to the simple systems diagram. It is called the rich picture (Fig. 12.3) (Checkland and Scholes 1990).

A rich picture includes the systems mappings, but it is much more.

First, a rich picture allows things to be unstructured. It can have structured and unstructured aspects to it.

Second, a rich picture does not try to be objective. It is meant to show people's perspectives of the system, how different people may see different systems, and even how emotion and biases may be evident as part of the system.

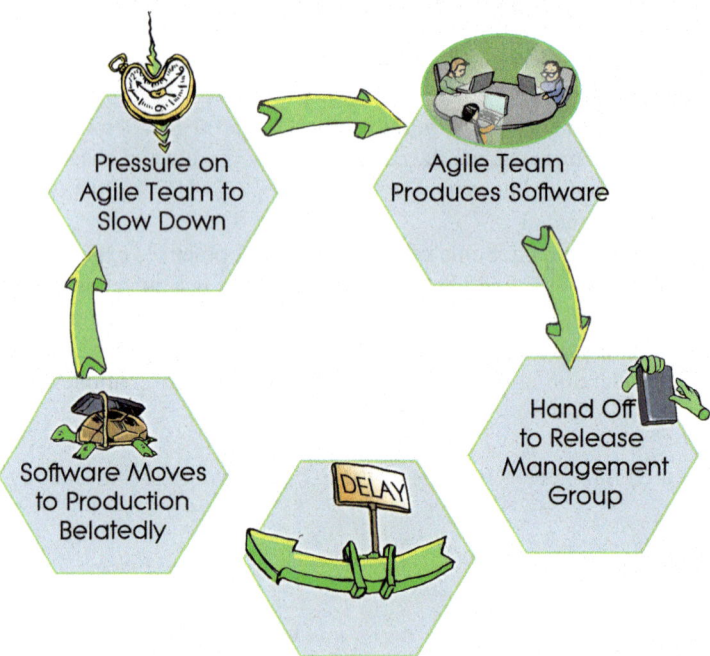

Fig. 12.2 Causal loop or systems diagram. © 2017 by Daryl Kulak and Hong Li—reprinted with permission

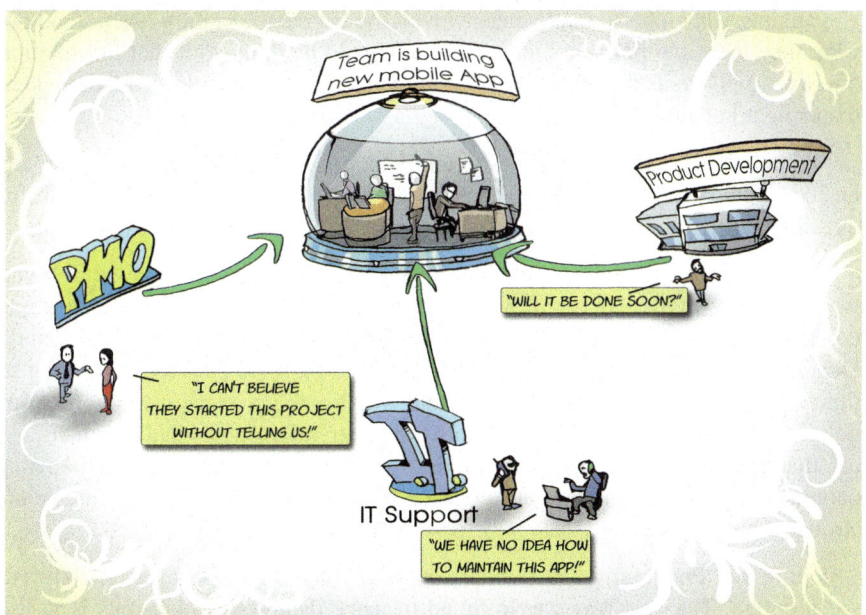

Fig. 12.3 Rich picture example. © 2017 by Daryl Kulak and Hong Li—reprinted with permission

If two vice presidents dislike each other, don't you think that will have an effect on a system of which they are both a part? Of course it will. And yet, we tend not to document this fact in any way, even though it is useful information.

You may say "I'm not documenting that because it would embarrass those people. They would pretend it wasn't true and they would think less of me if they knew I was writing this stuff down." That is quite possible.

Here is where you can find different roles for systems diagrams versus rich pictures. It might be that a rich picture is something you use for your own purposes but you don't publish it or show it to anyone else. The rich picture will still have a tremendous amount of value in this case, because it will help you structure your thinking about the problem situation. In some cases, a rich picture might be distributed among your stakeholders, but often it might never leave the hard drive of your computer. That's okay too. Let them see your systems diagrams and they don't need to know anything beyond that.

The rich picture can be a jumping-off point for your dialogue with the people in the system. You can ferret out information about people's perspectives, and people's perspectives on other people's perspectives. Remember, the people side of the system is where most of your potential for improvement lies, so don't disrespect this part of the work. It can be done with decorum and tact; it doesn't have to turn into a daytime talk show to be helpful to your work.

Planning what fixes to make means involving the people in the system. Find out what they think the problems are and what should be done. Pull that information into a set of systems diagrams and/or rich pictures and then look for places where fixes might be helpful.

We talk about "choke points" as potential places where you can begin to focus on fixing the system. Look for places where waste may be happening. Look for queuing, sorting or batching—these are common symptoms of waste occurring.

Also part of the planning is identifying a set of measurements that will tell you whether what you do worked or not. Here, the words of Deming and the concepts coming from inside Google, Inc. sound identical. "Base your decisions on data!" Deming encouraged managers to look at the data their teams were generating to figure out what needed to be changed, and whether the changes were working or not. Google is the same. They do A/B tests of different layouts of their products and use that data to make decisions on all kinds of issues. This drives user experience people nuts, because they want "creative license," but the Google ethic holds strong—"base it on data."

Part of the "Plan" activity is to figure out how you are going to measure things to see progress. The best way we've found to make data-driven decisions is to use behavior-over-time (BOT) graphs, which we discussed and provided examples of in Chap. 7—Business Value, Estimation and Metrics.

A big part of BOT charts is to put the focus on the data rather than a "problem person." Remember Principle #5—Blame the system, not the person. BOT charts can help shift the problem focus to "the system" rather than getting into the "blame game" of who is at fault.

12.1.1.2 Do

Making the changes is something you do in concert with the people in the system. You don't create the changes off by yourself and then come back and say "Surprise! It's fixed!" Instead, work with the team members[2] iteratively and refine your vision. By the end of the planning activity, you may find that your team is already making the changes you've been talking about all this time, which is great.

The "Do" part of the Shewhart cycle means "we measure." Conduct the measurements each day or week or whatever and look for trends. You can talk about the improvements (or lack of them) during the subsequent retrospectives and monitor the progress.

---

[2]One particularly competent Agile team we were coaching was like this. We would begin discussing some ideas we had about possible changes they could make with big, visible charts or continuous integration, and a few hours later we would see the charts going up and the integrations happening. It actually hurt our feelings a little at the time because we felt like they were stealing our thunder, but we quickly realized that this was the best possible consulting engagement!

You have to make the effort to keep the wall charts up to date. Most charts will need to be updated weekly, but depending on the chart you may need to make updates more often.

With one team, we had a problem where the product owner was not able to spend enough time with the team. The problem was brought up in the retrospective and the product owner acknowledged that he was not present often enough, but felt like he did not have the control to fix his scheduling issues. We decided to create a BOT graph that had a time scale of days and a y axis corresponding to the number of hours our product owner was able to spend in our team room each day. We also drew a horizontal line showing the number of hours the product owner was promised to the team each day. The product owner filled in the columns each day to show his hours. If he missed spending a day with the team completely, that column went blank.

One day the product owner's manager came into the team room and asked about the chart. We explained it to him. He was quite surprised and resolved to fix the problem. In a way, just the act of putting up the chart was the first step to solving the problem. Additionally, the other executives and managers asked about the chart and tried to find ways to help. We found that the chart was making our problem "big and visible," kind of proclaiming that we had this problem for all to hear, and then listening to see who could help us. The problem resolved itself nicely in just a few sprints. The chart did its job.

12.1.1.3 Study[3]

So, did it work? How do you know? Start to look at the data coming out from the measurements you decided upon when planning. Are the measurements trending positively? Great. The same? Or negative? Don't jump into action...yet.

"Don't just do something! Stand there!" Deming's worry was that, very frequently, managers were twiddling with their team's processes without allowing natural cycles to take place. Do you have enough data to say that the change didn't work? One sprint didn't go so well? Is that enough to kill the new change? No way. You need at least a few sprints (you judge how many) to understand the implication of your fix.

Further, you need to understand what Deming called "common cause" versus "special cause." In the graph below, there are certain variations that are simply part of the system. Don't jump all over them. Managers being overreactive causes instability in the system.

In Fig. 12.4, we have noticed that we have a problem with the number of times developers are checking in code that break the regularly scheduled build in the continuous integration stack. We create a graph that will allow us to analyze the situation with real data, not just vague problem statements.

---

[3]Often referred to as "check" in later derivative works. We prefer to use the original "study" verb to avoid this step seeming like we simply need to check off an item in a checklist.

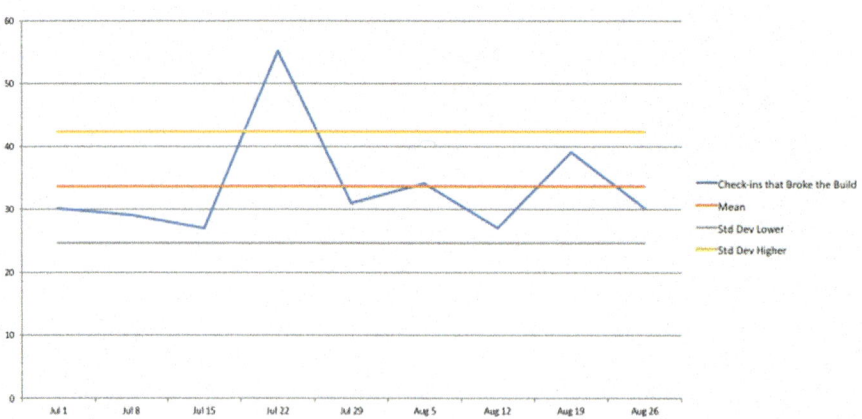

Fig. 12.4 Special cause, common cause. © 2017 by Daryl Kulak and Hong Li—reprinted with permission

Then we "study" the chart after a few weeks. We can see that the blue line, representing number of check-ins that break the build, jumps all over the place. But that doesn't have to be confusing. We add three additional straight lines to show the mean, standard deviation below and standard deviation above.

For those who do not enjoy math, those terms are probably a turn-off. But please don't abandon us yet. The mean is simply the average of all the points, in this case it's about 34 check-ins. Standard deviation above and below are markers for where the most likely deviations from the average will occur. It is about a 60% likelihood that any new point will exist below yellow line and above the purple line. Any behavior that is between these two lines is considered normal, or, in Deming's terms, common cause.[4]

So we have one point which falls outside these two lines that happened on the week of July 22. We had 55 check-ins that broke the build that week. That is interesting. That is worth investigating. What happened on that day? What was unique about those check-ins?

But, more importantly, the other points are probably NOT worth investigating. They fall within the purple and yellow lines and are therefore just variations within the system. Randomness, pure and simple. Noise. Nothing you can do about it.

And this is where well-meaning managers often go wrong. They will spend time analyzing why the bad check-ins rose from 27 to 39 from August 12 to 19. Yes, that seems like a big jump. But it's probably not worth investigating. It is within common cause variation.

---

[4] Finding data points above or below the standard deviation is just one factor in your investigation. We are oversimplifying here for the purposes of clarity.

But let's say that even an average of 34 check-ins per week breaking the build is unacceptable. Then we should try to find fixes that might bring that average down. Great! But we should not worry about the relatively small variations between, for instance, August 5–12 or August 19–26.

The danger of "fixin' what ain't broke" through poor understanding of common cause and special cause is that we will actually harm the system and cause productivity to go down further. Yes, we need to fix problems in the system. Yes, we should bring that average of 34 broken builds down to, hopefully, zero or close to it. But we shouldn't get distracted by common cause variation. That's a killer.

One example of a fixable problem would be if the team lacks training on a particular technology component, let's say Hadoop. This lack of knowledge is causing them to use Hadoop wrongly and causing lots of rework and hassles. It is a systemic problem, a problem in the system. We can fix it and the system will get better.

Another example is a team that has to rely on an outside group to do system testing. The team does their own unit testing and integration testing, but then must pass the code to a dedicated system testing group, who gives them feedback and defects to fix. If the team can convince their executives to allow them to do their own system testing (with their own testing staff), they may get some lift and the whole process might move faster.

For fixable problems, it is worth it to examine the problem, come up with solutions and implement them within the team.

12.1.1.4 Action

So now you have made your fixes, you have a pretty good idea whether they worked or not, and you can decide what needs to happen next. It could be that your fix is a failure (don't take it personally), and your fix needs to be retracted or perhaps fixed in a different way. Then identify that for your planning phase. Or it might be that the fix went great. Good! Congratulations all around and away we go again. What else can we do with this system?

Via Negativa!

Remember the Via Negativa principle as you're making improvements. Often, your first impulse will be to add something to fix the problem of the day. "We could set up a meeting!" Try not to. First, think of what you could subtract. Could we get rid of a standard/rule/constraint? Could we reduce the space between two teams who are not communicating well? Secondly, at least try not to add anything. Solve the problem without adding any new meetings, roles, rules or handoffs. And thirdly, as a last result, if you can't think of any other way to do it, add something to fix the problem.

Read more about Via Negativa in Chap. 5—Redefining Professionalism.

12.1.2 The Trouble with Self-Reinforcing Feedback

Most of the features of a systems diagram are knobs you can tweak that will make subtle or reasonably strong changes in your system. But there is one systems element you need to be very careful about. Watch for reinforcing loops.

A reinforcing loop is where more of A causes more of B, which in turn causes more of C, which causes more of A (Fig. 12.5). These can be extremely dangerous. They often cause instability in the system.

Another example of this comes to us from Gene Johnson, one of our colleagues in Agile software development. He often sees that managers don't trust their employees, so they create more structure, which breeds less trust. This is an example of a negative reinforcing loop.

Look for these loops in your systems, and pay close attention to them. At best, you can look for ways to balance them, perhaps by adding another factor which can slow down an escalation (or downward spiral) if it happens.

At worst, you can set up measurements to monitor for potential escalations or downward spirals and be ready to take quick action if something bad happens.

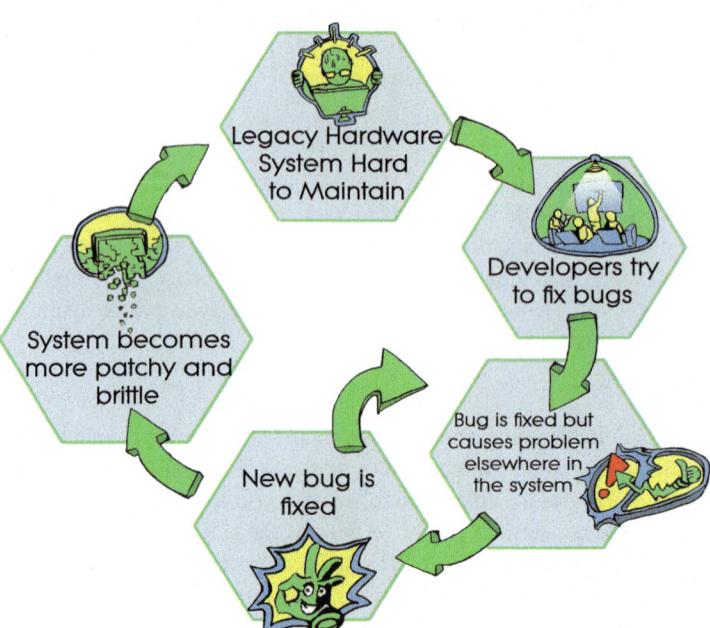

Fig. 12.5 Systems diagram with reinforcing feedback. © 2017 by Daryl Kulak and Hong Li—reprinted with permission

12.2 Where's the System?

When you think of "the system," you may automatically think of the way work is processed through your team. Requirements come in from the businesspeople, get coded, tested and features go out the door. Yeah, that is one system. But you have a bunch of others. Here are a few:

- Version control systems
- Code integration systems
- Team member orientation systems
- Meeting set up systems
- Change request systems
- Goofing off systems
- Big visible chart production systems
- Intra-team dating systems
- Smoke break systems
- Motivation systems
- People onboarding systems

Each system has its own rules, boundaries and participants. And each system can have an effect on the other systems.

Please don't think that you have to map all these as systems diagrams or rich pictures TODAY. You don't. But watch for systemic activity, and, when it's needed, take action on a system, any of these systems, and drop into your PDSA cycle.

12.3 How Long Is a Sprint?

There are people who feel strongly about sprint length and those who don't care. We care.

We think sprints need to be short. Part of the iterative/incremental lifecycle is to take a large project and break it up into small chunks. Why not really small? Our preference for sprint length is 1 week. It is a natural cycle (we have demos every Tuesday) that people can remember. But there is a much more important reason.

Let's say you have a 3-month project to get a product released. As we've said in earlier chapters, organizations should use the Cisco Rule where each team is releasing production software at least once every quarter.

There are several Scrum groups that encourage one sprint per month. In terms of retrospectives and improvements, how many cycles of improvement do you have?

Two, actually. One at the end of the first month, end of the second month, and then you're live in production.

Switch your thinking to weekly sprints and you have 11 cycles of improvement. You have 11 data points on your charts, 11 opportunities to take stock of what you've done so far and evaluate changes in direction.

And, most importantly, you are connecting with your stakeholders at the demos 11 times. Every opportunity to show people what you've done so far is valuable. You have less time to get off-track during a short sprint.

Why do some organizations use longer sprints? Most of the time, they use "overhead" as the reason. If we are running demos, sprint planning sessions and retrospectives every week, we are spending more time on these overhead activities and interrupting our developers' ability to concentrate on producing features and velocity.

This argument neglects the fact that a demo of 1 week's worth of code is shorter than 2 week's, usually by half. Makes sense, right? The other ceremonies are also much shorter because there is less to plan, less to retrospect.

Also, the thinking that these meetings are "overhead" is telling. If something is overhead, we should get rid of it. But these meetings should be critical to keeping the team on track and producing the best quality possible. The business world has twists and turns that do not occur on monthly cycles, they occur daily and weekly. The sprint teams need to keep up, and make changes quickly.

Our experience is that teams who use longer sprint cycles, even 2 weeks, experience more intra-sprint changes coming from the product owner. "Could you just fit this into the current sprint? I know I should wait, but I really need it now." This will always happen more with longer sprints. But with 1-week sprints, not as much. In fact, almost never. It is much easier for a product owner to "wait until Tuesday" to pop in a new idea, versus waiting weeks or months for the team to acknowledge the change.

Finally, team motivation is also a factor. In every sprint, there is a sag in productivity in the middle. With a month-long sprint, that sag probably lasts a week-and-a-half. But in a week-long sprint, there isn't much ability to sag. That is not to say the team is always anxious, stressed and overworked with 1-week sprints. You plan to do less because you have less time. But the work pace is steady without long sags in productivity.

For us, a month-long sprint is an eternity and fraught with risk. We have several clients who insist on 2-week sprints, which we can tolerate. But if we can possibly convince our clients to use a 1-week sprint cycle, we are happiest and least nervous.

12.4 Lightning Talks

> They think it's about the results. But it's not. It's about the team.
> Allen Smith, consultant extraordinaire

Lightning talks are a simple concept, but they can really help a team to gel and understand each other.

A lightning talk is a short speech made by one team member to their fellow team members on any topic whatsoever. The team can designate one hour each month to lightning talks and take volunteers to speak for 5–10 min on a topic that they are personally passionate about.

We've seen tremendous results from lightning talks. On one particular team, the developers coordinated a set of lightning talks to happen every second week. One developer had kept himself separate from the rest of the team (about 15 developers total). Let's call him Heinrich. Heinrich was working on a different part of the application than the other developers, and he was also quite shy, so these factors led to him being a bit of a loner in an otherwise social, loud team space. However, one day Heinrich volunteered to do a lightning talk on "squirrel fishing." He delivered it expertly and got lots of laughs and accolades. From that day forward, Heinrich and the other developers began to form a bit closer bonds, simply from having the lightning talks as a kind of icebreaker as an excuse to chat.

With lightning talks, you will learn a lot about your team mates beyond how they write code. You might even learn about their intentions and worldviews!

12.5 Learning, Improving

Learning and improving has very little to do with scheduling more training classes. In our experience, learning happens on the job and the lessons are often generated internally. To improve, we must do the work and have an intention to continuously improve what we do. The deadlines must not be so onerous that we feel we don't have time to improve. The team members must begin to understand one another's worldviews. And it helps to have people around who've been through this before (see Chap. 13—Getting Coaching That Really Helps).

> **Test Drive Your Knowledge Again**
> Answer the following questions with the knowledge you have after reading this chapter. Have your answers changed?
>
> 1. Once you've identified an action item in a retrospective, how do you go about fixing it, and making sure it is really fixed?
> 2. What's the best length for a sprint? Why?
> 3. What are some examples of "systems" in terms of systems thinking as it applies to your software team?

> **Try This Next**
>
> **For the executive:** Use the PDSA cycle to solve an inter-team issue that can be addressed in a fairly short time. Keep a big visible chart to track the improvement.
>
> **For the manager:** Set up a series of lightning talks to occur once a month at a time convenient for the team.
>
> **For the individual contributor:** Use the PDSA cycle on one of the retrospective items that you take ownership of. Keep a big visible chart to track the improvement.

References

Checkland P, Scholes J (1990) Soft systems methodology in action. Wiley, New York

Juran JM (1988) Juran's quality control handbook. McGraw-Hill, New York

Seddon J (2005) Freedom from command and control: rethinking management for lean service. Productivity Press, New York

Senge PM (1994) The fifth discipline: the art & practice of the learning organization. Doubleday, New York

Womack JP, Jones DT, Roos D (1990) The machine that changed the world: the story of lean production – Toyota's secret weapon in the global car wars that is now revolutionizing World industry, later edition available in 2007. Rawson Associates, New York

Getting Coaching That Really Helps 13

> **Test Drive Your Knowledge**
> Answer the following questions with the knowledge you have now. Then answer them again at the end of this chapter.
>
> 1. What are the pluses and minuses of the shu-ha-ri approach to coaching?
> 2. What are the aspects of an Agile transformation?
> 3. How are Agile certifications helpful or not?

13.1 Fighting Poverty in Rural China

James Yen[1] is a famous name in China. He accomplished a lot in his lifetime, even though he lived part of his life under the oppression of Mao Zedong's Communist Party.

Yen moved to the USA for his schooling in the early 1900s. He graduated from Yale in 1918 and formed a close relationship with the Young Men's Christian Association (YMCA) during his college years. His work with the YMCA led him to France, where he worked to support the Allies in World War I. The people he worked with were mostly from China, part of the Chinese Labor Corp. These Chinese were rural peasants who had come to France to dig the trenches of war and other back-breaking tasks. Yen had been, up until that time, an intellectual young man, full of himself and a bit condescending in his view of the peasants, whom the French called "coolies." But Yen found that he enjoyed teaching the peasants, and since most of them did not know how to read and write Chinese

---
[1]Be sure to read *To the People* (Hayford 1990) for James Yen's fascinating life story.

(much less French or English), Yen started in earnest with regular classes to help them learn. Yen relished the classwork and was very surprised at the capability of these "coolies" to learn given just a chance. They were highly motivated students and jumped at any chance to improve their own skills. Yen even began to teach the peasants bits of French so that the French officers could provide them with directions more easily, which, of course, helped the army's tolerance of Yen's classes.

Yen's metaphor for this process was that he was merely "unlocking the gold mines of people's minds." He saw that the coolies had many capabilities but that they were dormant until someone like Yen came along to unlock them. Once unlocked, the coolies could begin their own learning cycles and surprise everyone, including themselves, with their own creativity and intelligence.

This is significant. Here was Yen working with the most humble, most looked-down-upon people, and he was seeing that they were kind of "geniuses in waiting." What an insight.

Yen was so pleased with his interactions with the coolies in France that he started to do similar work in China when he returned after the war. Yen created the International Institute of Rural Reconstruction (IIRR) to tackle the problem of poverty in rural China. Yen recruited college students inside and outside China to work with him and help all Chinese benefit from better ideas and a better life. His focus was to help each village become more self-sufficient in agriculture, construction and self-governance.

Yen created a set of principles for the IIRR as follows:
Go to the people,
Live among them,
Learn from them,
Plan with them,
Work with them,
Start with what they know,
Build on what they have,
Teach by showing,
Learn by doing,
Not a showcase, but a pattern,
Not odds and ends, but a system,
Not piecemeal, but an integrated approach,
Not to conform, but to transform,
Not relief but release.

The Credo is poetic in its simplicity.

James Yen and the IIRR had to depart from China because of pressure from Mao Zedong's communist regime, which saw Yen as a threat to their grand plans.

However, the IIRR is thriving today. The headquarters of the organization is now in the Philippines, with projects throughout Asia and Africa.

13.2 How to Transform an Organization?

When companies contract a process coach, like an Agile coach, for instance, they are often looking for some element of organizational transformation.

The work that James Yen was doing with the IIRR in those villages was also a type of transformation.

And yet, most process coaches we've observed have a very different approach from Yen's successful approach with reducing poverty. They use another practice called shu-ha-ri.

13.2.1 Shu-ha-ri

> Oh my, how the world still dearly loves a cage.
> Tess Lynch, essayist

Many Agile coaches we've known use a process called "shu-ha-ri." This comes from the martial art Aikido, where students learn different parts of the art and pass through different stages in their own learning.

The students start with "shu." In this stage, you must obey your master without question. Learn the fundamentals but now is not the time to ask a lot of questions or even worry about why things are the way they are. The focus is on expediency, speeding up the learning process so you can move on to a more flexible state.

Next is "ha." Now you can start to learn the "why" behind things and start to make the practices your own. There is more flexibility now that students can grow into.

Finally is "ri." The student is now knowledgeable enough that they can change parts of Aikido and even break the rules, because they have a foundation on which they can stand safely.

There are several aspects of Shu-ha-ri that are interesting when applied to process coaching. In Aikido, there are a set of positions and movements that are static and the same for everyone. Everyone must go through the stages of learning them. Many coaches assume that software process is the same as Aikido. There are positions and movements to learn, you have to learn them like everyone else. "Best practices," you might say.

However, software techniques must be adapted to each situation. Software teams working in banks need to operate differently than in startups. Different things are important. Different practices are more or less relevant.

This is not the same as learning a well-established martial art like Aikido. There must be a process of adaptation. No "off the shelf" version of a software process (Agile, Lean or otherwise) will do.

Shu-ha-ri makes things very easy and simple. **For the coach.**

Putting the learners into a "shu box" by forcing them into a path without the ability to ask "why" is the most common mistake we've seen with unsuccessful process coaches. Remember principle #6—Treat people like people, not like machines. Forcing people into a situation where they cannot ask why or adapt the process to their needs causes them to feel like they are just a machine, executing orders. The Agile coaches who use shu-ha-ri are no better than waterfall project managers who are trying to control their subordinates.

Why do people need to ask why? It's because the people the coach is coaching might actually have some valid reasons why this particular practice might not work here, even though it has worked everywhere else. They might be right! They could be right and the Agile coach could be...gasp!...wrong.

But this frustrates some process coaches to no end. They want people to learn. They want people to change. They can't understand why people must resist so much. "You must be dumb to be unable to see the wonderful world awaiting you!"

Or.........maybe not so dumb.

13.2.2 The Alternative to Shu-ha-ri

Remember James Yen and the coolies. Yen and his IIRR colleagues were working with the poorest of the poor in rural China. And yet the IIRR credo reads "Live among them, Learn from them." Learn from these peasants? Imagine a young, college-educated IIRR worker's response to this idea. "What could I possibly learn from a poor person?"

Think of Yen's college grads as the Agile coaches. And the peasants are the employees of the company[2] receiving the coaching. What can the smart, quick-witted, Agile-experienced coach learn from these employees? He can learn the details of the company's own situation, the uniqueness of this particular industry and culture that might mean a new coaching approach is needed.

"Live among them, Learn from them."

Yen's IIRR Credo also says:

"Plan with them, Work with them."

Yen insisted that his college graduate "coaches" actually get into the game with the peasants. Get your hands dirty. Plant some rice. Lay bricks for the building. Feed the animals. Clean up the shit.

---

[2] In almost all cases, the employees being coached are just as educated, just as quick-witted as the Agile coaches. It is just the situation that puts the Agile coach in a more powerful position.

13.2 How to Transform an Organization?

Yen felt that there was only one way to really advise the peasants and that was to do the work right alongside them and subject yourself to the same hardships that the peasants deal with every day.

The same goes for coaching. We say that a coach has to be "in the muck" with our clients, dealing with the everyday crap that they deal with, before we can really understand how to help them. Offering advice from the sidelines is not helpful. A coach can preach "best practices" all day long, but the person the team members will really respect is the one who puts his own butt on the line with the team and experiences the highs and lows just like the team does.

For us, this is a serious deficiency in the world of Agile coaching and process coaching. Both of us have tried to play the coaching role years ago, but time and again we found that the effects did not last. Teams might comply with our words for a short time, but then they would relapse back to the bad old practices. Once we started acting like Yen's team in the IIRR, we achieved much better results, not to mention having more fun (because who wants to be the know-it-all on the sidelines, really?)

In James Yen's world, there was no shu-ha-ri cycle. He was not patiently doling out information to the peasants bit-by-bit like a wise teacher on a hilltop. He was rolling up his sleeves, kneeling in the dirt and solving day-to-day problems with them, learning and teaching all at once. As Agile coaches, we must do the same. That is, we need to change our own worldview, intention as we speak and take actions.

13.2.3 Scrum and Done!

So many organizations who bring in Agile coaches start with the Scrum practices, including cards on the wall, short sprints and frequent interaction with the business. These are great practices and they are a fine place to start. However, many organizations stop right there. They do not continue to include other beneficial practices, including ways to ensure valuable software as well as the software craftsmanship practices (discussed in Chap. 8—Flipping the Build/Run Ratio).

This is a real shame. Our own estimation is that a company that does "Scrum and Done" gets perhaps 20% of the benefit of an Agile transformation. Most of the benefit lies in the value practices (value stories, boundary critique, etc.) and the craftsmanship practices (test-driven development, continuous integration, etc.). Putting cards on the wall is great for transparency and the product owner role is great for pulling closer to the business, but there is a lot further to go to start getting big value from the team's efforts.

It makes good sense to start small, which might mean team room (re:Scrum) practices first. But organizations should persist in the other two areas (value and craftsmanship) before declaring victory.

13.2.4 Aspects of a Transformation

It makes sense to run an enterprise transformation the same way you run a software team. We put cards on the wall to show the transformation activities in the backlog and those underway. Generally, we run a Kanban wall for transformation. There isn't much need for sprints or demos as long as you groom the backlog regularly.

The place to start with a transformation is with "transformation value stories." (Read more about value stories in Chap. 7—Business Value, Estimation and Metrics.)

In other words, why do you want to transform? What are the business drivers behind doing this transformation work? How will you know when you've accomplished the transformation? What will be different?

Here are a few sample transformation value stories:

- As Organization X I want increased transparency into software development progress so that I can know where to continue to invest.
- As Organization X I want to decrease defects found in production code so that I can shift funds away from RUN and towards BUILD.
- As Organization X I want increased speed to market so that I can catch market opportunities that are currently passing us by.

Once the transformation value stories are known and prioritized, we can decide which one to work on first. For instance, if transparency is the most important value story, it makes sense to start with the Scrum practices of assigned product owners, user stories and card walls. If defects are the big problem, we should begin with some good engineering practices.

We've used the following categories of practices:

- Team room practices
    - Product owners, user stories, card walls, short sprints, frequent releases
- Engineering practices
    - Test-driven development, behavior-driven development, SOLID principles, continuous integration, devops
- Value practices
    - Value stories, Sprint Zero, prioritizing by value
- Enterprise scalability
    - Culture, HR agility, enterprise architecture, portfolio management

It may look like the list is all about "practices," but we sneak in the other parts of the noble paths under enterprise scalability. The first two categories focus mostly on the software teams. The value practices operate across multiple teams, and enterprise scalability happens with the connecting groups (HR, architecture, methodology, resource management, etc.) as well as the executives (changing the culture, intention and worldview).

13.3 Coaches Who Just Coach: NO; Extensive Training Sessions: NO; Certification: HELL NO

We've already explained our approach to coaches who just coach. Get rid of them, and find a team player who can teach by showing and learn by doing, like James Yen taught us.

How much can you learn about software process from a training class? Our opinion is that you can learn very little this way. Extensive training classes of a week or more are a waste of money, time and effort. There is a role for training, but it is limited.

Use training classes to get people oriented with **new terminology** and **new concepts**. Nobody is going to learn how to be a good product owner in a class, but you can give them the terminology and concepts around product ownership in just a few hours that will give them a foundation for learning. Then, the new product owner must be paired with a knowledgeable expert or coach, both of whom are doing the work together (i.e., not a coach who just coaches).

In particular, no one can really understand intention and worldview inside the bounds of a training class. No amount of "Agile mindset" training classes will get that across. It must be an examination, or better put a self-examination, that happens during the real work, day in and day out, unrelenting. And if you've got a knowledgeable team member (a coach) who is doing the work beside you, so much the better. Training classes can give you a boost of enthusiasm and self-confidence, but it quickly fades when you're once again confronted with real life. That is where hands-on coaching in the related context of real-life projects is needed.

The same goes for other roles. It is truly impossible to learn test-driven development (TDD) in a class, no matter how long the class extends (weeks? months?). But, in a class, you can give developers some vocabulary and concepts that will prepare them to be paired with other developers who can do TDD expertly.

The problem with trying to do extensive, lengthy training classes is that the training is fundamentally different from real life. Training exercises are bounded. Real life is not bounded. Anything could happen.

In a training exercise, the instructor will give the guidelines and rules for the exercise. "You can ignore the interfaces to other applications." "I'll act as the product owner and also the executive steering committee." The instructor has to do this otherwise the exercise may take too long and the participants might get off track too easily. But it is not real life.[3] Real life is much, much messier.

With training classes, we must exercise systems thinking principle #6—Acknowledge your boundaries. The boundaries of a training class include terminology and concepts, but exclude day-to-day competence.

So, the competence you build up in a training class is dependent on those boundaries staying intact. However, as soon as the class is over and you go back to your desk, you'll instantly run into a situation that wasn't covered in the training class. A new twist. A new complication. We call this phenomenon "train freeze." "But...but...but the class didn't cover this!" You thought you had the skill perfectly practiced in the class. But now, as you are faced with your day-to-day work, the skill breaks down and seems useless.

The boundaries we experience in the training class make our experience post-training to seem "not fair." It won't seem fair that our stakeholders change their minds or that our team composition changes drastically right at the wrong moment, or that the enterprise architect seems to be out to get us! The truth is, the training class was engineered to be "fair." But life outside the classroom is not fair. It never is. And dealing with unfair situations is the real skill that we all require.

This is not to say that training is useless. Not at all. But we should just treat it humbly. We shouldn't put too much stock into how far we will get with training. Much better to structure very short classes on bounded topics that are highly interactive, then move on to doing our day-to-day work in new ways, with help from experienced people who work with us shoulder-to-shoulder.

If a class promises that it gives you all the practical skills you need...**Warning!!** If a class is longer than a day...**Warning!!** If a class goes beyond vocabulary and concepts...**Warning!!** Steer clear of any of these types of classes.

Certification is, deservedly, a hot topic in the software field. Various Scrum and Agile certifications are offered by training vendors around the world. To tell you the absolute truth, in hiring, we pay absolutely no attention to certifications. If someone claims to be a "Certified Scrum Professional" we quickly skim past that and look for other qualifications that might be worth something. Most of our clients are becoming more and more similarly inclined. And yet, certification trainers continue to make lots of money offering their wares. Don't fall for this. Save your money to hire more good developers.

---

[3]You may think that you simply need to use real-life case studies in the class to overcome this problem. But you will still need to place artificial boundaries around that exercise, which will make it unlike what team members will face once they go back to their work.

Certification would be fine if the world only consisted of practices. But it does not. Worldview and intention play a bigger part in creating success, and you cannot certify those things. You can have conversations about them and you can improve them, but there aren't any certifications.[4]

To summarize: Holy shit! Certifications on processes or frameworks are beyond useless.

13.4 Talker+Doer

The best coach is one who is a "talker" and a "doer." For craftsmanship coaching, for instance, you need an individual who is able to speak eloquently about the concepts around craftsmanship, but who can also jump into the muck and get things done before the deadline hits. In our experience, most consultants are one or the other. Some consulting organizations, like large bodyshops, for instance, focus on the "doing." They can provide arms and legs who can code, but don't bother asking them for help in learning how they do what they do. On the other extreme, you have the coaching consultants, who will offer good-sounding advice all day long, just don't ask them to be part of the team and add velocity.

As a customer of coaching, you should always look for those consultants who can offer both, at least to a small extent. They will be the most help and will get the most respect from the team members.

13.5 Six Questions to Ask Your Agile Coach or Consultant

Q-01. Which Agile practices do you find need to be adopted at most of your clients?

Good answer: It is situation specific. There are a few that seem to be necessary in most organizations, but we tend to use practices to solve problems.

Bad answer: We always use the same set of Agile practices for every client. These are "best practices" that are proven to work. The practices are a complex web of activities that must be used together. If you take one out, you risk the whole structure falling apart.

Why is this answer bad? Consultants should not be trying to wedge their best practices into your problem domain. What the consultants bring is a variety of

---

[4]For more information on getting certified as a Senior Journey-Taker with the "Journey to Enterprise Agility" certification program, please have your credit card ready and go to the following website:

youknowwearekiddingright.com

perspectives based on the problems they've solved elsewhere. But a rigid set of best practices is only going to cause your internal team to have to follow them mechanically and, subsequently, be helpless after the consultant leaves.

Q-02. How do your Agile teams connect their work to business value?

Good answer: At the beginning of the project, we have a series of meetings with external stakeholders and the Agile team to determine how this project will be valuable to the company. In the best case, we will identify quantitative items of savings of expenditures or increases in revenue. Then we will use those statements of value to drive the rest of the project.

Bad answer: It is up to the product owner. Whatever they say is valuable is what the team treats as valuable.

Why this answer is bad: When a product owner becomes the single control point of value communication between stakeholders and the team, the product owner will become a single point of failure if the team relies on him exclusively. The team must truly understand the business problem they are solving and apply their own intelligence to it, not just be mechanical order takers for the product owner.

Q-03: What is the average length of the sprints on your projects?

Good answer: We try to use sprints as short as possible, to ensure that we are getting frequent feedback from the business. All sprints are the same length, the work stops at the end of the iteration, we never extend an sprint because the work isn't finished.

Bad answer: Many of our clients are not mature enough for short sprints, so we usually use one month sprints or longer. Iterations can vary during the course of the project, if the work doesn't get done, we extend the sprint until those deliverables are completed.

Why this answer is bad: Short sprints are necessary to ensure short feedback loops between the business and the Agile team. If the team goes astray for a sprint, which they will, much better for it to be a week lost than a month lost. Sprint length must not be variable. The heartbeat of an Agile team is what allows management to understand how much output the team can produce in a fixed amount of time, and it gives the team the much-needed motivation of accomplishing things regularly. The worst death march waterfall projects are those where the deadline keeps moving out into the future, making the project seem never ending.

13.5 Six Questions to Ask Your Agile Coach or Consultant

Q-04: What is the difference between a project manager and an Agile ScrumMaster?

Good answer: An Agile team leader, or ScrumMaster, or iteration manager, is very different from a standard project manager. The Agile team leader spends most of their time in the team room, while project managers tend to manage "by the numbers" from a distance. The Agile team leader understands the work they are managing deeply, while the project manager just sees tasks on a chart, unaware of what the tasks mean. Agile team leaders do not assign tasks, they spend time improving the processes. Project managers assign tasks and then request status. Project management is about control, the ScrumMaster role is about enablement.

Bad answer: Project manager and ScrumMaster are just two terms for the same thing.

Why this answer is bad: People who try to "project manage" Agile teams do not succeed because the teams are not able to self-organize, and progress is slow and mechanical. Project management has a different worldview than ScrumMaster (or delivery lead, as we defined it in Chap. 16—HR Agility).

Q-05: Does everyone have to be in the same team room for an Agile project?

Good answer: There are lots of instances of Agile projects with people who are not colocated and things work out fine. The issue is cost. A team that is colocated will be able to get more done for a lower cost than a team where team members are far apart from one another. It becomes a decision on whether it is worth paying the additional productivity cost for a team that is not colocated.

Bad answer: It doesn't matter whether the team is in a team room or in cubicles or far apart. It is all the same.

Why this answer is bad: This answer shows a lack of understanding of the costs of keeping a team separated. There are costs to a separated team, because questions and answers between team members will need to be batched and queued between locations, because side-stream conversations will not be overhead, and because the team members will not be able to engender trust with one another as easily or quickly.

Another bad answer: You cannot do Agile unless the team is colocated in an open space.

Why this answer is bad: The person is not willing to compromise to the realities of corporate life and will not be able to help you beyond spouting textbook Agile definitions. This answer shows that the person probably does not have much experience, and is over-reliant on Agile dogma.

Q-06: What sort of "best practices" will you bring to our organization?

Good answer: There are no best practices. There are good practices in certain contexts that we've seen, and we will most certainly share those with you. But the set of practices you need in your organization will be different than what other companies have successfully used. We'll examine your company's culture, your people's worldviews, intentions (to the extent possible) and speech. Then we'll fit the right transformations and practices that we think will help you most.

Bad answer: We closely follow (a) Scrum Alliance, (b) Scrum.org or (c) whatever other industry group.

13.6 People Don't Resist Change

> People don't resist change. People resist being changed.
> Richard Beckhard, American organizational theorist

Richard Beckhard was an organizational theorist at MIT, but he worked closely with a variety of organizations, including very small family-owned businesses. Beckhard's words have been ringing in our heads for several years now. How can he say that people don't resist change when we see that exact behavior every day?

Beckhard actually has a valuable insight. People need to decide their own way to change. They might not change the way you want them to, but that might be sensible from their perspective. Unless you are right there with them, in the muck of day-to-day life, you probably won't understand it. But if you are, you will.

You can probably remember instances in your company when people changed very quickly. Your company merges with another company. Do people change when that happens? You bet they do. They change quickly and decisively. They perceive it in their own interests to change, so change happens. But changes don't always have to be negative. Any type of change can elicit immediate results from people. They just have to be able to decide their own way to change. Which might not fit into the change agent's grand "change strategy." The change agent needs to adapt their strategy and move on.

> **Test Drive Your Knowledge Again**
> Answer the following questions with the knowledge you have after reading this chapter. Have your answers changed?
>
> 1. What are the pluses and minuses of the shu-ha-ri approach to coaching?
> 2. What are the aspects of an Agile transformation?
> 3. How are Agile certifications helpful or not?

> **Try This Next**
>
> **For the executive:** Institute the questions at the end of this chapter as part of the interview process for incoming Agile coaches and consultants.
>
> **For the manager:** Insist that Agile coaches are doers as well as talkers. Have them play real roles on the projects they serve.
>
> **For the individual contributor:** Ask the Agile coaches "Why?" they are offering the particular advice. Ask them to explain why their advice applies to this environment and situation.

Reference

Hayford CW (1990) To the people: James Yen and village China. Columbia University Press, New York

Capitalizing Software Investments   14

> **Test Drive Your Knowledge**
> Answer the following questions with the knowledge you have now. Then answer them again at the end of this chapter.
>
> 1. What is the difference between CAPEX and OPEX?
> 2. Which parts of the Agile lifecycle should be capitalized?
> 3. What are the benefits to capitalizing software investments?

14.1 Will That Be CAPEX or OPEX?

This chapter covers very basic information about capitalization of software investments. You may skip it if you are certain you know how an Agile lifecycle will affect your capitalization decisions. And please always consult your certified public accountant to make decisions regarding software capitalization.

When a corporation creates a software system, they are creating something of value. How that value shows up in the financial statements gets a bit fuzzy. In this chapter, we'll examine how companies have tackled the capitalization[1] issue for software.

Budgets for spending are generally placed into two categories: capital expenditure (CAPEX) and operating expense (OPEX).

---

[1]The authors of this book are not accountants. Therefore, we cannot offer accounting advice. Take this chapter as a retelling of how companies we've observed have managed capitalization of their software. Speak to a certified public accountant to get advice on your business affairs.

Capital expenditure is money spent towards the purchase or creation of an asset. This includes buying a building, a computer, a desk, etc. This money is not expensed immediately, but actually goes onto the balance sheet and is classified as an asset there. The expenses happen over a longer period of time, as the asset degrades. This degradation money is called depreciation expense.

Operating expense is money spent on day-to-day items that get used up and thrown away or services that maintain the status quo. Here you can think of printer paper, food for the cafeteria, parking lot snow removal, etc. Operating expenses go straight to the income statement as expenses; they do not become assets at all.

There are gray areas, but the Generally Accepted Accounting Principles (GAAP) and the International Financial Reporting Standards (IFRS) do their best to categorize money spent as either an asset or an operating expense (in excruciating detail).

14.1.1 CAPEX and OPEX Activities in Software Development

Here are some helpful guidelines that we've seen our clients use that help to classify CAPEX from OPEX:

Activities that can be CAPEX:

Software design
Software and environment configuration
Programming
Interface creation between applications
Hardware installation
Software testing
Creating the data conversion utilities for cutover
Project management
Hardware and packaged software cost
Consultant travel costs
Creating content for online help
Enhancements made to an in-production application
Hardware upgrades for an in-production application

Activities that should be OPEX:

Formulation, evaluation and selection of alternative hardware or software
Surveys of existing technology
Prototypes and proof-of-concepts
Data conversion activities (running the utilities)
Training
Post-production support
On-going hardware and software maintenance
Changes to the in-production application that do not result in new features

As you can see, all work that occurs in a sprint that relates to putting new features into production can be capitalized. Just maintaining existing applications needs to be expensed.

Once the capitalized software goes into production, that is when the depreciation can begin. The accountants will create a depreciation schedule that matches the guidelines from GAAP or IFRS and take the expense at regular intervals until the software reaches its expected lifetime. At that time, the software may stay in use or be sunsetted. But even if it stays in use, there will not be any more depreciation happening since the capitalized asset of software is completely depleted.

14.2 Why Capitalize?

If you are new to this topic, you may wonder why it is important to capitalize software, to turn it into an asset rather than just expensing it when you pay for it. We'll examine a few of the reasons why companies decide to do this.

14.2.1 Income Smoothing

If you are following the Cisco Rule that we introduced in Chap. 7—Business Value, Estimation and Metrics, you will be putting software into production often, at least every 3 months. That means you won't be waiting for 12 or 18 months to begin depreciating the capitalized asset, you will start a bit more depreciation each time a bit more software hits production.

This might be an advantage. A big reason that companies like to capitalize software and then depreciate it bit-by-bit over the subsequent months is to achieve "income smoothing." Income smoothing is a way to take the big jumps in expenses and spread them out so that the reports of net income (to Wall Street or any other type of investor) are fairly predictable from quarter to quarter. It's not good if net income jumps around—investors don't like that. They want to see their investment as a nice, predictable moneymaker. If income jumps around, it's almost as bad as if income goes down; it's disruptive (and not in a good way).

So company executives figure out ways to smooth income. Depreciating capitalized assets is one way to do this. But with more frequent releases, the smoothness becomes even smoother! Smaller chunks of software being depreciated sooner. It can be effective, but the decision really sits with the CFO of the company. There are many strategies.

Putting software into production frequently may be the most important Agile financial principle. If you do accomplish that, all the other practices simply support that objective. All team members should feel the need to put software into production. They should all feel itchy and twitchy if they know the code they're currently building isn't destined for production anytime soon.

14.2.2 Ratio Analysis

Many CFOs decide to use bank loans or lines-of-credit as an additional tool to add liquidity for growth spurts. That means dealing with banks, who have opinions on how the business should be run that might conflict with the company's own vision. But it is often worth the trouble.

Part of how banks analyze a corporation's creditworthiness is to use a "ratio analysis." The bank looks at all the company's assets and compares them to the liabilities. Should we loan this company more money, given their existing debts? It can make sense, as long as the assets owned by the company are substantial as well.

Capitalizing software can be a strategy to make a company's ratio analysis look better for the banks. If a CFO is wanting to increase assets in order to lobby for a higher set of liabilities, capitalizing software can be an effective way to do that.

So, if a company defaulted on its bank loan, could a bank just as easily foreclose on its software the same way it could foreclose on a factory? Unlikely. Banks apply various factors to the assets to account for this, but software is still an asset and can help produce a better financial picture.

The ratio analysis can also be useful for startups that have outside investors. Those investors will be eager to see assets being built up, rather than just a stream of expenses. For most stakeholders in a business, the equation is Assets = Good, Expenses = Bad. In a situation where a company is trying to reduce its tax burden, they might actually look favorably on being able to expense things sooner, but in most cases, the above equation holds true.

14.2.3 Reduced OPEX

If a team is using Agile practices and is running short sprints instead of waterfall phases, the amount of OPEX analysis is reduced. Some activity will take place to decide what to accomplish, which will be OPEX, but then the team will move quickly into sprints, which include design, programming, testing and deployment, which are all capitalizable. In Agile parlance, the early analysis phase is often referred to as "analysis paralysis" and teams try to avoid taking too long to figure everything out up-front. This can help to reduce OPEX activities which may take a significant portion of a waterfall lifecycle.

14.3 Creating Financial Projections with More Confidence

When software teams are using Agile, especially releasing software more frequently, it can help a CFO to create financial projections with more confidence. One factor is that the more frequent releases mean that a capitalization cycle will not last many months or years before the capitalized asset is realized, as often

14.3 Creating Financial Projections with More Confidence

happens in waterfall lifecycles. Secondly, because Agile teams are breaking the work up into manageable releases, the "trainwreck" style of large waterfall releases is also minimized. If a CFO has been capitalizing software for a waterfall team over a course of months, and then realizes at the time of the release that the whole project has failed, all that money will have to move to the expense column and the investment is lost. This is embarrassing for the CFO and the entire management team and will have to be stated to investors as a problem. But if teams are diligent about releasing frequently and adopting an Agile intention and worldview, the CFO can be more confident in projecting the success of future (small) releases.

> **Test Drive Your Knowledge Again**
> Answer the following questions with the knowledge you have after reading this chapter. Have your answers changed?
>
> 1. What does it mean to capitalize a software investment?
> 2. Which parts of the Agile lifecycle should be capitalized?
> 3. What are the benefits to capitalizing software investments?

> **Try This Next**
> **For the executive:** Talk to your certified public accountant to create a set of guidelines that can help you determine which parts of the Agile lifecycle should be capitalized or expensed.

Integrating Enterprise Methodology and Architecture with Fast-Moving Development Teams

15

Test Drive Your Knowledge
Answer the following questions with the knowledge you have now. Then answer them again at the end of this chapter.

1. How can an Agile team connect effectively with a waterfall PMO?
2. How can an Agile team supply the necessary information to an enterprise architecture group?
3. How can an enterprise architecture group transform itself and stay relevant?

15.1 The Organizational Legacy

We've been talking about how the industry "best practices" tend to focus on the end-game, the beautiful "city on the hill" that we can all aspire to. But they miss something important. They miss the fact that it is a long, arduous road to get to that shining city.

In this chapter, we are surveying two important groups who may not initially connect to new Agile teams very well—corporate methodology and enterprise architecture.

We'll look at two aspects for each corporate group. First, we examine how the Agile teams can "play nice" with the external group. It is not acceptable for Agile teams to say "Oh, we're Agile, we don't have to talk to you." We offer ideas on how the Agile teams can work with methodology and architecture.

Next, we provide some thoughts on how the methodology and architecture groups themselves can transform in a positive way. In each corporate transformation we've been a part of, methodology and architecture groups struggle to remain relevant once the teams start to move to Agile, and this can be a net negative unless these groups learn how they can contribute to the success of the development teams.

15.1.1 Playing Nice: Avoiding Process Illth

Teams experimenting with new development processes, whether Agile, Scrum, Lean or other varieties, always risk encountering resistance from enterprise groups, especially as related to methodology and architecture. In this section, we'll examine ways to "play nice" with these enterprise groups and provide the needed "adapters" to help everyone prosper even as things evolve.

Remember illth from Chap. 1? Illth is an old term used to mean the opposite of wealth. A new change to a society, town or company may bring wealth, in the broader sense meaning money, richer relationships between people and overall happiness. But that very same change may also bring ill effects, like pollution, unfairness, superficiality and even poverty (for other people). Those ill effects are "illth."

When development teams start using new software processes, the same thing can happen. The team might experience a boost in productivity, better morale and a closer relationship to the business. But they might also create problems for other groups, making their lives harder and straining relationships between people who have different objectives than the team has.

Some Agile coaches we've seen approach this issue very one-sidedly. The development teams doing the new, cool stuff are the "good guys" while the dastardly, stuck-in-the-mud enterprise groups are the "bad guys" who are trying to stop progress and make life miserable.

This is not helpful.

Instead, what we've seen with multiple successful transformations is a two-step process. First, the development teams experiment with new ideas and processes, but they still need to fit in with how the enterprise continues to operate. We'll call this the "Play Nice" phase. Then, after a few teams have been successful with the new processes and mindsets, the enterprise starts to take notice and there are decisions coming from the executives that the enterprise-level groups (methodology, architecture, HR, etc.) need to transform themselves to make way for the new normal. We'll call that the "Transforming Worldviews."

15.2 How Development Teams Can Play Nice with Corporate Methodology Groups

Enterprise methodology groups often do not appreciate development teams experimenting with new processes and mindsets. Most big companies and government departments started creating their corporate methodologies in the 1970s and

15.2 How Development Teams Can Play Nice with Corporate Methodology Groups

1980s when the waterfall cycle was the predominant view. From our observation, most companies have not changed their corporate methodology very much in the intervening decades, or perhaps have added an "Agile track" to their existing waterfall cycle, often losing all the benefits of the new processes by doing so. And certainly any change in people's worldview or intention has completely escaped the corporate methodology purview.

So when a "rogue" development team starts to experiment with new practices, either Agile, Lean or whatever, this presents a problem for the group who is responsible for the corporate methodology. The enterprise group is hoping to achieve compliance with the current methodology and so having people experimenting with new ways of doing things is going to cause questions and problems.

In our experience, this is a problem but not unsolvable. We've used a mapping process to show how the new process can satisfy the intent of the corporate process and how the two can work side-by-side. This chapter is dedicated to those mapping artifacts that have been helpful for us in the past and may be helpful for your experimental teams inside a larger enterprise.

15.2.1 Stage Gates

Stage gates were used in waterfall processes to ensure a project was staying on track throughout its lifecycle. For each of the phases, there is a "stage gate" at the end of it to ensure that the team has gone through certain activities and produced certain documents before they can proceed to the next phase. Someone outside the team, perhaps an executive or someone in corporate methodology, makes a judgment call as to whether the team is allowed to proceed.

We've shown an example here (Fig. 15.1) of how we mapped the various stage gates[1] of a waterfall process to a Scrum cycle. You can see the phases across the top (Project Initiation, Product Scoping, Product Validation) across the top and the stage gates (After Project Initiation, After Product Scoping, After Product Validation, etc.) along the bottom.

As with most waterfall lifecycles, the Scrum cycle may not begin until the second or third waterfall phase. There can be meetings among stakeholders where business cases and ROI are discussed. But even once the Scrum team is engaged, the stage gate process can still be satisfied.

---

[1] Thank you to Jill Tubaugh, Leo Gilbert and the rest of the team who cocreated this diagram over the course of many meetings.

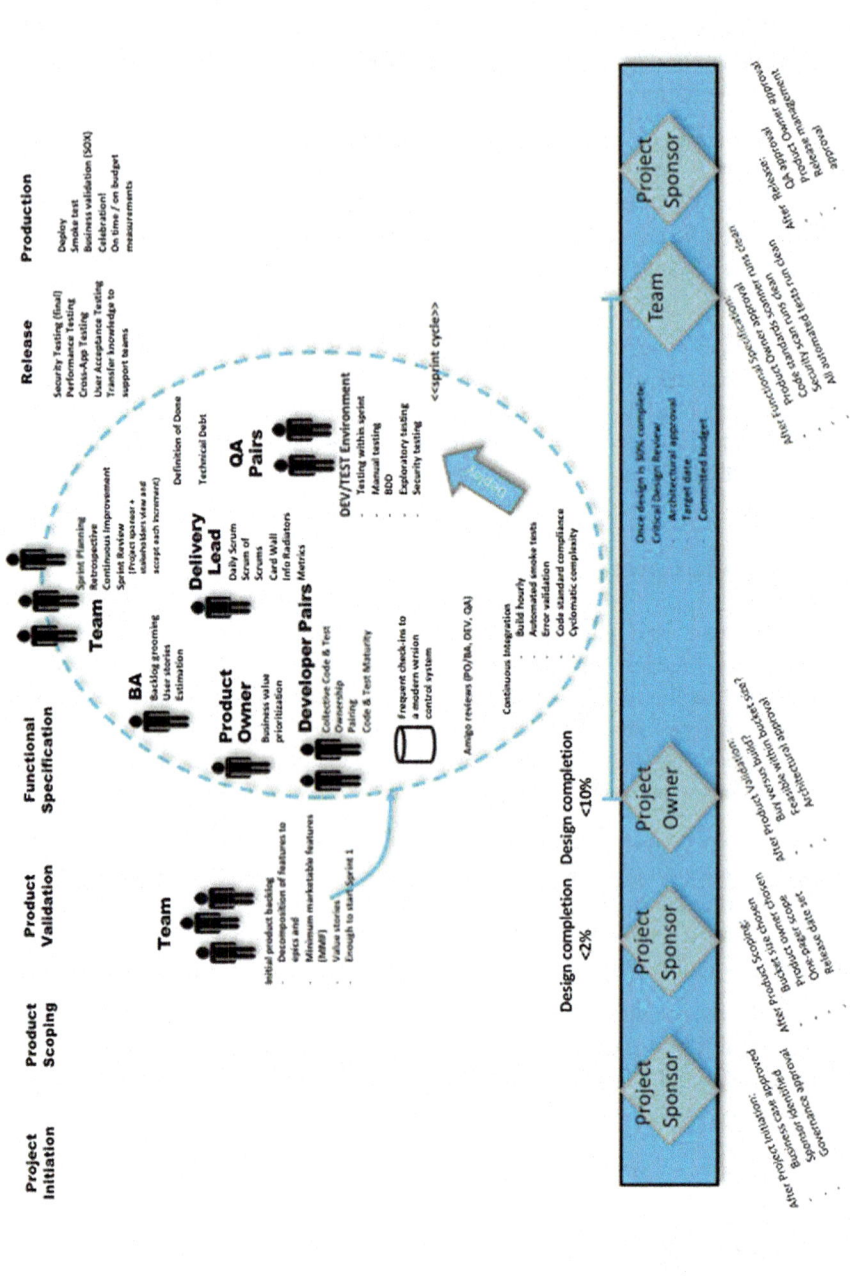

Fig. 15.1 Mapping Agile practices to a legacy SDLC and its associated stage gates. © 2017 by Daryl Kulak and Hong Li—reprinted with permission

In the waterfall phase labeled "Functional Specification" the team must produce the following documents:

- Design document
- Test plan
- Project schedule
- 30% project completion
    - Architecture approved
    - Target date
    - Committed budget

An Agile/Scrum team can produce such documents to satisfy a stage gate meeting. That's not to say these documents have tremendous benefit for the team, but they can produce them to avoid creating illth for the methodology group, certainly. The goal is to take a light touch with each document, producing something at a very high level that gives the methodology group the minimum of what they need and also does not distract the team from producing the code.

Our way of getting the documents done was to break them into cards and run them through the card wall just like the rest.

The Scrum team plans the number of sprints they will run before each of the stage gates and plans to complete those required documents before that point.

15.2.2 Project Plans

Probably the biggest mismatch between Agile/Scrum teams and the corporate methodology group (not to mention the PMO) is how to report progress. Agile teams tend to use burndown charts, but the corporate methodology usually uses a work breakdown structure and GANTT charts. Here we'll show how we've created the mapping between an Agile team's progress and the necessary reporting mechanisms for the enterprise.

GANTT charts can be at several levels. You could build a GANTT chart that shows one task per sprint that lasts 1 week (the length of the sprint), and then the next task for the next week, etc. Or a GANTT chart can show the tasks that individuals are accomplishing within the sprint, and the dependencies among those tasks, etc.

The right level of GANTT for your Agile project is the higher level, that is, one bar on the chart for each sprint. Resist any efforts by your managers to delve into a lower level of detail on your GANTT charts. Not only is it a waste of time, but you do not want to be tracking people's activity at that level, your team is meant to be self-organizing to that extent.

What is interesting, though, is that each sprint provides a neat "milestone" to report progress to your superiors. You can say that something (working code providing list of features) was delivered on this date and either we did it or we didn't.

The areas where we've seen projects get into trouble with "Sprints = Milestones" are as follows:

- Agile teams that overlap sprints with one another, where the requirements people are doing current sprint plus 1 and the testers are testing current sprint minus 1 means that you have multiple sprints going on at once. This can be confusing when explaining this to a non-Agile manager. Overlap to them might mean that things are out of control. Whether you believe overlapping sprints is a good idea or not (many people think it is bad), you may want to avoid them for reporting reasons alone, if nothing else.
- Agile teams tend to work on a set of features for a particular sprint and then, partway through, feel free to drop some of that scope (in cooperation with the business) to hit the date of the end of the sprint. That is the Agile way. However, to a corporate methodologist, that may seem like unprofessional behavior. To them, you cannot say you "made the date" if you did not include all the scope. There are several steps to get over this roadblock. First of all, does the team have the ability to change the scope committed to at the end of the release cycle (going into production)? If not, then it really is a problem to miss a set of features on a certain sprint. In this case, missing one sprint's feature set should automatically bring up the conversation of what to do about the production date that is now in jeopardy. This should not be taken lightly. The Agile team should not say "Oh, we'll make it up in future sprints." No. You probably won't. So let's have the conversation now. What should we do? Move the date? Remove functionality/scope? Add to the team (often a questionable idea)? Agile is meant to bring up the hard issues quickly, and it will as long as you let it. Bring your dirty laundry into the open and discuss it. In the other circumstance, however, where the scope could potentially be slipped from the upcoming production release date, that is a good thing. Notify the appropriate stakeholders (and upstream/downstream teams) and then look for ways to improve in the next sprint to make sure further slippages don't have to occur.

In the corporate methodology, it may be that each team is expected to keep a project plan (generally a GANTT chart) to show its progress. Yet, Agile teams don't tend to use GANTT charts; instead they focus on burndown charts and velocity measurements.

The reality is that the team will need to maintain a GANTT chart and the various big, visible charts in the team room (burndown, velocity, etc.). But the good news is that you should be able to produce the GANTT chart with little effort, and it should not change too much over time.

Here is what you can do.

Set up one bar on the GANTT chart to signify each sprint. Make the bar 1 week long (or whatever is the length of your sprint). Produce the bars in waterfall fashion, with each new sprint ending where the last one completed (do not overlap sprints). Add dependencies into the plan if you wish (and if they are mandatory). Assign the entire team to each sprint bar.

Avoid breaking down the sprint activity/task into smaller units. The corporate methodology may want you to do this, but resist. Hey, you're going through the effort to produce a GANTT chart for them, which is more than most Agile teams would probably do. The least they can do is to let you reduce the level of detail, right? Negotiate!

Instead, you can offer them a standard breakdown of the tasks inside each sprint, showing that some requirements finalization is done, some design, some coding, some testing, some data work and some management time. Tell them this standard breakdown applies to all your sprints. But hopefully you don't have to put those individual tasks into your project plan, because that will infinitely complicate your status reporting. Instead, your team members should all code their time to the sprint activity/task, and their estimates-to-complete (ETCs; see below) should always be zero at the end of each sprint.

15.2.2.1 Defined Minimum or Maximum Hours Per Task

The problem here is that we generally want our project plan (i.e., GANTT chart) to be at the sprint level, so there will be one BIG task on the plan that contains every team member's hours for the 2-week period, which could be 400 or 1000 or 2000 h, which usually exceed any arbitrary maximum of hours per task.

The solution is to document your need for an exception to this policy. If the methodology is anywhere near modern, it should have some type of customization tool or document, so use that to document what your project's maximum hours/task will be and why. And the "and why" cannot just be "because we're Agile, dude." You are creating a way for the team to satisfy changing business requirements and that is why you're requesting an exception on this policy.

15.2.2.2 Certain Deliverables Recommended on All Projects, Agile or Not

Certainly, you should evaluate whether those prescribed deliverables add value to your customers or not. If they do, you can work them into your sprints. The way we've found most useful is to tag the deliverables or associated activities (in the project management tool) as applicable to one of the following:

- first_sprint (something to be done in your Sprint Zero or before the regular set of sprints start)
- last_sprint (something to be done in your Sprint N or after your regular set of sprints is completed)

- most_sprints (something you expect will be needed in most of your sprints, whether control activities, logs, change request activities, etc.)
- set_of_sprints (something that you expect will take more than one sprint, but not the entire release cycle, like say, an operations manual)

15.2.2.3 The "Triple Constraints" or "Iron Triangle"

As we've discussed previously, the iron triangle, or triple constraints, from the PMI are scope, time and resources. The idea is that, you can fix any two of the three, but the other must remain variable. For example, you can fix time (a deadline) and scope (requirements) but then you'll need flexibility on resources (how much money you can spend to get that scope done by that date).

With Agile, there is a predetermined view of the triple constraints. Agile projects focus on a fixed time parameter and fixed resources (budget, team size), with scope being the variable. As it happens, this is usually what the businesspeople want as well. So, with triple constraints, your Agile project will likely focus on fixed time, fixed resources and variable scope.

15.2.2.4 Baselines

A baseline in project management terms is a point-in-time snapshot of the project plan and schedule. Having a baseline allows a project manager to see if and how much things have slipped over time. It is a very useful tool in waterfall projects, because it is easy to slip a little here and there but before you know it, you're 3 months late.

To tell the truth, baselines are pretty much useless in the Agile world. Your project plan is a set of 1 week sprints. Each sprint lasts 1 week. That's how you plan it, that's how it happens. You don't extend the end date of your sprint in Agile.

So how do you bridge this gap? Well, the big thing is to keep the definitions of your sprints at a very high level. Sprints should generally have a theme, so keep that theme pretty general. Have a sprint to accomplish "multiple UI changes" or "accessibility features" and leave it at that. That way, your project baseline will hold up amazingly well. All your waterfall friends will be jealous. However, if you try to be too specific on your sprint themes, then if you need to leave something out, the traditional project manager will consider that sprint to be "late," even if you finished your sprint on the date scheduled and cut scope accordingly. This is a major mismatch between Agile and most corporate methodologies. So it is best if you have some way to keep your sprint themes vague, or, if you have to, abandon sprint themes completely and just refer to them by number (Sprint 01, Sprint 02, etc.).

15.2.2.5 Estimates-to-Complete (ETCs)

A big part of input into a corporate methodology is estimates-to-complete (ETCs). This is a measure of how much time an individual contributor believes is left on his current task to get it to complete. Ideally, a corporate methodology hopes to collect ETCs from every individual contributor on every task being currently worked on. The idea is that the project plan is becoming more and more accurate as time goes on because we're getting a better view of the time that each task-in-flight will actually take.

There are several problems with ETCs on waterfall projects. First of all, people don't fill in their ETCs. This is a chronic problem. Secondly, when they do fill them in, the numbers vary widely from what ends up being the final "true" number of hours. The old adage of a task being 99% done for weeks and weeks creeps in to wreak havoc with ETCs. A developer might think that they've almost got this technical problem fixed this week, and then next week comes and it still hasn't progressed towards completion.

The process of creating the single task per sprint is the solution to the ETC problem for Agile teams. Each team member has an ETC that takes them to the end of the "sprint task" and they use up the time exactly at the point where the sprint ends. Your ETC compliance will be perfect!

15.2.2.6 Overlapping Sprints

Overlapping sprints, where part of the team in the room is working on Sprint n+1 (one sprint ahead), most of the team is working on Sprint n (the current sprint) and part of the team is working on Sprint n−1 (one sprint behind) can cause a lot of problems in the translation to the corporate methodology.

The problems it creates is that you, as an Agile team, may want to call the sprint complete when development is complete, but your corporate methodology may not want to allow that because testing hasn't finished yet. In a way, they are right.

The solution to the problem is to define what "done" is for your team. Is the work "done" when development is complete or when system testing is complete? Most teams, once they look at this, decide that the code must be system tested to be considered complete. But the reality is then that you actually have 3 or 4 week sprints which overlap, if you include system testing time and requirements (which often happens before the "real" sprint). You should strive to have 1 week sprints that do not overlap, so this is something your team may want to fix. Overlapping sprints are usually caused by specialized roles on the team, for instance, business analysts who don't code, or testers who are not developers.

15.2.3 Corporate Methodology Is Not the Enemy

What each software development team needs to understand is that you are building a change-ready, anticipatory team. That applies to each and every challenge and roadblock during the course of your project's life. In the same way, it applies to how you deal with your corporate methodology and project management standards, policies and restrictions. Those are just things for you to work on, like environment problems, faulty equipment and recalcitrant co-workers. And thinking of working with the corporate people as "feeding the beast" won't help. You need to understand what it's like to be in their shoes. They have good reasons for wanting standardization and compartmentalization. They're not wrong. It is just that their needs from your project and your method of delivery don't particularly match up well at this point in time. So change it. Fix it so it does match up and everybody can get what they need.

15.3 How the Corporate Methodology Group Can Transform Its Worldview

Corporate methodology groups that we've seen prosper during a transformation are those that focus on coaching and concise communication.

A corporate methodology group does not need to be large. After all, the goal is to push decision-making as close to the work as possible, so there should not be an outside group dictating the standards to the development teams. However, in a large enterprise, it does help to have a handful of people who act as coordinators and facilitators for the methodology as it emerges.

We've seen a coaching philosophy is helpful in a corporate methodology group. As long as those coaches are willing to roll up their sleeves and work with the development teams, putting themselves on the line towards the team's success. The same coaching rules apply as we outlined in Chap. 12—Getting Coaching that Really Helps.

The corporate methodology group should have a strong focus on how to communicate the standards concisely. The idea of a "methodology binder" or a "methodology website" should cease to exist. Your corporate methodology should not be a series of documents. It should be a set of principles and practices that people can remember. The easiest way to state this is that the corporate methodology should be able to fit onto one poster. Think of a wall poster that has the central ideas of the methodology printed on it. In big letters, not a tiny font size.

The methodology should be communicated in pictures more than words. If you must build a website dedicated to the methodology, fill it with stories. Stories communicate the connection between worldview, intention, speech and action far more efficiently than lists of documents.

Think about how you can help people understand more than just the actions (practices, documents, etc.). How can you communicate the worldview that best suits the enterprise?

And then there is intention. If people are creating the documents "just to get them out of the way" then your methodology has failed. How do you communicate intention? How do you answer the "Why" questions behind the parts of your methodology?

We've been a part of corporate methodology groups in large enterprises. It isn't easy. But it can be a very helpful role if the methodologist uses a coaching mindset and focuses on concise communication of worldview, intention, speech and action simultaneously with each engagement with the teams.

Documentation should be approached with a "Via Negativa" worldview. (For more on Via Negativa, go back to Chap. 5—Redefining Professionalism.)

That is to say, we should ask "Is there any other way we can accomplish our goal besides creating a new document?" We are not saying teams should never create documents, but if a conversation or short meeting could suffice, why not use that? Our bias should always be towards more lightweight communication methods (i.e., face-to-face) rather than an ever-increasing pile of documents.

15.4 How Development Teams Can Play Nice with Enterprise Architecture

Enterprise architects and experimental development teams often run afoul of one another. One way is that development teams would rather not have to conform to an enterprise architecture; they often feel that they should get special exceptions to make it easier for themselves. And enterprise architects can often be bullies, holding the development teams to standards that were created in a vacuum and are not helpful to the teams or even the enterprise in the long term.

In this section, we'll focus on how development teams can play nicely with enterprise architecture groups. There is a time and a place when enterprise groups must change with the times, but for this section, we'll assume that the development teams do not have the momentum or political capital to do that. Transforming the enterprise architecture group will have to wait until the next section "How Enterprise Architecture Can Transform Its Worldview."

15.4.1 Architects: Come to Our Demos!

Our advice to any development team experimenting with new processes is to invite the enterprise architects to their weekly demos. This has the effect of starting a trusted relationship. People who regularly attend demos are able to get a sneak peek into what the team is really building, rather than looking at documentation that reflects the real thing.

From the architect's perspective, a demo (with the ability to ask questions afterward, of course) can be better than an architecture document. This is because a demo is "closer to the metal." The team is demonstrating what they are really building, not showing a document of what they intend to build. Very often, there is a difference between the two. The architect should be looking at the real product, and offering advice and guidance based on that, rather than a document that the team may or may not follow.

"But I need to catch the team before they build anything the wrong way," the architect might say. If the sprints are short enough, the architect can "catch" the team's mistakes or lack of compliance very quickly and can bring them back to the standards with hardly any lost effort at all.

This is a different worldview, to be sure. And if the team must create an architectural deliverable before they start coding, so be it. Create the document in the Sprint Zero activity and get it approved through the right channels. But most teams we've worked with have an easier time with architecture groups because they provide complete transparency to them and are open to a dialog on the best approach. Architects can be much more empathetic with development teams when it is a question of code being written today, rather than philosophical discussions of what might happen someday. That is the goal, to make that switch in intention.

For those documents which must be created and approved, the team needs to schedule those into their own sprint cycles and create cards for each deliverable, just like they would for any other stakeholder. The team must leave enough lead time for the approvals to take place and be able to work around any delays or rework required.

15.4.2 Volunteer to Be an Early Adopter for New Architectural Capabilities

Agile teams have an advantage in that they can try new things without damaging their production schedule too much. The iterative approach allows teams to give something a try without committing to it for the long term. This means that Agile teams can volunteer to be an early adopter for architectural components (e.g., new security API, new caching mechanism, etc.) that enterprise architects are wanting to introduce. This accomplishes two things. First, the Agile team might benefit if the new architectural component is helpful. And second, the beta testers will get the attention of the enterprise architects and be able to begin building a positive relationship once the architects can see a benefit of the Agile lifecycle for their own role.

15.5 How the Enterprise Architecture Group Can Transform Its Worldview

Now let's examine the thorny question of how enterprise architecture groups need to transform as the IT organization moves to a new process holistically.

15.5.1 Architects Who Write Code

The days of the "PowerPoint architect" have come to an end. Anyone who works as an enterprise architect (or solution architect or application architect) must not only be able to code, but must involve themselves in coding at least a few times a week.

15.5 How the Enterprise Architecture Group Can Transform Its Worldview

It is true that architects may spend a lot of time attending meetings and drawing charts, but they must get down to writing code to make sure that their knowledge is staying up-to-date. Teams who are using the pair programming practice (mentioned in Chap. 8—Flipping the Run/Build Ratio) have an easier time with this. Architects can easily come into a team room and start to pair with one of the existing developers on the team, undoubtedly learning some things about the specifics of that application, and also providing insights and leadership with their greater contextual knowledge of the other teams and groups. Every architect should have a goal of writing code for some amount of time each week, either scheduling it on the calendar ahead of time or visiting team rooms spontaneously.

This can also be difficult for the architect. If the architect does not know a particular technology well, they may feel embarrassed to put a spotlight on their ignorance. But the architects will need to get past these feelings and take the plunge in order to stay relevant and continue to offer helpful advice to teams.

15.5.2 Setting Standards

> The level of conformity in an organization is in inverse proportion to its creative ability.
> Russell L. Ackoff (Ackoff 2007)

Some enterprise architects are very focused on setting standards for the development teams and then enforcing those standards. "Why can't people just follow the standards?" is a famous lament of architects.

If architects are not writing code regularly, they may be getting out-of-date with their technical skills (reading magazines and creating PowerPoint slides just won't cut it), and they may also be creating standards that "sound good" but really don't help the teams at all.

Here is a good worldview on enterprise standards:

What you standardize, you fossilize.

That means that whenever you set a standard for the company (or even just a department), you are effectively putting up a sign (Fig. 15.2) that says "No innovation here."

That sounds very negative, but we don't mean it to. Maybe an example will help.

Let's say that the enterprise architect sets a standard that states that all automated unit tests for Java programs should be written in JUnit. Seems reasonable, because JUnit is far and away the most popular unit testing tool. Then a team member on one of the development teams has some frustrations with JUnit and decides to use his personal time to fork the JUnit code (it's open source, so why not?) and builds his own alternative to JUnit. This standard will keep this innovative team member from using his new module. The standard has forced out the creativity in this corner of the world.

Fig. 15.2 When you standardize something, you are asking people to avoid innovating in that particular area. © 2017 by Daryl Kulak and Hong Li—reprinted with permission

Now, as we've debated with teammates many times, fossilizing can be a good thing in a variety of circumstances. If there is a high cost to deviation of a standard (compromises security, etc.) or if there really isn't much need for creativity in an area (what color story cards should we use?), then fossilizing is perfectly acceptable. We're not saying fossilization is bad. We're just saying that fossilization happens when you have standards. If the development teams can accept that, then it is a good standard. But if the enterprise architects are finding they are constantly fighting the developers on a particular standard, it is probably a fossilizing standard put into the wrong area.

15.5.2.1 Electric Cars Need a Standardized Battery, Right? or No?

This probably wasn't always true, but electric cars being produced these days are so cool. Nissan has the all-electric Leaf. GM, Toyota and other companies have very compelling hybrid electric vehicles that are practical and energy efficient. And, of course, Elon Musk has created a whole new car company called Tesla that is churning out 100% electric cars that look beautiful and perform like the best sports cars. Tesla is even starting to place their "supercharger" units around North America, Europe and other regions to make it easier to take your electric vehicle out onto the open road, rather than sticking inside the city limits, close to your home charger.

Unless you've been following the industry closely, you might not know that the charging units for different manufacturers are incompatible. The same is true for the batteries. You cannot take the battery unit out of a Tesla and place it into a Chevy Bolt. They are completely different. Incompatible across the board.

So we should standardize, right? Think of the benefits. Instead of needing to charge the battery that is sitting inside your car, you would just slide the battery out, take it into the gas station (or whatever we will call it) and they will exchange it with a fully charged battery. Instead of taking 30 min or an hour or whatever to charge your battery, you are in-and-out in the time it takes to hit the bathroom.

Problem solved? Wait a minute. The electric car industry is in its very early stages. Everything is up for grabs. So much is unknown. How will these cars perform after 10 years? What safety issues might they have? What technologies will come along that increase the capacity of batteries by a factor of ten? Or one hundred? Or one thousand?

We don't know. We can't predict.

By standardizing things now, we risk bottling up the creativity that could give us the breakthroughs we need in shortening charging time, improving safety or reducing cost. If we standardized the battery size or electric connection or design, we would be placing a big sign on the battery industry "No creativity allowed here." And that move would potentially kill the electric vehicle industry in its tracks.

Again, this is not to say that standards are universally bad. We are instead saying that standards are not universally good. And we're saying that standards and creativity are not compatible.

In fact, it is accurate to say that if an executive is hoping to get more creativity out of his development staff, the first thing he should consider is which standards to get rid of? Are the standards holding back valuable creative initiatives that my staff might otherwise be pursuing? It's a worthwhile question.

For each area of technology and methodology, we have to look at how important innovation is. If we don't care about people innovating in a particular area, we can standardize things there without worrying about stifling creativity.

But in **most** areas, innovation is important. We want developers constantly thinking about how to write code that accomplishes more in fewer lines of code, has fewer defects and is easier to maintain. We want testers to be automating their tests in ways that run faster, visually show results (pass/fail) and that show the "why" of the application. In operations, we want creative DevOps engineers who are thinking about ways to reduce human intervention and get things to run faster.

Our message about standardization is not "don't standardize." Instead, we are saying that standardization has a downside, a big downside. Acknowledge that, tread carefully with standards, and talk to the people who will be affected by the standards.

15.5.3 Emergent Architecture

One of our systems thinking principle is #5—Bring decision making as close to the work as possible.

An extreme example of a manifestation of this principle is called "emergent architecture." Emergent architecture is when a development team cannot say exactly what their technical architecture might look like until after they start to write code. Only then will they make architectural decisions (use this framework, conform to this industry standard, use a package for this function, etc.) because then they know that it is truly called for.

The emergent architecture movement has been getting a bit of a bad name. This is perhaps because it is a knee-jerk reaction against the "big architecture up front" of the past. We feel it is right to rebel against having to define an architecture in detail before ever writing a line of code, but the purist emergent architecture approach probably goes too far in this rebellion.

The answer is somewhere in the middle. Development teams should probably create some form of architectural vision in Sprint Zero. That vision should be driven by their current understanding of the value stories. It should also be extremely high-level and not involve any hardcore details. But producing such a document before coding is not a crime. It can be a helpful way to get all the team members thinking about the way they might design this application and the compromises they might need to make sprint-by-sprint. And no one should hold the team to the quick-and-dirty architecture from Sprint Zero.

The way we think of these models is that they should be created "quickly and humbly." We shouldn't assume too much about our own knowledge at this early point, and we shouldn't really commit ourselves to one stated direction. But it is helpful to talk things through and take a shot at moving forward with a diagram or two.

Architecture models that are put together quickly, that are messy and don't contain too many details are the best kind of models. But that is not to say we should have zero up-front architecture and only build it "emergently." That is taking things too far.[2]

15.5.4 What's That Sound? Is Your Architecture Screaming?

Screaming architecture[3] is a term that comes to us from "Uncle Bob" Martin, whom we introduced in Chap. 8—Flipping the Run/Build Ratio. Uncle Bob states

---

[2]The same is true for standards. You can keep them light and messy, but relying only on "emergent standards" is not good either.

[3]bit.ly/BobScream.

that, whenever you look at an architecture in an enterprise, it should "scream" the application that it supports. For instance, if this is an architecture meant to support financial applications, the architecture should "scream" financial applications as you look at the way the modules are structured and the way things are named.

Uncle Bob is trying to get us to move away from thinking of generic architectural frameworks that are absolutely application agnostic. In fact, he is pushing us to the opposite extreme. He is saying that architecture should explicitly support the applications and be tied to the applications, and not try to be separate and isolated.

We think this is good advice, although definitely extreme (as is Uncle Bob's tendency). Most enterprises are hobbled by their overly generic enterprise architectural frameworks. In most cases, these frameworks make development more difficult, not less. They reduce productivity. They cause (and often contain) more defects.

The momentum in the developer community is away from complicated enterprise frameworks and towards "the simplest thing that could possibly work." This is a positive step, but it also can be taken too far, because a development team cannot operate in isolation, producing "the simplest thing that could possibly work, given the needs of my team alone." There needs to be a view of what is best for the enterprise, not just the team. Still, this is a positive step.

15.5.5 Test-Driven Architecture

Using the lesson from screaming architecture, architectural components needs to have a reason to exist. The best way to express those reasons are with automated tests. It makes sense that architectural components are subject to the same type of test-driven mentality as applications. Using this approach, architecture can become more relevant, less wasteful and lighter-weight.

15.5.6 Being an Architect Is Not the Desired Career Path for Every Developer

The best software teams don't have many architects. They do have very, very, very senior developers. But don't call them architects,[4] because they code a lot and they have no PowerPoint ability whatsoever. (We've seen their PowerPoints, they are terrible.)

This is not to say that there is no place for enterprise architects in large organizations. They do have a place. But their goal must be to push decision-making as close to the work as possible, and also to keep themselves connected to the code being created.

---

[4]Linus Torvalds, the creator of Linux, probably sees himself as a developer, not an architect. He does make final decisions on what features go into the kernel, but he doesn't put himself above the people creating those features.

However, an enterprise should not have a single career path where developers can only be promoted to someday become architects. There needs to be a way for developers to stay developers. Yes, architects have their place, but there should be equally senior people inside the teams who are actively contributing to velocity every day, mentoring their team members and teaching by example. This career path is vital for any organization that hopes to achieve competitive advantage with the software they produce. Your best coders should continue to code and a few, only a few, might go on to become architects who attend meetings and help collaboration across teams. But most of the best-of-the-best should keep creating code all day long. (Which is what they really want to do anyway.) We'll speak more about this in Chap. 15—HR Agility.

15.6 A Word About Bimodal IT

The Gartner Group, the best-known trend-watcher in our industry, has missed a number of major trends over the years. However, they seem to have latched on to, and even clearly defined, a very helpful concept called "Bimodal IT."

For many years, new innovations have been stopped in their tracks by parts of the IT group who actively worked against those innovations. As we have explained here in this book, those working against the innovation are not anti-innovation, they are just trying to accomplish their own responsibilities and see the particular innovation as a hindrance to that.

Gartner's idea of Bimodal IT is that every large enterprise essentially needs two IT groups, what they call Mode 1 and Mode 2. Mode 1 is responsible for "keeping the lights on," maintaining up-time of existing applications and infrastructure. Mode 2 is where the innovation happens, and it is kept separate from Mode 1. Generally, Mode 1 reports to a CIO, Mode 2 reports to a CDO—Chief Digital Officer. Each IT employee reports to either the CIO or CDO—but not both.

Some people see Bimodal IT as a temporary stop on the way to becoming completely Mode 2. But that is not the case. The goal is to find a way that Mode 1 and Mode 2 can work together effectively, in the short term and the long term.

15.7 The Corporate Immune System

Often, when an Agile team that is internally successful encounters external groups who seem to be trying to defeat the team, the team responds "Oh, it's just the corporate immune system trying to kill anything it doesn't understand." But, from what we've observed, it usually isn't that simple. Really, the Agile team is causing illth for other groups that is making their lives difficult. If the Agile team instead responds by mapping their Agile processes to what the external groups need, it can be productive and enjoyable for everyone. The work being done by Agile teams is often less risky, better connected to business needs and making faster progress. But the teams need to prove those benefits to the external groups, like methodology and architecture, to ensure the success and transformation towards a better work life. The most successful projects usually make the best contributions to enterprise architecture, methodology, and practice.

> **Test Drive Your Knowledge Again**
> Answer the following questions with the knowledge you have after reading this chapter. Have your answers changed?
>
> 1. How can an Agile team connect effectively with a waterfall PMO?
> 2. How can an Agile team supply the necessary information to an enterprise architecture group?
> 3. How can an enterprise architecture group transform itself and stay relevant?

> **Try This Next**
>
> **For the executive:** Ensure that corporate methodology and enterprise architecture employees are evaluated based on their effective support of Agile teams. Consider reducing the size and power of these groups to push more decision-making into the development and operations teams. Evaluate Agile teams on how well they work with the corporate groups.
>
> **For the manager:** Ensure Agile teams are supplying the needed information and compliance to the corporate groups. Do not allow Agile teams to duck their responsibilities, but instead find ways to map the Agile artifacts and processes to the spirit of what is being requested corporately.
>
> **For the individual contributor:** Keep the intention of being a good team player with corporate groups. They are just people trying to do their jobs, although they may have different worldviews than you do as an Agile team member. You are not "feeding the beast," you are being a servant leader.

Reference

Ackoff RL, Addison HJ, Bibb S (2007) Management f-LAWS: how organizations really work. Triarchy Press, Axminster, Devon

HR Agility   16

> *We trained hard—but it seemed that every time we were beginning to form up into teams, we would be reorganized. I was to learn later in life we tend to meet any new situation by reorganizing, and a wonderful method it can be for creating the illusion of progress while producing confusion, inefficiency and demoralization.*
>
> Petronius Arbiter, 65 AD (There is some disagreement as to whether Petronius Arbiter actually said this or not. Either way, we like the quote as a shot across the bow of corporate reorganization philosophy.)

Test Drive Your Knowledge
Answer the following questions with the knowledge you have now. Then answer them again at the end of this chapter.

1. What are the aspects of HR that may need to change to accommodate Agile teams?
2. What are the pluses and minuses of goal setting?
3. What is the one true motivator for people?

The title of this chapter is not to be confused with the "Agile HR" movement inside the human resources industry, although we don't have any particular problem with what they espouse.

16.1 Why Did Churchman Quit the Field He Pioneered?

One of the founding fathers of systems thinking, and one of the scholars of our book, C. West Churchman, was a pioneer in another field first—operations research. Churchman, after having served in World War II, worked at Case Institute of Technology in Cleveland, Ohio, and played a major role in improving operations research as it was used in the US military. After tremendous success in the OR field, including establishing the first master's and PhD programs, writing the first OR textbook and hosting the first series of conferences, Churchman left the field of OR and moved on.

Why would he do that? He was lionized and highly regarded throughout the field of operations research.

Churchman grew up in a deeply Catholic household in Pennsylvania in the 1910s. He also attended a Quaker school, where he learned the importance of humility and service to others. Churchman took this to heart. When he was only seventeen and an undergraduate at the University of Pennsylvania, he wrote in his journal that he had decided to dedicate his life to bettering humanity.

This is the background for Churchman's decision to leave the field of OR behind. Churchman could see that OR was fast becoming a community of scientists who were focused on perfecting their sets of mathematical models, rather than people who were looking for ways to improve society. He saw that scientists were distancing themselves from murky ethical dilemmas, and instead retreating to their crisp, clean equations. For Churchman, this was cowardice. He needed to continue to find ways to put academic science to use in the service of humanity.

Churchman's way of doing this was to switch from OR to the field of general systems theory. GST had been begun by Ludwig von Bertalanffy, an Austrian who came to North America and had been proclaiming how science and ethics had to be united as one. This fit Churchman's worldview very well, and Churchman, along with Russell Ackoff and Leonard Arnoff, became one of the most important bright lights in the systems thinking revolution of the twentieth century.

We believe, like Churchman, that ethics cannot be detached from science or technology. The biggest ethical breach we have today is when we try to wedge living, breathing, feeling people into a mechanical organization. Doing this, we suck out the "life" from the organization, we make the people unsatisfied with their jobs, and it is bad for business. A mechanical organization cannot innovate. It cannot hold the attention of employees and will therefore just churn through the most creative people, leaving only the people behind who are willing to suffer the monotony of life inside a big corporation.

Sucking the life out of organizations, by making them mechanical, is the cause of most of the unethical behavior that occurs in the business world today.

It doesn't have to be that way.

Many technology startups have a lively culture and are fun places to work. But they're new and small. It's easier to be lively and fun when you're small. Our goal is to help establish that big companies can be lively and fun too. And central to that shift is the HR function. There are many new ways of looking at things that can help the HR professional flip a culture to become more like a startup—interesting, collaborative and purpose driven.

Human resources departments play a crucial role in helping the IT organization to change and improve. In this chapter, we'll examine ways that HR can help, ways it can harm and ways for HR to transform itself to become more responsive in the new worldview.

16.2 Changing Your HR Worldview: People Aren't Your Resources

Recall back to systems thinking principle #6—Treat people like people, not like machines.

It is inconsistent with systems thinking to refer to people as "resources." When we think of resources, we think of paper and photocopiers and workstations and servers and ladders and hammers. Those are resources you might need to get a job done.

But people are different than resources. They have intelligence that resources don't have. People have creativity. They perform better or worse depending on how they feel about the job, the corporate vision and the people they work with. When you make the big announcement that you've just merged with Federated Evil, Inc. your resources aren't affected. But your people are.

By using the right speech, we can encourage a bit better working environment. Calling people "resources" is a bit like what happened to the students who were the prisoners in the Stanford Prison Experiment story we told in Chap. 5—Redefining Professionalism. The pseudo-prisoners were given identification numbers and embarrassing clothing by the pseudo-guards to help dehumanize them. And it worked. Just by making those changes, the guards started to see the prisoners as "less than human" and their treatment of the prisoners devolved accordingly. "Don't worry about it. They're just resources!" Words matter.

What might happen if you lose the "resources" term?[1] It's worth a try. Maybe use "people" instead? Chief People Officer is a pretty common title in newer corporations.

---

[1] Whatever you do, please don't replace "resources" with "human capital." It's just as bad. The good news is that you're not a pair of pliers. The bad news is that you're worth only as much as we can monetize you.

Here is a story about how a set of companies in the Netherlands (Laloux 2014) started treating people as resources, and then how one small startup fixed the problem and got back to treating people as people.

16.2.1 The Neighborhood Nurses

Since the nineteenth century, the Netherlands has had an interesting system of "neighborhood nurses." The idea was that there was a small group of nurses that took care of the people in a specifically defined neighborhood. If someone got sick, they could call the neighborhood nurse and be cared for. The nurses could help with many, many small problems, and they were also deeply involved once a person became chronically ill or also as people became older and did not have family members close by for assistance. As a patient's condition escalated, the nurses were able to arrange for a prompt hospital visit.

In the 1990s, these small groups of nurses started being aggregated into larger companies, and efficiency experts established call centers, specialization among nurses, centralized route planners and time limits per service (10 min to dress a wound, 2.5 min to change a compression stocking, etc.). The new corporations also increased the number of nurses a particular person might see, so there was little or no continuity or familiarity for the people being served.

As you might imagine, neither the nurses nor the patients were happy with this situation. Nurses felt like they were not taking good care of their patients, and the patients vociferously agreed. These mechanized procedures took the "life" out of the neighborhood nursing program, reducing the patients to machines. The nurses were technically doing all the right things, but were forced to leave out activities that they knew really mattered for the holistic health of their patients, as if any of the health issues of the patients should be simply treated as isolated mechanical defects.

In the old program, a nurse would get to know her patients in her neighborhood and remember the nuances of their lives and their fears and joys. She would gladly stay for a cup of coffee after the treatment. She would be a familiar face to elderly patients, who might be confused or fearful of unknown people coming into the house.

But with the efficiency changes, these human benefits were removed, leaving only the cold comfort of the rushed medical procedures and unhappy nurses and patients everywhere. As resources, the neighborhood nurses were being efficiently allocated. As people, life sucked.

One of the unhappy nurses, Jos de Blok, decided that he had had enough of the mechanical system and started his own neighborhood nurse company which he called Buurtzorg. He reverted back to the older system of personal care and familiar faces and took out the offensive time restrictions and specialization that caused the problems. He also trained his nurses in some effective self-organizing techniques, so that each small group of nurses could manage themselves, rather than being micromanaged by a distant bureaucrat.

The results were stunning. Ernst and Young studied Buurtzorg against its competitors and found that Buurtzorg required 40% fewer hours of care per client, even though they were being much more generous with their time (having coffee, chatting, etc.). The study also found that Buurtzorg patients stayed in care only half as long, healed faster and became able to care for themselves more quickly. Hospital visits were 30% fewer with Buurtzorg and hospital stays were shorter.

With these benefits, plus the happier nurses and patients, Buurtzorg made quick work of the neighborhood nurses industry in the Netherlands. After starting the business in 2006 with only ten nurses, de Blok now employs over 60% of all nurses in the country. His organization became the obvious destination for any nurse who cared about doing a good job, and the neighborhoods benefitted from better care and provably better healthcare results.

HR departments should be constantly looking for ways to treat people like people. How is your organization treating employees like machines? How could you fix it?

16.3 Evaluating People

Changing your HR mindset means that you'll have to evaluate your technical people differently than before. Here are a few items that may help with evaluations.

16.3.1 Reduce the Document Focus

We cannot evaluate people based on which documents they've successfully written anymore.

> *I've done seven requirements analysis documents, four business rules catalogs, and three logical data models. I should be promoted!*

The documents are not the most important thing. The working, tested software is the most important thing.

This means that performance appraisals should not focus on which documents a person has written, or how many, because the Agile teams should be focusing less on writing documentation and more on being part of a team that produces working, tested software.

16.3.2 Performance Appraisals

W. Edwards Deming (1992), one of our systems thinking scholars, had nothing good to say about the annual performance evaluation:

> *It nourishes short-term performance, annihilates long-term planning, builds fear, demolishes teamwork, nourishes rivalry and politics. It leaves people bitter, crushed, bruised, battered, desolate, despondent, dejected, feeling inferior, some even depressed, unfit for work for weeks after receipt of rating, unable to comprehend why they are inferior. It is unfair, as it ascribes to the people in a group differences that may be caused totally by the system they work in.*

Deming wrote these words three decades ago. Many managers pledge allegiance to Deming's systems thinking (and the Lean derivatives of his work), and yet almost all companies still do some form of performance evaluation!

Habits are hard to change. It seems to come back to a need for measurement. If we don't measure performance through a manager's evaluation (or 360 degree review or whatever), how can we know where our employees' skill levels are?

Let's go back to Deming for more on the problems with performance appraisals:

The idea of merit rating is alluring. The sound of the words captivates the imagination: pay for what you get; get what you pay for; motivate people to do their best, for their own good. The effect is exactly the opposite of what the words promise. Everyone propels himself forward, or tries to, for his own good, on his own life preserver. The organization is the loser. Merit rating rewards people that do well in the system. It does not reward attempts to improve the system. Don't rock the boat.

Peter Scholtes (1998), Deming's preferred specialist on people performance, provides some interesting **assumptions** that we make that can lock us into the thinking of needing performance appraisals:

- An employee is motivated to improve after being evaluated.
- An employee has control of the results of their work.
- The employee's own contribution can be separated from the contributions of the system in which he works.
- Processes that look the same are the same.
- Evaluators can be objective.
- Evaluators are consistent with one another.

These assumptions are, unfortunately, wrong as hell. Every one of them. Evaluators, being human, are not objective. They are influenced heavily by their own impressions of the people they are reviewing.

16.3 Evaluating People

It may sound incorrect to say that an employee has no control over the results of his own work, but this is an assertion of systems thinking under Deming. The system within which the employee works has a much larger impact on the results than the employee's individual performance. So why do two employees in the same situation performance differently? Because they are not truly in the same situation. There are variations in the system everywhere, sometimes difficult to tell by an onlooking manager.

Deming states that the best reaction to a poorly performing employee is for the manager to examine the systems of the company and find out what is causing the problem, rather than immediately questioning the employee's skills, motivation or ethics. This goes back to a manager being a "systems scientist." Each manager is spending time examining the system around his people and finding ways to improve the system.

So, what should we do instead of performance appraisals? Scholtes says that it requires a change in our thinking. It also requires an unbundling of the features that we think performance appraisals bring us. **We do performance appraisals today because we think they give us:**

- A way to identify and respond to outstanding performers (outstanding in statistical terms, much better than normal or much worse than normal)
- A basis for pay
- Feedback to employees
- Direction and focus to our team
- Identification of career goals
- Identification of education and training needs
- Identification of candidates for promotion
- Identification of candidates for layoffs (now or later)
- Communications between employees and managers
- A paper trail that may be necessary in dismissals, demotions or disciplinary actions
- Conforming to regulatory requirements
- Motivation for employees

By unbundling these into other activities, we can actually get rid of the performance appraisal with no loss in information.

When we bundle the items in the list above, the items affect each other negatively. For instance, giving a person feedback on their performance in the past year will not be well received if the person knows it is linked to their salary increase or promotion. The person is incented to deny the problems and to persuade their reviewer that those problems never actually existed and it must be someone else's fault. All the stuff that makes giving feedback so difficult in the first place, and now we are reinforcing the wrong behavior.

Scholtes says that each item can be unbundled into a separate activity. Identifying and responding to outstanding performers (positive and negative) can occur when the data shows the outstanding figures as team performance. Career goals can become the providence of the employee themselves, which is more appropriate. The vast majority of managers are not trained or disposed to effective career counseling. And all of us who have received performance evaluations know that they are NOT motivating to the person being evaluated.

We are delving headlong into Deming's quality theories here, and that is not our intent. The topic of performance appraisals and how to improve them (or eliminate them) is fascinating. Please read Scholtes' work (Scholtes 1998—Chap. 9 specifically) for the details of how to rid your organization of performance appraisals. There are also some very good books dedicated to the topic of abolishing performance appraisals (Coens and Jenkins 2002; Culbert and Rout 2010).

16.4 Rewarding People

This section looks at new ways of approaching rewards for people who do excellent work. We'll have to examine the patriarchal corporate mindset and shift it into something new to create a workplace where people will thrive.

16.4.1 Goal-Setting and Specific Targets

Goal-setting has been a hallowed practice of management. "Set specific, measurable goals for your team and then reward them once they've achieved them."

What could possibly be wrong with setting goals?

Every management book espouses goal-setting. However, a landmark paper written by Lisa Ordóñez of the University of Arizona in 2009 with coauthors from the University of Pennsylvania, Northwestern and Harvard, contend that goal-setting is like a drug that has been "overprescribed."

Their paper, humorously called "Goals Gone Wild: The Systematic Side-Effects of Overprescribing Goal Setting[2]," shows how goal setting has limitations, and how the practice of setting goals for others should carry a "warning label" like a powerful drug.

They give an example of Lee Iacocca's leadership at Ford. The charismatic executive gave a clear, specific goal to a product team at Ford. "I want a car that weighs less than 2,000 pounds and costs less than $2,000." (Yes, new cars were a lot cheaper back then.) He also gave them a deadline: have it ready for the 1970 model year.

---

[2]bit.ly/GoalsGoneWildQ.

The team did exactly that. They produced a car that was inexpensive, lightweight and ready on time. Check. Check. Check. The marketing group decided to give it a flashy horse name, like other Ford performance vehicles before it. The Ford Pinto.

Iacocca must have been pleased with his team and also pleased with himself for being so clear in his direction. He was very likely not pleased when the Ford Pinto became known as the "exploding[3] Ford Pinto." The team had decided that the extra shielding between the rear bumper and the gas tank would have added extra cost (true) and extra weight (also true). Plus, with the tight deadline, the safety inspections on the design were trimmed back, and no one caught the dangerous design flaw before the vehicle went into mass production (sorry, no time). It wasn't until people started dying in the car, due to gas tank explosions, that Iacocca and the team understood the implication of meeting their goal. Fifty-three people died and hundreds of people were injured.

Goal-setting proponents will object. "Well, Iacocca should have added a safety goal along with the others." But there is a problem with that too. The team would have found another way to satisfy the four stated goals, while marginalizing some other, unstated area. In fact, Iacocca could have stated 500 goals and the team would have met those 500 criteria, while marginalizing the 501st thing.

For anyone familiar with tax codes, these strategies are called "loopholes." You can always find loopholes that are technically legal, even though they violate the spirit of the law. And the more laws you create, the more loopholes you create. The violators don't even have to be criminals or lowlifes. You just have to want to succeed. And you can succeed. Just make sure you meet the stated goals and use the other areas (unstated) as the places where you can leverage and shortchange.

So are goals a terrible thing? No. Just overprescribed, as Ordóñez says. Teams can set goals for themselves. The big problems arise when anyone who is not on the team sets the goal for the team. Whether that is a manager, PMO, methodology group or CEO, it is just plain dangerous for outsiders to set goals. Sometimes it can help, like that powerful drug, but please read the warning label on the bottle before you prescribe goals for other people.

16.4.2 Tangible Rewards

> Initiative, creativity and passion are gifts. They are benefactions that employees choose, day by day and moment by moment,to give or withhold. They cannot be commanded. If you're a CEO, you won't get these gifts by exhorting people to work harder, or by ordering them to love their customers and kill their competitors.
> Gary Hamel (Hamel 2012)

---

[3]We genuinely apologize for our apparent obsession with gas tank explosion stories. What is wrong with us??

Every time you reward one person, you kill the motivation in everyone else. "What am I, chopped liver?" is the thought that crosses every mind that worked hard, worked smart and yet, received diddly. Was that your aim in rewarding people?? (Kohn 1993)

Whenever you use the carrot or the stick, you are breaking the trust with your workers. When you break the trust with your employees, you are stuck with a mechanical organization instead of an organic one.

Our corporate culture built around rewards comes originally from B.F. Skinner, the famous psychological researcher and author. Alfie Kohn wrote that "B.F. Skinner could be described as a man who conducted most of his experiments on rodents and pigeons and wrote most of his books about people." (Kohn 1993). Skinner's theory is known as "behaviorism."

The prevailing view in the corporate world is that, as Tom Peters puts it "Get the incentives right and productivity will follow. If we give people big, straightforward monetary incentives, the productivity problem goes away." This falls directly in line with Skinner's behaviorism. But this simply doesn't work. Here are the problems with an incentive-based workplace:

- It is very difficult to base the incentives on the right measurements. If we base incentives on subjective evaluations (a manager's opinion), then people will rightly complain that the manager is biased in one way or another. If we base incentives on objective measurements, it is usually the case that the competing employees can game the system to increase their scores by finding the ever-present loopholes.
- Incentives often pit one team member against the other (or one team against the other). As soon as this occurs, those people (or teams) have no reason to want to help each other, and, in fact, are better off if their neighboring teams do poorly. (Sabotage, anyone?)
- Incentive plans are extrinsic motivation. Motivation, if it's going to work, must be intrinsic, coming from inside the person.
- Rewards rupture relationships. Incentives mean that cooperation between peers will be reduced to zero, and that relationships between subordinate and boss will be reduced to a stream of numbers (what's being measured) as the subordinate tries to effectively game the measurements. Collaboration will diminish and information will be hoarded.
- Incentives discourage risk-taking. Why innovate when it might jeopardize your incentive? Just keeping doing it the old way and churning out the numbers.
- Incentives ensure that "it" will get done, but they change how people do "it." There is a difference when a person is doing some work because they know it is the right thing to do, versus doing it to ensure that they receive a reward. Rewards define success in a way that is external to the individual. It becomes "What does the boss want?" rather than "What do I think is right?" Qualities, or unmeasured qualities, rather, fall by the wayside. The more unmeasured

qualities you can find to trample on, the more likely you will reach your incentive goal!
- Incentives undermine interest. Have you noticed that, once you've been extrinsically motivated to do a particular type of work (let's say woodwork), you are no longer interested in doing it as a hobby afterward? Incentives break the connection between a person and their joy of work. It becomes "work."

Deming (1992) put it best when he said that, if you set targets for people, they will achieve them, even if they have to destroy the enterprise to do it.

Show Me the Money

As a manager, you can effectively set the tone for how the team will behave in certain ways. One way is to focus on money. If you try to squeeze every dollar's worth of productivity from your people, then you can expect a similar response coming back. "Hey, if you're going to ask me to show you the money, Mr. Manager, then I'm going to say the same thing when it comes time for salary increases." And, if anyone approaches me from the outside to offer a higher salary (or better bonuses, benefits, promotion possibility, etc.) I am gone. I'm outta here. Eat my dust.

Show Me the Money management begets Show Me the Money employees.

16.4.3 Work That Is Challenging, but Not Overwhelming

Edward de Bono, one of our scholars, in his book *The Happiness Purpose* (de Bono 1979) showed how happiness is created in the workplace or anywhere else. We are at our happiest when we have situations that are challenging enough, but not overwhelming. He uses the terms lifespace and selfspace, where lifespace is what is being asked of us and selfspace is the amount we can handle easily with our current competence and confidence. In Fig. 16.1, we can see how lifespace and selfspace compare and how we can work in a happy way.

On the left is when we feel overwhelmed. Our lifespace, what is required of us, is too large and our selfspace, what we are capable of, is much smaller. We can't keep up and we feel inadequate. We are unhappy.

In the middle, we can prosper when our selfspace nearly matches our lifespace. Most often, this happens in our hobbies. We become very good at a craft, say knitting or painting action figures, and we enjoy living in that space of pure competence. From a work perspective, though, it doesn't work as well. We become bored easily. If our selfspace is too close to our lifespace, we will probably leave that job for something more challenging.

And finally, on the right, we have a balance. We have a job that challenges our abilities, that stretches us to our limits, but not too far past them. As an HR professional, you should constantly be looking to position each person in a way

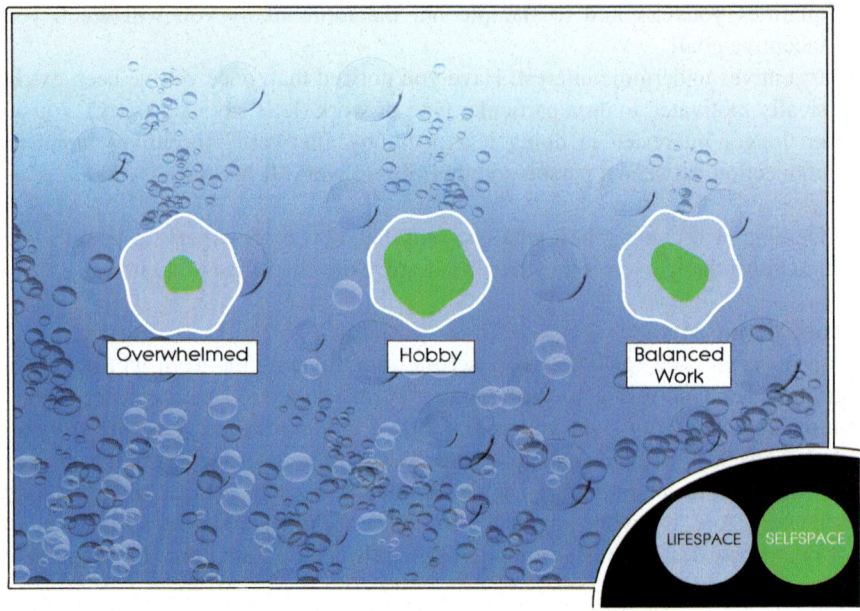

Fig. 16.1 Lifespace and selfspace—de Bono's diagrams for finding happiness in work. © 2017 by Daryl Kulak and Hong Li—reprinted with permission

that gives them the right lifespace–selfspace proportion and helping the employee and their manager to fix the imbalances. You can use de Bono's simple lifespace–selfspace diagrams to work with people and understand where they are.

"Draw lifespace–selfspace for how you feel about coding in Ruby/Cucumber. How about working in Hadoop? Scala and Spark?"

Another aspect of control over one's work is the type of work we are choosing to do. What if I am being perfectly challenged life-space versus self-space, but I don't feel that this work is contributing towards my own goals?

That is also a problem. Here, you as a manager need to help the person connect their own goals to the work at hand necessary for the project. This means that both of you jointly look for ways that this current work can be some sort of stepping stone towards the person's own career goals. Haven't you had those situations in your career where you were put into a situation that you thought you'd dread, or that actually was unpleasant as it was in progress, but that you looked back to as a stepping stone? That's the type of connection you need to help your employee make. If the work is total drudgery, far below the employee's capabilities, then it becomes tougher (again, a life-space/self-space problem), but if the work does have some challenge, you should be able to make some tentative connection.

16.4.4 The Fun Committee

HR departments are notorious for trying to create "fun." Apparently, what the HR people think is fun and what everyone else thinks is fun are quite different.

In our experience, fun is usually spontaneous. Any "annual company picnic" or "release celebration party" are usually boring, awkward time-wasters. Maybe it's just us.

Or maybe not. The book *How Google Works*, written by Eric Schmidt and Jonathan Rosenberg, says something quite similar (Schmidt and Rosenberg 2014). At Google, they consider spontaneous trips to the movie theater fun, but they try to avoid heavy-handed social events with management speeches and well-wishing. Googlers consider Sergei's nerdy jokes as fun, but they do not pine for a weekly company newsletter with its related Dilbert comic strip. If you've heard something too many times, it isn't funny[4] anymore.

It's worth trying to rethink the "fun committee." How can "fun" become less drudgery and more "fun?"

16.5 Teams Competing Against One Another

Over-enthusiastic managers often state that they would like to have their newly Agile teams compete against one another to increase everyone's productivity. "Competition is good for the company!"

Do you see any problem with this?

It is certainly true that competition is a vital part of a capitalist society like we have in the USA, Canada, Europe and other places. Even communist China has found a way to inject capitalism and competition into its own economy, pushing the country's growth levels to astonishing heights.

Competition is good for an economy so it must be good within a company as well, right? Actually, no. The difference is that people within a company are working towards the same goal, while competitors in an economy have different goals (my goal is for my company to succeed, your goal is for your company to succeed, if you disintegrate, that helps me).

This difference matters a lot. If you set up teams to compete against one another, and maybe even offer prizes for the victor, you are ensuring that those teams will not collaborate.

---

[4]Except for Abbott and Costello's "Who's on First" comedy routine, which is funny. Every. Single. Time.

Competitors do not collaborate.

This mindset sees that teams need to focus on their own performance, not the performance of the larger enterprise. The larger enterprise is not their concern. The deliverables of their "competitors" are not their concerns either. If the team takes some action that helps themselves, but damages the other teams, that is actually a great thing in a competitive culture. Your goal is to beat the other guy, so the more he loses, the more you win.

Competition for storypoints[5] is obviously the most ridiculous. Storypoints are relative measures of complexity. Their sole purpose is to reduce the wasted time of detailed estimation. To have teams compete to produce more storypoints than one another will simply motivate the teams to reduce the size of each storypoint so they can pump out more (itty bitty) storypoints.

You should treat any ideas of competition among software teams as suspect. Try to think how the competition might hurt productivity, especially as it relates to collaboration between teams, hoarding information, and prioritizing team success above enterprise success.

16.6 Promotion Paths

Even promotion paths will need to be altered as IT organizations transform to improved processes.

The most important promotion path is for developers. Developers should be able to continue writing code no matter how long they've worked in the software industry, how long they've been at this company, or how gray their hair happens to be.

The path for developers in most large organizations is that a "senior developer" needs to continue on to become an architect or a manager. You cannot really just keep coding and expect to get raises and keep your job.

But a truly technical promotion path needs to be available. It is helpful to have names for senior level development roles all the way to the top. Here's an example of a popular structure.

The lowest level,[6] most inexperienced developers are called "apprentices."

The next level of developers are called "journeymen." Then we have more experienced "craftsmen." Finally, at the very top are the "software artisans" who

---

[5]For more detail on storypoints, see Chap. 7—Business Value, Estimation and Metrics.

[6]We (mostly) follow the structure from Dave Hoover and Adewale Oshineye in the book *Apprenticeship Patterns* (Hoover and Oshineye 2009).

are often equal to the executives in the company and may, in some cases, report directly to the CIO. In IBM, these folks used to be called "technical fellows."

All levels stated above write code. Every day (or at least a few times a week). The higher you get, the more you get paid and the more you're expected to mentor (and pair with) more junior people. You are also expected to be highly productive as a coder. And you are expected to be able to deal with political problems that crop up inside or outside the team space. But you still get to code.

16.6.1 Leadership Promotion Paths

You should not push delivery leads out of the team space, any more than you should push developers to stop coding. People can be very senior delivery leads, but they may still choose to lead teams in team spaces day to day rather than being involved full-time in back-office activities.

Also, increases in responsibility and pay do not need to directly equate to team size. There is no additional prestige involved in leading a team of twenty versus a team of ten. This is most likely because we know that complexity increases exponentially with team size, so we always try to keep our teams quite small. We don't want our delivery leads to be obsessed with increasing the size of their direct reports on a team just to show that they deserve a raise. If we did that, we'd be incenting people to think of reasons to create larger projects with larger teams, which, because of their size, are always at more risk of failing.

16.7 There Is Only One Motivator

> Too many organizations—not just companies, but governments and non-profits as well—still operate from assumptions about human potential and individual performance that are outdated, unexamined, and rooted more in folklore than in science. They continue to pursue practices such as short-term incentive plans and pay-for-performance schemes in the face of mounting evidence that such measures usually don't work and often do harm.
> Daniel Pink in "Drive" (Pink 2011)

Not to directly contradict the common wisdom[7], there is only one way to motivate team members.

Let them control their own work.

That's it.

The rest is just window dressing and happy talk (at its best) or nonsense (at its worst).

---

[7]We're looking at you—*1001 Ways to Energize Employees* (Nelson 1997) and *1001 Ways to Reward Employees* (Nelson 2005)!

Control over one's own work is such a powerful motivator because it creates a feeling that you are a trusted member of a team, that you know what you're doing and you need to be listened to when it comes to issues of x, y and z. That feels really good and it's meaningful, unlike pizza lunches, trips to the zoo or showers of confetti on your desk.

So a manager's main job is just to leave team members alone? Of course not. But just know that every intrusion you make into a person's sphere of control over their own work, no matter how small, is a notch against their motivation.

Motivation is a product of the system. Fix the system and you'll fix the motivation problem. Hire a person to throw confetti on your workers and motivation will stay the same or even decrease.

This is one more reason why systems thinking principle #4—Bring decision making as close to the work as possible—is so important.

16.8 Recruiting, Interviewing and Contracting

Now let's look at our intake process for new employees. We'll examine the importance of diversity in a workforce, recruiting tips and also speak to the effective ratio of contractors to employees.

16.8.1 Diversity and Inclusion

Having a diverse workforce is good for business. The companies that figure this out now will have an amazing competitive advantage over those who don't.

Let's define the two words: diversity and inclusion.

Diversity refers to the ways that people are different from each other. It can mean differences in gender, ethnic background or age. It can also mean differences in life experiences, like people who have lived or traveled around the world, veterans of wars and people with experience in government or nonprofits.

Inclusion is the act of bringing diverse people together and doing something positive with the richness of ideas, backgrounds and perspectives.

We talk about innovation and creativity in this book. If you've got people from various backgrounds who have different perspectives, you cannot help but have more creativity. It comes for free. But it can also be squashed, even unintentionally.

Here's how it gets squashed. If you have a company culture that favors one particular perspective, let's say the educated, white male in his twenties, then the people who join the company who are not white males may self-censor their unique perspectives and your company will never get the benefit of them. Silicon Valley has many companies that suffer from this lack of variety in perspective.

Carol Dweck is a researcher of motivation in the workplace (Dweck 2006). She posits that there are two mindsets that people can adopt: fixed and growth. The fixed mindset people think that we are all as smart as we're ever going to be, and there isn't much point in trying to improve. The growth mindset people assume that people (including themselves) can learn anything and are always looking for ways to grow themselves and the people around them.

It is important to take a growth mindset when hiring people. Hire people for their potential rather than the list of skills they happen to have at the moment.

You want to create a team that "thinks together" effectively. You also want a team that has a fast learning curve. Notice that we say that the "team" has the learning curve, not the individual team members. Don't put pressure on individuals to learn fast, but instead ensure that you have a diverse, inclusive team, which presents the benefit of a fast learning team.

In systems thinking, there is something called the "Law of Requisite Variety," coming from one of our scholars, Ross Ashby. A system must be diverse itself in order to handle the diverse set of problems that get thrown at it. Likewise, your team must be diverse to handle the problems they will face and to be able to come up with creative solutions that draw from a diverse set of life experiences, cultures and gender perspectives.

Here is one small way you can help to increase the gender diversity in our technology field. If you are a speaker at a conference, insist that the organizers have a "code of conduct" that outlines that women and minorities must be treated respectfully at the event. The code[8] can say what type of behavior is required and what will happen if any person does not act respectfully.

16.8.2 Don't Fetishize Technical Skills in Interviews

> *I worked as a consultant delivery lead on a large project at a medium-sized corporation. The larger project was already underway so we were adding some velocity to the team. The technology stack included JavaScript, node.js and Protractor as an automated testing tool. My team of consultants started on real work very quickly and soon began contributing velocity as expected.*
>
> *A few weeks into the engagement, I was in a meeting with some of the client executives. They were planning to hire some new developers as full-*

(continued)

---

[8]Here is an excellent example of a code of conduct for a conference that we spoke at in Bratislava, Slovakia: bit.ly/ScrumImpulz.

> timers, and they knew they could find people with JavaScript but they also knew that the Protractor experience would be a lot tougher.
>
> "We'll have to set aside some training time and expense for the new people coming in," said one of the executives. I didn't think much of it at the time.
>
> After the meeting, I went back to my consultant team. They were busy coding and testing. Wait a second, I thought, my team didn't know Protractor either! And yet none of the developers even made the slightest mention of it. That's strange. So I asked them about it.
>
> "No, none of us had used Protractor before. But it is similar enough to R-Spec, which we have used. It wasn't any big deal."
>
> Even though I held these particular developers in high regard, I had underestimated their ability to pick up new tools drastically.
>
> This is something I've noticed often. Let developers use new tools and don't get too hung up on how long it will take them to learn them. This mindset has served me well with developer tools, but not as well with other products. For instance, it might not be good advice for a team getting started on a new ERP or CRM application, for example. Maybe it's because open source developer tools are written by developers for developers, and are therefore more intuitive. The last thing anyone could say about a gigantic ERP or CRM tool was that it was "intuitive." Who knows.

It's best if your recruiters think of tools in families. For instance, if a developer knows R-Spec, it won't be very tough for them to pick up Cucumber or Protractor. If they know JavaScript and backbone.js, then learning angular.js won't be a big deal. Once they know Ruby and Closure, learning Scala will be pretty smooth. And so on.

As a recruiter, you are really hiring for potential more than x months or years of a specific technical skill. Hire people who can learn and you won't have to restock with new employees once your technology stack shifts.

It is important to distinguish between technology tools that require deep knowledge and those where similar skills might provide a headstart. For instance, Hadoop has so many pieces to it that it is difficult to learn and even a bit nonintuitive even for developers who have worked with NoSQL in other contexts. There you might need a special "Hadoop expert." But, as in our example above, you won't need to find a Protractor expert if you've got people who know RSpec. And there are lots of examples where those equivalences are the case. Ask your technology people to map it out for you.

Once you've gotten past fetishizing technical skills, there is another trick we have to share with you. Remember that diverse teams are creative teams. Now you can focus more on putting together a diverse team and lessen your focus on getting the exact right set of technology skills. Build diversity first. Then use the practices of pairing and TDD (described in Chap. 9—Flipping the Build/Run Ratio) to quickly spread the knowledge of the tools and utilities. It may be helpful to have at least one person who can answer questions quickly on the new tools, but even that may be unnecessary (see the Protractor example above).

16.8.3 The Use of Contractors and Contracted Services

We discuss software vendors and contracting in Chap. 10—Better Vendor RFPs and Contracts, but it is worth looking at the picture from an HR perspective. People are people. They are not interchangeable parts in a machine. They can feel more or less connected to their employer, their boss and the vision of the company. Contractors, by definition, cannot feel that connection. We're not saying that companies should never use contractors, but they should find ways to use them for specific improvement projects (build this app, help us improve our practices, help us scale up temporarily, etc.) and try to minimize general contract staffing whenever possible. Full-time employees are just that much more likely (no guarantees, of course) to buy into your vision and operate with their whole hearts and minds towards the goals of the company.

For several years, books like *Free Agent Nation* (Pink 2001) have glorified the use of contractors, giving a view of short-term contracts between liberated individuals and free-flowing corporations. Pink and his colleagues are dead wrong. This is a mechanical view of people, seeing them as interchangeable parts, and a corporation that has too many contracted staff will not be able to execute as quickly or creatively as one that encourages long-term employment.

Having a majority of contracted staff also makes it difficult to encourage a corporate culture with diversity and inclusion. One more reason to limit contracted staffing if you can.

The most productive companies we've seen with staff to contractor ratios have been around 80/20. This is a large enough pool of full-time staff to hold a culture together that emphasizes the right aspects and intentions. The ratio may go up when there are large projects that require temporary help from consulting firms, but should drop again once the projects are complete.

16.9 Changing the Culture

If an executive decides that the corporate culture needs to change to fulfill one of her objectives, she will, no doubt, assign that task to the HR department. But how the heck do you change a culture?

16.9.1 Look! I'll Change the Culture by Replacing the People!

Sometimes executives think that the way to change the culture of their organization is to replace the "bad people" with "good people" who really get their vision. But it isn't actually that easy.

Think of the Ohio State (OSU) football team. (American football, not soccer. Apologies to the rest of the world.) OSU has had a winning team for decades. As we write this, OSU has had 875 wins, 320 losses and 53 tied games since their first season in 1890. That's a 72% winning percentage. Year after year, they win almost every game in the regular season and often go on to win major national titles in the bowl games.

So they must have great players, right? Sure. But not the same great players. After all, we're talking about 1890 until 2016. It can't be the same players all that time. In fact, it is a university, so the players are only on the team for, at maximum, 4 years. Then they're gone. There is a completely new slate of players every 4 years.

Okay, so great coaching, right? Sure. But the current coach (as of 2016), who helped the team win the national championship in 2014, just joined the team in 2011. The OSU team was good before he got there. Very good, in fact. So it isn't just the coach.

Well, good decision making in the executive offices, then, right? Yes, but those folks change too from year to year.

And on and on we go. The fact is, we've replaced every single piece of the team many times over the years and yet we still have a winner. How is that possible.

It is possible because the real winner is the "system." The Ohio State football program is where the winning comes from. It can't be documented in a binder. It isn't a person who sits in a chair. There is a culture of winning beyond all the people, where the winning formula resides. Speech, intention and worldview all intertwine to create the OSU football program.

As an HR professional, this is what you want for your team. You want to build a program, a system, a culture that helps people "win" at software development. Look for the small decisions, the contributions to right speech, right intention and right worldview that can encourage the creation of something special beyond what's documented in company brochures.

16.9.2 Being a Student of Corporate Culture

As we discussed in leadership principle #8 in Chap. 11—Servant Leadership—we all must become conversant in corporate culture. It is not enough to say "We have a command and control culture" or "We need to have a Silicon Valley culture." We must know the dimensions of culture, as defined by the Cultural Intelligence Center (Livermore 2013):

Individualism versus collectivism
Power distance
Uncertainty avoidance
Cooperative versus competitive
Time orientation
Direct versus indirect
Being versus doing
Particularism versus universalism
Neutral versus affective
Tight versus loose

For HR executives and managers, it is even more important to know the dimensions of culture, to know the status quo of your organization and to have a plan to improve the culture in specific ways.

For more details on corporate culture and how to change culture, refer to Chap. 11—Servant Leadership.

16.10 How Team Roles Change

> I always wanted to be somebody, but I should've been more specific.
> Lily Tomlin

As teams move to doing project work in short sprints and using advanced engineering practices (like those described in Chap. 8—Flipping the Build/Run Ratio), the composition of the team is likely to change.

The easiest way to visualize the changes is to think in terms of the team's velocity. What roles add velocity to a team? The only role that increases velocity is when you add developers. The rest of the team members are there to support development. This may sound like an insult, but it's not meant to be.

16.10.1 Thinner Management Layers

Management roles may even be reduced if the teams are standing teams who know how to work together and can self-manage. With most large enterprise teams we've worked on, there are three types of management roles.

Delivery Lead
Inside the team space is the "delivery lead." It refers to a combination of what people called ScrumMaster (improve the team process), project manager (track

metrics, progress, budget) and resource manager (handling people problems, vacation schedules, career, etc.). Delivery leads are responsible for all these things inside the team space. One delivery lead should be able to handle a team of up to 12–15 people.

Delivery leads[9] are generally full-time in a particular team room. If two teams are small (fewer than five developers), a DL might be part-time across two teams, although this is not ideal (see time-slicing section later in this chapter).

Tech Lead

A tech lead writes code as much as any other developer, but is also the go-to person when questions come up about how to use the engineering practices, which practices apply to this project, coding standards and architecture issues. The tech lead is a full-time person on the team. They are not time-sliced across multiple teams.

Project Manager

Yes, project managers still exist! What we've found is that we need a person to coordinate work between team rooms when certain projects require it. For instance, if a project comes up that is meant to modernize the user interface on all Web applications simultaneously, then the teams who are dedicated to each Web app need to take their portion of the user stories for that project, but the overall project still requires some coordination over-and-above what occurs in each team room. This is a job for a typical project manager.

16.10.2 User Interface Designers

We have seen every possible permutation of involving user interface designers into development teams. We've seen where designers participate full-time and sit inside the team room. We've seen where designers are time-sliced across several teams. We've seen where development teams work with external design teams who pass the work back piece-by-piece, sprint-by-sprint.

Our preference is to have the design talent in the team room full-time. They may be full-time for a while but they might not be permanent. That is, the design work may be concentrated in the first 30–40% percent of the sprints, early in the release cycle, so maybe that is when the designer(s) are full-time. This role has been much tougher for us to figure out the best type of involvement. It is probably more guesswork based on the corporate culture of design work as well as the existing structure (one centralized design group versus floating designers on development teams).

---

[9]One of our clients refers to this role as "value lead" which is also a great role name.

16.10.3 Generalizing Specialists

> A human being should be able to change a diaper, plan an invasion, butcher a hog, conn a ship, design a building, write a sonnet, balance accounts, build a wall, set a bone, comfort the dying, take orders, give orders, cooperate, act alone, solve equations, analyze a new problem, pitch manure, program a computer, cook a tasty meal, fight efficiently, die gallantly. Specialization is for insects.
>
> Robert Heinlein, science fiction writer

There is a term called "generalizing specialist" that is being used more and more in the software realm. It means that a person can play one role particularly well, let's say front-end Web developer (html/css/JavaScript) and they are a very good specialist in that role. However, they are also able to switch to several other roles, perhaps back-end Web services developer, BDD spec developer and workflow package customizer. This person is known as a generalizing specialist. They are a specialist in one thing, but can switch to other roles when it is necessary. They probably have a preference to stay within their own specialty, but they are willing to move around to benefit the team when there is a bottleneck to be busted through.

Your goal, as an HR person, is to maximize the number of generalizing specialists on all the IT teams. Can the developer move around to code in different areas? Can the developer also play the role of a BA? Can the BA also act as an exploratory tester? Can the delivery lead also do a bit of testing?

Without some element of generalizing specialists on the team, each sprint devolves into a mini-waterfall. The developers cannot get started until the business analysts have done their work. The testers can't start testing until at least some of the user stories have been developed. And so on. The waterfall delays are lessened from the giant waterfall cycles, but they still exist and they're still wasteful. Try to encourage people to become generalizing specialists.

However, from an HR perspective, there's a problem with generalizing specialists. How do you evaluate people? In most large organizations, job descriptions are fairly well defined. You are a developer. I am a tester. We each need to do our job, as it fits our job description.

Doing work outside that job description doesn't help you meet your goals. In fact, it might be looked on negatively by the HR department. "If you're a developer, why are you doing work in these other roles? You should focus your energies. Think of your career."

The HR department needs to have a strategy for dealing with generalizing specialists. Each person might be evaluated on their ability to do their own work (the specialty) as well as how much they were able to help other roles when the bottlenecks appeared (generalizing). Otherwise, if the promotions and salary increases are stacked against the generalizing specialists, the team rooms will be stuck with mini-waterfalls and wasteful sprint time.

16.11 Allocating People's Time

The next aspect of the HR worldview has to do with how we allocate people's time. Once we move away from the waterfall lifecycle, the phases of analysis, design, development and testing are no longer the times when it makes sense to allocate certain roles to projects. With Agile iterative/incremental lifecycles, analysis, design, development and testing occur all at the same time for the life of the release cycle. HR departments and managers will need a new view to match the Agile lifecycle, which we address in the following section.

16.11.1 Competency Centers

By competency centers, we are talking about groups that fit a certain role, like the "Business Analysis Competency Center" or the "Quality Assurance Competency Center." These groups are external to the development teams but provide support in terms of swapping team members between the teams, as well as ensuring that their members (all the BAs, for example) get the appropriate training and attend conferences that are worthwhile for them. The competency centers probably have meetings once a quarter to share stories, ideas and provide mutual support.

If you examine these job titles closely, you will see that they align very well with waterfall phases. Business analysts align with the requirements and analysis phases. Developers align with the development phase. Testers align with the testing phase.

Waterfall projects provide certain guidance for competency centers. When a new project starts up, the competency center knows that the project will need some BAs. A bit later, they will need architects and designers. After that group is done, developers can move in. Then later still, testers can come in and finish the job.

People who work full-time inside a competency center might be called "resource managers." (There's that "resource" word again.) The resource manager needs to get very good at scooping up people after they are no longer needed on a particular project and finding new homes for them on the next projects. It is labor-intensive.

When IT organizations move to a "standing teams" model and towards short sprints, the role of the competency center changes dramatically. People from every role are assigned to standing teams and then they stay there, doing bits of business analysis, design, development and testing every day and every week. Instead of specialists moving in and out of a project phase-by-phase, the whole team sticks together and delivers a small chunk of functionality every week. No more swapping and trading people (or at least less of it).

Our advice to resource managers inside competency centers starts with the situation where some of the enterprise's projects are done using a waterfall cycle and some are done using short sprints (Agile).

Bring your people across one-by-one to the Agile side. Once a person is doing short sprints on a standing team, they stay on that side. Don't time-slice anyone partly waterfall and partly Agile if you can possibly help it. Move the whole person across the waterfall-Agile boundary.

The waterfall projects can be staffed as they've always been—phase-by-phase. The Agile teams require 100% dedication from all roles and the teams stay static for months at a time.

That is not to say that people should be stuck on one team for a lifetime. It makes very good sense to move people around between teams, synthesizing knowledge, spreading expertise and multiplying working relationships. We just shouldn't be swapping them every day! Use a time-frame that makes sense in your organization. Do you look at transfers between teams once every 6 months? Once a year? Every 18 months? Most high-performers get bored if they are dealing with the same codebase for too long. Keep teams together for at least 6 months, but consider whether teams should keep all their team members for even longer than that. And don't break teams apart. Remove only one person at a time. So, for instance, if you have a team of eight people, consider moving one person to a different team after 6 month, then another person off the team 6 months after that, and so on. Respect the fragility of the personal relationships and the productivity of teams who have already been through the forming-storming-norming-performing cycle.

16.11.2 Time-Slicing People Is the Biggest Productivity Killer in the Known World

What usually happens in waterfall IT shops is that people not only move from project to project after each phase (e.g., BAs move off the project once analysis is done), but in fact the employees are time-sliced across multiple projects all at once.

As an example, Rhonda the tester is working on the invoicing project (20%), the UI enhancement project (30%), the tax project (20%) and the super secret project (30%). Rhonda is expected to attend meetings for all the projects, get a little bit of work done on each project every day.

Would you like to be in Rhonda's shoes? Do you think Rhonda has gotten to know the team members of each team? (Remember, her teammates are also probably time-sliced across projects too. "Are you on one of my teams? I can't remember!")

Multitasking in short bursts is extremely unproductive. A study[10] published in the August 24, 2009 issue of *The Proceedings of the National Academy of Sciences*, done by a team at Stanford, looked at student's ability to multitask. The results? One researcher, who was fully expecting to find a "secret ability" among the frequent multitaskers, exclaimed "The multitaskers were just lousy at everything!"

---

[10] bit.ly/MultitaskersLousy.

Doing two things at once, for example, talking on the phone and driving, and switching between several projects during the course of the day, require the same ability. It is called "context switching." And, according to the research, our brains are absolutely terrible at context switching.

IT projects are complex. They require a lot of background knowledge. They have multiple levels of details. They often have hundreds of thousands of component parts. The greater the complexity, the longer it takes to context switch.

There is a quick exercise to show the productivity hit involved in context switching. It comes from the Potential Project,[11] a consulting firm in Denmark.

Ask someone to time you for each of the two following exercises.

The first exercise is as follows:

- Write the complete sentence below on a whiteboard or piece of paper:

I am a great multitasker

- Then, once you're finished the sentence, write the following numbers:

1 2 3 4 5 6 7 8 9 10 11 12 13 14 15 16 17 18 19 20

Stop the timer and write down the amount of time it took.

The second exercise is as follows (start the timer):

- Write the first letter of the sentence, then switch to writing the first number
- Then write the second letter of the sentence and then the second number
- Continue until the sentence and the stream of numbers are complete (they are equal)

Stop the timer. You will find that the second exercise took perhaps double the amount of time as the first. Yet the results are the same. That lag time is due to context-switching. And this is very simple work, writing a short sentence and some numbers. Imagine the context-switching costs when you are moving from one complex IT project to another. It can be measured in hours lost per week, not seconds. Those hours are waste.

For this reason, we strongly suggest standing teams doing short sprints. Standing teams, where all team members are 100% dedicated to one common goal, provide amazing productivity benefits, just by dedicating[12] people to a task rather than time-slicing them.

---

[11]bit.ly/PotProj.

[12]For teams who are responsible for maintaining lots of small applications, one team might need to provide coverage for several hundred systems. In this case, of course, one developer will need to multitask among dozens of goals. However, managers should constantly try to optimize work among developers to minimize the multitasking and distraction for each developer.

Try to limit developers' involvement in external meetings. The delivery lead and tech lead might need to consult with external groups and figure ways around political issues, but the developers should be allowed to concentrate on their work for hours at a time. That is not to say there has to be silence in the team room. We are instead saying that the developer pairs should be engaged in conversation with each other, and be communicating to the other pairs freely, but all focused on the job of building the next increment of code, not the various political blow-ups surrounding the team room at the moment. It is a balance between "Don't bother them! They're working!" and "Team rooms should be collaborative."

16.12 HR Is a Big Part of an Agile Transformation

As you can see from the past few dozen pages, there is a lot for the HR department and managers to do when a culture is changing towards Agile. Agile teams do tend to break a number of HR processes, so it is important to know how to match HR offerings to what is most helpful for the Agile teams. Some parts of HR, especially the performance appraisal, are due for a change anyway.

> **Test Drive Your Knowledge Again**
> Answer the following questions with the knowledge you have after reading this chapter. Have your answers changed?
>
> 1. What are the aspects of HR that may need to change to accommodate Agile teams?
> 2. What are the pluses and minuses of goal setting?
> 3. What is the one true motivator for people?

> **Try This Next**
> **For the HR executive or IT manager:**
>
> - Remove references of people as "resources" in all documents and day-to-day language.
> - Unbundle the performance appraisal system using Scholtes (1998—Chap. 9); Coens and Jenkins (2002); and Culbert and Rout (2010).
> - Reduce the emphasis on goals and rewards, especially monetary rewards for behavior. Instead, look for ways to increase autonomy for people. Read Pink (2011).
> - If there are instances where teams are encouraged to compete against one another in work (we're not referring to charity drives, etc.), stop this immediately.

(continued)

- Educate hiring managers on the true business benefits of diversity and inclusion.
- Reduce or eliminate time-slicing across multiple projects and codebases whenever possible (obviously difficult when one person is maintaining several small applications in production).
- Become a student of corporate culture using the cultural dimensions from the Cultural Intelligence Center.
- Create promotion paths so that people can write code for the rest of their lives and continue to receive reasonable increases in compensation.

References

Coens T, Jenkins M (2002) Abolishing performance appraisals: why they backfire and what to do instead. Berrett-Koehler, San Francisco

Culbert S, Rout L (2010) Get rid of the performance review! How companies can stop intimidating, start managing – and focus on what really matters. Hachette Book Group, New York

de Bono E (1979) The happiness purpose. Penguin, New York

Deming WE (1992) Out of the crisis. MIT, Cambridge, MA

Dweck C (2006) Mindset: the new psychology of success. Random House, New York

Hamel G (2012) What matters now: how to win in a world of relentless change, ferocious competition and unstoppable innovation. Jossey-Bass

Hoover D, Oshineye A (2009) Apprenticeship patterns: guidance for the aspiring software craftsman. O'Reilly, Sebastopol

Kohn A (1993) Punished by rewards: the trouble with gold stars, incentive plans, A's, praise and other bribes. Houghton Mifflin, Boston

Laloux F (2014) Reinventing organizations: a guide to creating organizations inspired by the next stage of human consciousness. Nelson Parker, Brussels

Livermore D (2013) Customs of the world: using cultural intelligence to adapt, wherever you are. The Great Courses, Chantilly

Nelson B (1997) 1001 Ways to energize employees. Workman Publishing, Victoria

Nelson B (2005) 1001 Ways to reward employees, 2nd edn. Workman Publishing, Victoria

Pink D (2001) Free agent nation. Hachette Book Group, New York

Pink D (2011) Drive: the surprising truth about what motivates us. Riverhead Books, New York

Schmidt E, Rosenberg J (2014) How Google works. Grand Central, New York

Scholtes PR (1998) The Leader's handbook: making things happen, getting things done. McGraw Hill, New York

Buy Versus Build   17

> *No trumpets sound when the important decisions of our lives are made. Destiny is made known silently.*
>
> Agnes de Mille

Test Drive Your Knowledge
Answer the following questions with the knowledge you have now. Then answer them again at the end of this chapter.

1. What question do you need to ask about your IT department before you make a buy versus build decision?
2. Can software be a competitive advantage for a company that does not sell software?
3. Are there other choices besides just buy or build?

17.1 The Character of Your IT Shop

A CIO often faces the question—should we buy prepackaged software to solve a business problem or should we build something custom? And does our IT group even have the ability to build custom software at scale?

Often IT groups go through layers of budget cuts, and in the process they become less capable than they were.

A top-level internal IT organization is truly able to accomplish software development. They understand the business side and they are on top of the latest innovations in technology and process. But after enough cuts and lack of focus, they can become nothing more than a service bureau. They can respond to small changes requested by the business, but with any major initiative or any kind of large change, they need help from the outside.

Think of a car manufacturing plant and a service station. The service station can provide you with very good service, including gasoline fill-ups, oil changes, tire rotation, check-ups and brake replacements. But you could never ask that service station to build you a car! It would be very expensive, low quality and would probably be years late in delivery.

The same with an internal IT shop that has become a service bureau. It can't be expected to deliver anything substantial. This isn't a knock on IT shop service bureaus, but it is something that they must know about themselves.

In our experience, it is not a matter of size. Certainly, if an IT shop is very small, it is difficult to be a true software development organization. But there is no connection between being a large IT shop and necessarily being good at software development. We have worked with very large IT departments that were capable of nothing more than service bureau-level support of their business. And yet, unless they know that about themselves, they will encounter failure after failure with their own projects. They must bring in a strategic partner, consulting firm or whatever, to help them accomplish big projects.

Now back to the CIO's criteria for placing projects. Can we do it in-house or not? To answer that question, step back from looking at the problem to be solved and look inside instead. What type of organization do you have? Is it a software development organization or just a service bureau? Don't fool yourself. Ask the question honestly.

What do you want your IT group to be? If you are a service bureau now, but you want to become a software development organization, ask why. Why make this expensive shift? What will you accomplish? Is there an appetite for this type of investment in the C-suite? Amongst the shareholders?

Not every IT shop should be a true software development organization. Not every IT shop has to be a service bureau. You just have to know what you are, and then make good decisions based on that knowledge.

17.2 To Buy or to Build?

Buy or build? The salespeople from the package vendors definitely have an opinion, but the CIO has to think about what is best for his own department.

There are several factors to the buy/build decision that we'd like to offer in this chapter. Hopefully this can serve as a framework for CIOs and decision-makers when looking for new applications.

17.2.1 What Business Are You In?

The authors being consultants, we get to see a lot of industries. It's quite exciting. We've worked inside manufacturers, banks, insurers, distribution companies, healthcare providers, retailers, utilities, nonprofits and government. In each case, they have a dedicated "IT department" that is meant to provide services to the other departments.

One type of company is structured differently. Software product companies do not have an IT department.[1] The whole company is the IT department. We devote an entire chapter to the differences between software product companies and internal IT departments (Chap. 19—Differences Between Software Product Companies and Internal IT). But for now, suffice it to say, these types of companies don't have the same problems.

The internal IT shop provides services to a larger organization. The amount of money spent on technology is often a fraction of the overall corporate budget. For manufacturing firms, we've seen amounts as small as 1% of the budget dedicated to IT. For banks, it is often closer to 5%.

This provides a different vibe for internal IT shops. Software projects are not usually the biggest projects around (except when they go badly over budget), and often not the most important to the executives either. Plus there is another factor that the internal IT shop must understand.

What business are we in? If our company sells cars, then we are in the automotive business, not the technology business, right? If we are a bank, then we are a financial services business, right? Right?

17.2.1.1 But We're a Bookstore!

Borders bookstores were a familiar sight in the Midwestern USA in the early 2000s. They were a thriving bookstore in the USA and Canada and were expanding into other countries. They saw Barnes & Noble, B. Dalton and Chapters as their competitors. But an unlikely competitor lurked outside their purview called Amazon.com.

The executives at Borders saw themselves as people who sold books in brick-and-mortar stores. They did not see themselves as technologists. The executives at Amazon saw the world differently. They were a company who used technology to sell books (at the time) but could really sell anything else using the same infrastructure.

In just a few short years, Borders closed their doors permanently. Barnes & Noble purchased Borders' customer list, but there wasn't enough of a company left to even purchase. Borders had underestimated the speed at which people would

---

[1] Actually, software product companies do have an internal IT support group that handles the help desk and small issues. But this group is not our focus here.

embrace online book buying. At one point, Borders even outsourced their customer-facing website to Amazon, which did nothing to differentiate Borders from their aggressive online competitor and was kind of like having the fox guard the henhouse.

It was good that Borders' executives had the answer to the question "What business are you in?" it is just unfortunate that their answer was their undoing. They saw technology as something separate, something they could outsource and not worry about. They did not see technology as an opportunity for competitive advantage.

We often see this with our clients. They are all cognizant of the question "What business are we in?" but they often answer the question too narrowly. And there are competitors lurking in Silicon Valley and elsewhere who fully intend to use technology to disrupt every industry we now think we know so well.

Let's start with insurance. "We are a financial services company." True. Each insurance company has a property and casualty offering, perhaps also auto and life insurance and maybe even health insurance. Also, each insurance company has some way to profit from the money that their insured clients pay each month, so they have a group focused on investments.

Is an insurance company a technology company? Certainly not in the traditional sense. An insurance company offers insurance policies, not packaged software. But, thinking more broadly, how much does information technology enable insurance? After all, what is an insurance policy, if not information? And if one insurance company enables better access to information than the others, will they find greater profits?

With insurance, we've seen some answers to these questions. A Midwestern insurance company called Progressive Insurance made big bets in the 1990s on using technology to enable better access to information. They were among the first to offer insurance quotes on the Internet. They pioneered mobile phone apps to take pictures of accidents and provide instant payments to insured customers at the site of the accident in some cases. Other insurance companies were caught flat-footed and took years to catch up.

Financial services companies who see themselves as technology-enabled financial information providers sometimes have a strategic advantage over those that see technology as a "cost center."

17.2.1.2 Products "Wrapped in Information"
When American Airlines built their SABRE airline reservation system back in the 1960s, it was one-of-a-kind. Their new software had the ability to make reservations on any American flight, and then track the passenger as they checked in their luggage, boarded the plane and got to their destination. No other airline had anything like it.

17.2 To Buy or to Build?

American began using their software to book flights for other airlines. Soon, the SABRE corporation was a profitable service arm of American Airlines. At one point, American toyed with the idea of selling SABRE to gain some cash. They started getting lucrative bids from prospective buyers.

Looking at those bids, the executives at American Airlines realized something. SABRE was really valuable. In fact, it was more valuable than the parent company. To be more precise, the information about an airline passenger seat was actually more valuable than the revenue generated by the seat!

This must have floored the executives. They had discovered that information has tremendous value.

Each corporation today should be operating by that same principle. The information about your products or services might be as valuable, or more valuable, than the products and services themselves. Are you capitalizing on that information?

The way to think of your products and services is this: The most valuable product/service is one that is wrapped in information. If the product/service is wrapped in exactly the right information, you can double or triple the value.

For instance, if a company is shipping steel to its customers, what could be more commoditized, right? Wrong. Wrap that steel in information. What is the chemical composition of the steel? What is the expected delivery date? Is the trend of this particular type of steel going up or down in terms of shipments across the customer base? Where was this steel fabricated? What is its tensile strength? How was it shipped? Where was it stored and for how long?

Farms and grocers are finding that it is valuable to have the "pedigree" of the food being sold. Shoppers like to know where a food was grown, get information about how it was shipped and find out how long ago it was picked from the vine. Pedigree information is also tremendously valuable for food safety. The ability to trace the origins of food can help with recalls due to bacteria infestations or unsafe levels of chemicals present in the products. Wrapping food in information can add value.

Find out what information your customers want wrapped around the products and services they are already receiving from you. Anticipate new types of information that they might never even realize they need.

If the software package you are considering allows you to collect new information that you can use to wrap your products, all the better. If it does not, you might need to write additional software that facilitates collecting that information that will increase the value of your offerings.

17.2.1.3 Software as a Competitive Advantage

The next factor to consider is whether this new initiative is meant to be a competitive advantage for the company. Will the software be a "cost of doing business" or something that simply keeps things running, or will it need to provide a leg up on the competition by creating something new and different—something no one else has?

This is line of thinking that has been around a long time, ever since Michael Porter wrote his book *Competitive Advantage* in 1985 (Porter 1985). But it gets confusing when deciding whether or not a piece of software you are about to have is a competitive advantage or not. The problem is that every application could potentially be a competitive advantage.

What could be more banal than supply chain management? Certainly that would be a cost of doing business, right? And yet, Walmart has effectively used a custom-built supply chain management system to their own competitive advantage for decades now. And you might too.

It can be hard to decide whether an application is a competitive advantage for your company or not. But go back to the corporate strategy. Each company must excel in their own specific niche where they continually beat their competitors. The company who is "middlin'" in all categories is the one who will go out of business the fastest.

What is your company's secret sauce? What are you known for among your customers? Do you offer the lowest prices? Are you the fastest to embrace new technology? Are you first in customer service (measurably, not just a slogan)? Are you a specialist in a niche market?

We have one client who is an insurance agency. What could be more bland than an insurance agency? But they specialize in classic cars, motorbikes and boats. They have risen to become a billion dollar company (remember this is an agency, not an insurance company), simply by being ultrafocused on this unique marketplace.

Having sorted out your competitive advantage, it becomes a question of whether this software serves your company's strategy. If you are the low price king, does the software lower costs, like Walmart's supply chain software? If so, you may consider the application to be a competitive advantage and you'll want to develop it in-house or with a partner. If you are customer service focused and the software elevates your service capability through technology, then build it, don't buy it. And so forth.

17.3 It Might Not Be Buy Versus Build: It Could Be Buy and Build

Something many companies forget is that buy versus build does not need to be an either/or decision. You don't necessarily need to go with a package that the vendor insists will solve all your problems. And you don't necessarily need to start with an empty whiteboard and begin drawing class diagrams.

There are options down the middle.

One of our clients wanted a very customized chat application that the executives could use in-house that had a number of functions no existing chat software vendor could provide. At first, the executives were thinking "buy versus build" and having a terrible time making a decision. But then they realized that the company was already using a chat program in-house from Microsoft called Lync. This product had a very comprehensive SDK (software development kit), which allowed developers to write custom software[2] that communicated to Lync. In effect, Lync was able to do the heavy lifting of basic chat functions (user registration, sending messages, security, various platforms, etc.) and the team was able to build additional functions on top of Lync that gave the needed features that executives were asking for.

In each situation, the company should consider buy-versus-build as a continuum, not an either/or decision. Many enterprise products from IBM, Oracle and Microsoft come with an SDK that makes it possible (although not usually easy) to build on top of these complex products.

17.4 Where Are You on the Emotional Spectrum of Packaged Software?

It is hard not to get drawn into the emotional aspect of packaged software. Packaged software vendor salespeople are experts at making it all "sound easy." They can draw in naive executives with their promises of low costs and amazing automation. It's easy to buy on the emotion. There is even a term for executives making silly IT decisions based on very little information—"airline magazine syndrome." Executives read an article about a success with packaged software in an industry similar to their own, and they immediately start a process to bring that same package into their company. The only trouble is that the article only interviewed one or two people from the client company and those people subsequently hired on to the package company (none of which was mentioned in the article).

On the other end of the spectrum, crusty IT people are often emotional against packaged software. Almost every IT group has experienced a disastrous package implementation that provided none of the vendor-promised benefits and cost much, much more than if the developers had just written a custom solution from scratch. *CIO* magazine puts out a yearly article chronicling the ERP failures of just the past 12 months. They have enough volume of stories of gigantic failures to produce a list every single year! And yet, executives continue to choose large packages. The good

---

[2] A note to executives: Ensure that the enterprise package you are considering has an SDK (software development kit) and have your best technical people try writing code against it to see if it works well (before you buy the damn package). Having the option to add your own custom software onto the base package is an insurance policy that you will be glad you thought of before taking the plunge.

can outweigh the bad, but it requires a careful approach and a depth of knowledge into the risks. Hopefully this chapter has provided an open door onto those risks and offered some unique solutions that your friendly neighborhood package vendor might not have mentioned in the sales pitch.

> **Test Drive Your Knowledge**
> Answer the following questions with the knowledge you have after reading this chapter. Have your answers changed?
>
> 1. What question do you need to ask about your IT department before you make a buy versus build decision?
> 2. How can software be a competitive advantage for a company that does not sell software?
> 3. Are there other choices besides just buy or build?

> **Try This Next**
> **For the executive:** Document and communicate your corporate competitive advantages. Identify areas where software could provide a new competitive advantage by wrapping an existing product or service in information.
>
> **For the manager:** Insist on provision of an SDK being an important criterion in selecting software packages.
>
> **For the individual contributor:** Examine your own biases for or against packaged software solutions. Be looking for ways your company can wrap its products or services in information and make suggestions to do so.

Reference

Porter M (1985) Competitive advantage: creating and sustaining superior performance. Free Press, New York

A Brief Note About Using Offshore Teams 18

> **Test Drive Your Knowledge**
> Answer the following questions with the knowledge you have now. Then answer them again at the end of this chapter.
>
> 1. What's the right way to decide which parts the offshore team should tackle?
> 2. What's the highest bandwidth communication method between two people? The lowest?
> 3. What is something you can do to reduce communication problems with people of other cultures or gender from you?

18.1 Mind-Body Separation

In this chapter, we'll tackle solving the myriad difficulties of physically distributed teams, including offshore.

Our first leadership principle—Bring decision making as close to the work as possible—is an important one. We've looked at how separating the decision-making from doing the work can be harmful to motivation. We've begun to understand how it just isn't possible to know the implications of a methodology or architecture decision unless you have to live with it.

You can think of this as the danger of separating the mind from the body. Remember Rene Descartes from Chap. 1? Smart dude, to be sure, but he continues to cause us problems because he agreed to separate the mind from the body to satisfy the Catholic church.

But mind-body separation doesn't serve us when structuring a large team. It doesn't work when the "mind" of the team is in Ohio and the "body" is in Bangalore. We'll examine the root causes and systemic problems in the following pages.

We (the authors) have had our own experiences with large, distributed teams. But our experiences with offshore teams have been decidedly mixed. So, for this chapter, we relied on several of our acquaintances to help us with stories of how the offshore Agile model can really work well. Nish Gandhi and Kevin McCann both helped us significantly with the information in this chapter. Nish has managed teams spread between the USA and India, and Kevin has worked with software product teams in a variety of locations, including the USA, Brazil, Ukraine, UK, Russia, Germany and Croatia.

Adding to Nish's and Kevin's experiences, we'll include our own experiences, with teams from USA, Canada, India, Singapore, Germany, UK and Macedonia.

18.1.1 Slice at the Thinnest Part

If we should not cut our teams apart when they need to communicate a lot, how can we possibly use the offshore model? Doesn't everyone have to communicate to everyone else?

Actually, it is a matter of degree. Every large team must be broken down into smaller teams. Everyone does this. But the ways we decide to break down the teams is so important. In the waterfall worldview, we would, of course, break teams down by IT function. One team to do analysis, one team to design, one team to code and another team to test. But we know how problematic that breakdown model is.

So how about using our architecture as the model? We could have a multifunction group of business analysts, designers, developers and testers who work on the user interface layer, another to work on business logic and another for data access. Again, this model will be cumbersome. All the risk will be in the interfaces between the teams (connecting a UI widget to the business logic, etc.) and integration will be a nightmare.

How about by technology? One team that does Java, another does DataPower, another that handles html/css. Again, we will have lots and lots of interfaces between teams, lots of room for botched integrations that happen too late and too many business assumptions made differently among the teams.

Fourth try—how about slicing by business function or subsystem? This is better. One multifunction team can build the membership function, another can do benefits and another one can handle invoicing. Yes, the teams need to talk, but the interfaces between teams will be reduced versus the functional or architectural breakdown models above. You can see how one product owner could be focused in the benefits area, another one in membership, etc. The interfaces are fewer and less complex.

So, to summarize, it makes sense to segment the teams in a business way, not technically. We call this "slicing at the thinnest part." It means that we want to create each team so that they will need to communicate to the other teams in the program less. Not that we discourage inter-team collaboration, not at all, but since we need to break up a big program, we want to break it up along the lines where we will do the least damage.

Now think about the offshore teams you've been involved with. Pushing part of the work offshore is the biggest possible slice you could have between teams. One part of the program is thousands of miles away, different time zone, different native language, different cultural background—so much that's different and removed and could easily get in the way of communication. Now where were those teams sliced? Very often, the offshore team will write the code, while the onshore team has product owners, business analysts and testers. What madness is this?? We have effectively cleaved the team apart in the very area where the MOST communication is required.

Remember the Agile Manifesto? "Business people and developers must work together daily throughout the project."

Agile projects don't work if business people and developers are at arm's length from one another. Yes, you can set up chat sessions and video conferences between the US team and the offshore work site. But those are stop-gap measures, low bandwidth, just bandaids. You need fast, efficient, constant, high bandwidth communication between those particular roles, and whatever blockages you place in between will most certainly harm the team.

Many Agile luminaries see this problem and simply state "Agile cannot be done with an offshore team." In their comfortable little world, this might be okay. But in the real world, we have to figure out ways to make it work.

Slicing in a Different Way
Nish Gandhi, our colleague, used a different method to slice his team structure in a way that worked well in the long term. He had a 20-person team in the USA, and another 20 people in India. The entire team needed to collaborate to achieve one business objective together. So Nish broke the work up along business lines and assigned part of the work to the offshore team. Nish was working with an offshore vendor, so they were surprised when he told them he needed business analysts and product owners as well as developers and testers. But the offshore vendor complied, providing people who could fit into those roles. Nish was working in an insurance company at the time, so it was not likely that the offshore vendor could find a knowledgeable product owner to insert into the offshore team. Instead, Nish had a different idea. He brought the designated offshore product owner and asked them to work closely with the onshore product owners for several months. This collaboration helped the new Indian product owner get a sense of the insurance business and begin to provide that function to the offshore developers and testers.

The onshore team in the USA also had developers and testers—lots of them. Nish was careful to staff both teams similarly in terms of roles. Both locations had a product owner, business analysts, developers and testers. And the two teams had mirrored card walls. Everyone in the USA was able to see card-by-card what was being done in India and vice versa. For Nish, it was important that the Indian team did not feel subservient to the American team. Both teams felt equal, and everything Nish did was to try to reinforce that feeling of equality. Nobody was giving orders to anyone else.

You could say that Nish was in a good position in several aspects. First, Nish was originally from India, so he knew a lot about Indian culture and could navigate traps that an American-born manager might have fallen into. And second, Nish had access to a travel budget to bring the Indian product owner to the USA and better integrate him with the other product owners. But Nish had to fight for that budget; it was not handed to him on a silver platter. Nish knew that it would be harder to succeed if he did not slice the program in the right way, and if the offshore team did not have minute-by-minute access to someone who could make business decisions in their assigned business module.

Nish actually went even further with promoting team collaboration. He brought developer pairs from India to the USA for several weeks at a time to get them accustomed to the engineering practices (test-driven development, continuous integration, etc.) that the US team was using and bring those ideas back to the Indian development site. Nish sees these moments as crucial to the success of the program. Amazingly, Nish's program was able to reap the cost reduction of the offshore model without experiencing the quality problems that plague so many offshore teams.

18.2 High and Low Bandwidth Communication

Just like communication networks can be high bandwidth or low bandwidth, so can human communication be. If you send an email to a colleague, a lot of subtlety and context is completely lost. This is a low bandwidth communication method. However, if the two of you are standing in front of a whiteboard, face-to-face, and are able to exchange ideas, ask questions, clarify and respond, this is tremendously high bandwidth human communication. Body language, facial expressions, flashes of emotion—everything is available to be absorbed and interpreted. It is much less likely that your message will be misinterpreted in a face-to-face conversation versus an email.

When we slice teams apart, we often reduce the bandwidth of the human communication. Even if part of the team is on the fifth floor and another part is in the sixth floor, you've reduced bandwidth. Now I have to climb the stairs, or pick up the phone, or write an email to ask a quick question. Reduced bandwidth, more likelihood of communication problems.

This is why Agile people are so fanatical about open workspaces and keeping the team together. But even in a perfectly open workspace, problems can still arise. Why?

There is another aspect to human communication bandwidth problems. Even if it is a situation where two people are at a whiteboard, if those two people are from different cultural backgrounds or even from different genders, we now introduce additional bandwidth problems. Like it or not, bridging gaps between cultures and genders is tough. It takes effort and directed thinking. It doesn't come automatically just because we are at a whiteboard.

18.2.1 Those Tricky Metaphors

One group of researchers we met at a systems thinking conference looked at corporate cultures and tried to find ways to identify one culture from another. To a large extent, they relied on metaphor usage. Do people in the company tend to use war metaphors? "We are fighting for every inch of territory in this market!" That may be a sign that this company values competitive spirit and devalues collaboration.

Prevalent metaphors can tell a lot about a person or a corporate culture. It is good to be conscious of the metaphors you use. Sports metaphors might seem universal, but they are unlikely to connect with people of different cultures and even genders. A detailed metaphor about American football might be very confusing to an Indonesian team member who is crazy about badminton. Sports metaphors might be very motivating to male team members but might be fairly meaningless to a female member of that same team who sees watching sports as a great way to waste a weekend.

It's not to say that we must cleanse our conversations of all metaphors. But we must think of our metaphors in the context of the audience. Try to find out what your team members are interested in and find metaphors that fit into those interests. Making assumptions about what they're interested can also be problematic. "Oh, you're a woman so I'm sure you like to clean house and cook." That might do more to alienate your female colleague than anything else. Even if she does enjoy cleaning house and cooking, she probably won't appreciate you making a blind gender assumption about it.

Metaphors are tricky. Be careful about using them, and try to tailor them to the person you are conversing with. This goes double for when you have an offshore team. Take extra time thinking about your message and using metaphors that might work well and avoiding those that will fall flat under different culture. The wrong metaphors can actually reduce your human communication bandwidth.

18.3 Large Distributed Teams Can Work

We've all seen plenty of disasters using large distributed teams, but it is possible for them to work. If you get assigned to a project that has an offshore component, or as part of a very large team, don't assume that it will necessarily fail. There are practices and intentions that can help it succeed. Influence the structure of the team as much as you can and fight to get the right pieces into place for each location and team.

> **Test Drive Your Knowledge**
> Answer the following questions with the knowledge you have after reading this chapter. Have your answers changed?
>
> 1. What's the right way to decide which parts the offshore team should tackle?
> 2. What's the highest bandwidth communication method between two people? The lowest?
> 3. What is something you can do to reduce communication problems with people of other cultures or gender from you?

> **Try This Next**
>
> **For the executive:** Structure your next offshore team along business lines, rather than function (product owner in the USA, developers in India). Don't put the mind of the team in one location and the body in another. Or avoid using offshore completely.
>
> **For the manager:** Work towards getting enough travel budget on each offshore project so that team members can visit one another and learn how to collaborate more closely, even across distances and time zones.
>
> **For the individual contributor:** Look at the way you use metaphors that might be alienating your team members of other cultures and gender.

Highlighting the Differences Between Software Product Companies and Internal IT

19

> **Test Drive Your Knowledge**
> Answer the following questions with the knowledge you have now. Then answer them again at the end of this chapter.
>
> 1. How are value stories different for a software product company or an internal IT shop?
> 2. How does the Scrum product owner role differ from a product manager role?
> 3. How does a non-software company take the role of software more seriously?

19.1 The Role of Software in Your Organization

As we've mentioned in previous chapters, software product companies are quite different than internal IT shops. In this chapter, we will expand on that comparison and highlight how both types of organizations need to approach software creation in their own unique way.

We're describing software product companies as those that generate more than 80% of the total company revenue from the sales of software. We recognize that many companies are blurring the line between other types of products and software products. For instance, Cisco is known for producing routers, so they are a hardware company, right? Well, that's not how they see themselves. They produce high-quality router software, and also products that use routers (like Telepresence), which makes their routers even more valuable. Many companies are starting up their own software companies inside the larger entity, blurring the lines even more. We will share an example that we've seen of this later in this chapter as a case study.

Internal IT shops we will define as IT departments that exist inside corporations that do not see themselves as primarily software revenue-driven. For instance, a railroad company might have a lot of software developers working for them, but their primary business is moving railcars down the track carrying goods for customers. Software helps them do that, but it is not a primary revenue generator.

19.1.1 Making Money by Selling Software Versus a Software Cost Center

In Chap. 7—Business Value, Estimation and Metrics—we introduced the idea of value stories. Value stories are often quite different for software product companies versus internal IT shops.

19.1.1.1 Revenue Value Stories

Revenue value stories are those that we expect will provide the enterprise with additional revenue. Expense value stories will provide a reduction in expenses, either bankable or nonbankable (more on that later).

In software product companies, since software is what we sell, most value stories are revenue related. We are developing feature after feature in hopes that it will help us sell additional licenses to customers. It's often hard to quantify that a particular feature was responsible for some number of additional licenses sold. But we need to make a guess, so we tie some financial amount to each value story (if we can). Remember, we don't have to go full-on Thurmanator on ROI, we just need to make an educated guess that a particular feature might help us gain financially.

We worked with a very innovative software company that sold its products to county and state governments to help automate back-office processing in human services offices (welfare, child support, etc.). They responded to RFPs (requests for proposals) from the various states and counties by explaining how their software would fit the bill for what the customer needed. In many cases, they could see that certain features were being requested more and more often in RFPs, and so they had some type of estimate for the amount of revenue they could gain if they would build those features. But it was no guarantee. They might build the feature in a different way than the customers were expecting/hoping, or they might build the feature only to lose the RFP for some other reason. But it was at least a way to relatively prioritize value stories based on expected future value.

For companies that produce shrink-wrapped software, this becomes an even more difficult estimation of value. How can Microsoft or Symantec know that if they add this additional feature that they will suddenly boost their sales volume by X amount? Again, they don't know, but they can guess. If they see a competitor gaining market share, and that competitor's products have a feature that is missing in their own product, they can guess that they must add the feature themselves to keep up.

Revenue value stories are often big dollar amounts. Even for small companies, one particular revenue value story will often represent several million dollars. Sales figures are always larger than expense figures (at least you would hope so).

With some companies, we've seen them focus their value stories on profit generated rather than revenue. Net profit might be difficult, because it is hard to determine which elements of SG&A (sales, general and administrative) should be allocated to a particular product, but you can use gross margin, which only subtracts expenses in the "cost of goods sold" category. This can be a more meaningful metric for value stories, since you don't want to spend $1M on a development effort, gain $2M in revenue but then boost profits only by a few hundred thousand. The total profit must be larger than the original investment. We're not advocating using sales, gross margin or net profit in particular, just be consistent among the value stories with one or the other.

Internal IT shops may also have a significant number of revenue value stories. e-Commerce applications are built to boost company revenues (and profit).

To summarize, revenue value stories are often big dollar amounts, but they are also very subjective and fuzzy. It is hard to calculate exactly how much revenue you will produce.

19.1.1.2 Expense Value Stories

Expense value stories are where the team is building software for the purposes of reducing cost. This might be creating a tool that will speed up an essential process or cutting out steps in a long process that is taking too much time.

We divide expense value stories into two categories: bankable and nonbankable. Bankable expense value stories offer reduced expenses that will show in the quarterly financial statements. For example, if the new software will render an old application unnecessary, and the old application has some recurring costs (let's say a license fee), then that savings will drop to the bottom line and will change the company's profit for the quarter. Another example of a bankable expense value story is one which will result in reduced headcount in a department. If the team is building call center software that will make the customer service representatives more efficient, the company may be able to lay off some number of those people and thereby see a true reduction in expenses for those salaries.

Obviously, there are certain aspects of bankable expense value stories that are attractive, in that the CFO can tell shareholders about the software project in terms they will really understand. There are certain problems with bankable stories, where one team is creating a tool that will cause other employees to lose their jobs.

Nonbankable expense value stories are where the team is creating value, but it is not quite so clearly connected to the financial statements. For instance, one software team we worked with created a tool that made contract analysts much more efficient when they needed to enter new products into a product catalog. But the introduction of the software did not cause the contract analysts to lose their jobs. It merely meant that they were able to focus their time on more important tasks, like analyzing contracts for potential savings (they were contract analysts, after all).

We could not take the movement of the contract analysts from a less efficient task to a more efficient task as a definitive savings to company, because their salaries stayed the same. It is possible that you could guess at the productivity of the analysts once they had more time to analyze contracts, but we did not do that. The CFO of the company wanted to make a clear distinction between value stories that he could explain to shareholders versus those more fuzzy ones. He understood the value of both types, but he did not want complicated explanations of nonbankable value stories, he just wanted them in a different category from the bankable stories.

19.1.2 A Software Subsidiary

We've worked closely with a large healthcare distribution company for the past several years. They've taken a very innovative path with their approach to software. Healthcare distribution means that you are the company that moves healthcare products around, from manufacturers to warehouses to doctors' offices and hospitals. That could mean quantities of drugs, gloves or paper tissues all the way to large MRI machines. In some cases, the company found that it made sense for them to manufacture certain products on their own that didn't exist in the marketplace. For those machines and devices, software was often a component.

Initially, these "software product teams" were intermixed with all the other internal IT teams in the vast IT shop. But then they made the decision to separate the software product company that they had inside them and put it in a separate building, about two miles down the road. They put great care into the look and feel of the new place, instituting new dress codes (casual), a new philosophy and new software processes. The experiment has been a success and mirrors what has happened in other large IT departments that are seeing the need to take a different approach for their software products, rather than good ole IT.

Software product companies are different in many aspects than internal IT shops. In this chapter, we've attempted to outline some of the most important differences and also to show that both might exist in the same shop, in which case it can help to separate them and encourage unique cultures for each.

19.2 Product Managers and Product Owners

Software product companies usually have a role called "product manager." This is a person who focuses on a certain set of software products and tries to plan where that product should go in the future and how to make it more relevant to customers' needs. Product managers often report to the marketing function in the company.

When a software team is trying to identify the Scrum role of product owner, the product management group is a natural place to start. After all, why not connect to the person who is responsible for the market success of this product for direction in the team room?

From our experience, the product manager usually does not become the product owner. Instead, someone more junior, who perhaps reports to the product manager, becomes the full-time product owner.

There are several considerations for this. One is that the product manager's job is often on-the-road. Product managers who stay in the office most of the time are not usually good product managers. They must be going on sales calls, attending conferences, speaking, and talking to customers one-on-one. The product owner role is quite different. The team needs constant access to the product owner. Sure, the product owner may leave the room now and then to attend meetings or be out in the field, but they need to be accessible to the software team members for questions, clarifications and planning. In any case, this usually does not fit any senior executive being a product owner, but especially product managers.

We've seen some movement in non-software companies towards the product management philosophy. As many industries become more and more entrenched in technology, why not have product managers for those important pieces of software? In a manufacturing company, a product manager was assigned responsibility for their customer-facing order system. In a bank, product managers exist for consumer savings accounts, wealth management accounts, mortgage accounts, etc., all of which could be considered software products. When you get a mortgage, you expect there will be online software to support your needs. The better that software, the happier you are as a customer of the bank. We find ourselves choosing vendors based more on their maturity of technical applications than other factors. Even gas stations need to have fully functional software on their gas pumps that get customers filled up and on their way quickly.

19.3 Selling Software or Just Using It

Software product companies are quite different from internal IT shops in the way software is valuable. If you are producing software to sell, you have a different way of measuring value than if the software is being built in support of another type of product or service. But in both cases, it helps for the software teams to have a deep understanding of the value stories and to be prioritizing their work and frequent releases by value.

Test Drive Your Knowledge Again

Answer the following questions with the knowledge you have after reading this chapter. Have your answers changed?

1. How are value stories different for a software product company or an internal IT shop?
2. How does the Scrum product owner role differ from a product manager role?
3. How does a non-software company take the role of software more seriously?

Try This Next

For the executive: Clearly understand the extent to which your corporation relies on software sales versus non-software. Also understand the direction the CEO wants to go with this ratio. Then communicate this path forward clearly to your staff.

For the manager: Help teams create revenue and expense value stories that are appropriate for the type of organization.

For the individual contributor: Ask about the places where the executives intend to use software as a competitive advantage.

Conclusion

Our Hope

That's the end of our tirade. We hope you've learned something valuable, even if it was just a practice or two that you can try in your own environment.

It is our fervent hope that this book can start an international dialog where we can begin talking about intentions and worldviews as much as we discuss action. Where we can relent a bit from our focus on the details of practices and our thinking that any practice could be "best."

And, most of all, we look forward to a time when others are proposing different models from what we have here, either building on what we've done, or starting anew in competition with us. That would be the best of all possible worlds.

From what we've seen, very few books talk about Agile illth. Very few examine how we have an outdated view of professionalism and how that can hurt an Agile team and the entire adaptive enterprise. And we haven't seen enough focus on how to meld the work of fast-moving Agile teams with groups like the PMO, enterprise architecture, corporate methodology and HR.

We felt like it was time to provoke a dialog about all of this. Changing how we develop software is hard. But we must improve our industry track record. And we must come to terms with reality that "Software is eating the world," as Mark Andreessen stated a few years ago. If so many businesses in so many industries are going to rely on software as a competitive advantage, we'd better be producing very high quality test-driven software, and we'd better be as responsive as heck in changing to match the business. Currently, we're not there, but we can do it.

This is a long book. You're amazing for having read this far. Thanks for picking this book up and going through it.

We've created our website **EnterpriseAgile.biz** to continue the conversation, so please feel free to let us know what you think and what the next steps should be. Now it's your turn.

CPSIA information can be obtained
at www.ICGtesting.com
Printed in the USA
LVOW01*0013170417
531016LV00001B/1/P